Gregory Yeoman

~~~

RIDING INTO THE SUNRISE

Recollections of a Bicycle Journey Across Russia

First published in Great Britain 2013

Copyright © Gregory Yeoman 2013

The Author asserts the moral right to be identified as the author of this work.

ISBN 9781471652158

All rights reserved. No part of this publication may be reproduced, stored in a retrieval system, or transmitted, in any form or by any means, electronic, mechanical, photocopying, recording or otherwise, without the prior permission of the author.

This book is sold subject to the condition that it shall not, by way of trade or otherwise, be lent, resold, hired out or otherwise circulated without the author's prior consent in any form of binding or cover other than that in which it is published and without a similar condition including this condition being imposed on the subsequent purchaser.

For information about the author and all his cycling expeditions go to www.red-line.moonfruit.com

Acknowledgments
Thank you to all the Russian people we met along the way, who helped make this such a memorable journey, especially our co-cyclists Vladimir, George, Eugene, Yuri and Sasha. Special thanks to Kate Leeming, whose initial phone call provided the impetus for me to get out and do what I had been thinking of for some time, and led to further cycling adventures. Early drafts of this book were read by Benedict Yeoman, Julian Dobbins and Michael Zeidler, who each provided useful comments with welcome frankness, and the maps were created by Philip Normington. Finally, thank you to all the sponsors of the Trans-Siberian Cycle Expedition – go to page 242 for the full list.

All photos were taken by Gregory Yeoman, Kate Leeming or someone using their cameras.

Cover photo: Why take the Trans-Siberian Express when you can go by bike? The author and Sasha heading towards Tu on Day 133.

To my children, Izaak and Nancy.

The world is full of wonder and adventure;
it is for you to seek it out.

Contents

Introduction	1
Section 1 – Settling in: St. Petersburg to Ryazan	5
Section 2 – Ryazan to the Urals	35
Section 3 – Across the Steppe	63
Section 4 – Around the Sayan Ring	83
Section 5 – Breakdowns, Baikal and Buryatya	117
Section 6 – Tackling the Swamp	163
Section 7 – Land of the Tiger	215
Epilogue	238

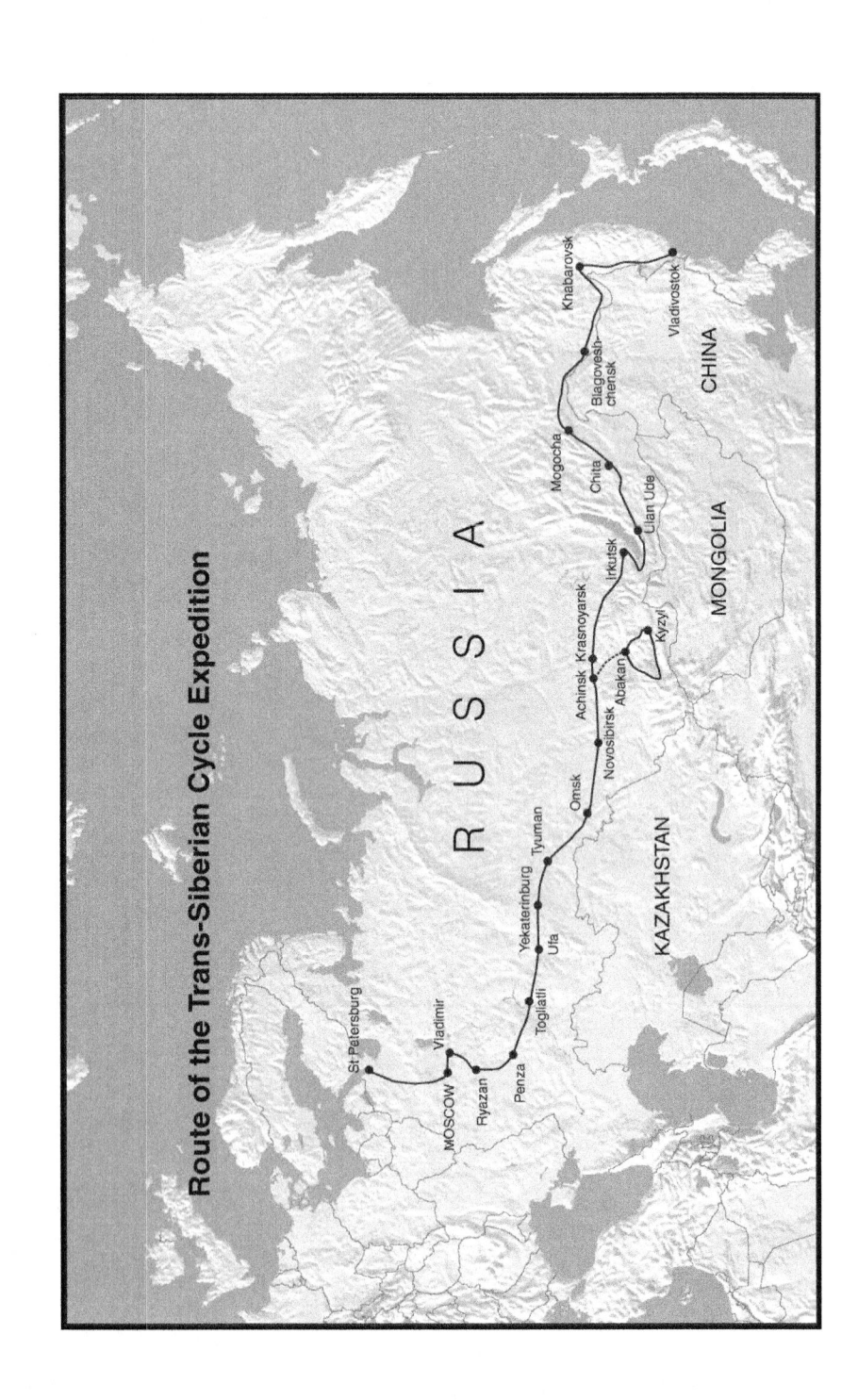

Route of the Trans-Siberian Cycle Expedition

INTRODUCTION

~~~

"Oh, just take the whole bloody lot and sort it out yourself!" I exclaimed, thrusting all my remaining dollar bills through the grille at the stony-faced woman. Our immediate fate lay in her hands.

I was trying to leave Russia, and it was not going very well. I had thought *getting* here would be the difficult part, securing invitations and visas for a six-month visit during which it would be impossible to say where and with whom we would be staying, and when. But here I was, struggling to convince this hangover from a previous (though clearly still-too-recent) era that my money was good and would she please just sell me the tickets for the flight.

The problem, apparently, was the paper. Not the issue dates of the bills – we had been careful about that and only had 1991 issue or newer. It was something about the quality. In front of the woman on her desk was a small black box with a narrow slot in the side. One by one, each note was carefully placed in the slot and the machine pulled it in hungrily. A split second later it spat it out, and either a green or red light would flash, indicating whether or not the note met the machine's requirements. The process was tediously slow, and we had rather a lot of notes to get through – tickets for Kate and me cost $335 each, and those for Sasha and Valera $100. Over the previous six months we had grown accustomed to the many annoying aspects of bureaucracy (offices not being open when they should be, decisions made according to the person's mood rather than the facts, generally abrupt behaviour) and had developed some sort of coping mechanism. Plus, of course, there was the fact that we had chosen to visit the country to experience all that was different about its culture and way of life, and we had chosen to do it in a way that meant we would be here for a long time. If we had not liked it, there were two options: go back home early, or deal with it. Complaining was not going to achieve anything and would only obstruct our view of the country and the people who live there.

However, I had now reached the end of my long trip. I had successfully cycled across the biggest country in the world, and now I wanted to go back home and experience decent food and a comfortable bed. I felt justified in becoming more than a little peeved with the impervious cow looking back at me from her position of strength on the other side of her desk. $690 were, apparently, acceptable. The other $80 had been rejected. Even some that the machine *had* accepted had been turned down by the human element in the process. On the basis of what? The notes had the wrong smell? Clearly I was not about to be initiated in the dark art of dollar acceptance, and despite my protests that I had no more money I could tell that she was not going to give any ground at all. Reluctantly I took the money back and endured the eight-mile return trip in the packed trolley bus to the flat we were staying in, where I picked up all of our remaining cash. Back in the Aeroflot ticket office the process began again. With a bigger pile of money this time I was confident we would crack it. Slowly, the pile of dollar bills that met the company's tough selection criteria grew. Things were looking good. We were through the $700 barrier. $750 came and went. A fair number of bills lay forlornly on the reject pile, denied their birthright to be used in the ages-old tradition of financial dealings, and the pool of spares was disappearing fast. $760; surely we were home and dry. $765; visions of the green pastures of southern England floated before my eyes. $769; I could feel the crunch of my first juicy apple in six months between my teeth. $770. Yes! We had made it! I reached out to accept the tickets, already feeling the surge of the plane's jets lifting me into the skies above Vladivostok. But wait! What was this? Suddenly I was back on the runway. Worse than that, the plane was still in the hangar. I did not have a ticket in my hands at all. I had a dollar bill. One single dollar. $769 was on the clock and she had rejected the last dollar! And this time it really was the last one; I had brought all of our money from the flat. This was too unbelievable for words – words that could be repeated in polite company at any rate, somewhere I clearly did not believe I was at the time. Although she spoke no English I reckon the woman behind the desk got the gist of what I was saying.

 One dollar. One lousy dollar. This country was on its knees. The rouble, or as it seemed more appropriate to call it, the rubble, was going through the floor. Russia needed dollars; here I was doing my best to give them some and they were being thrown back at me. I thought it best to quieten down as it became obvious my behaviour was doing nothing to break down these tenacious remnants of Iron Curtain intransigence. Valera, who had been standing beside me patiently throughout, stepped in to sort things out. I was not sure if he wanted to apologise for me and restore cultural relations, or if he realised that it was also his ticket home that was hanging in the balance. Whatever his motivation, he managed to persuade the woman to retry some of the notes. At last she found a one-dollar bill that passed muster.

I took the tickets before she had a chance to change her mind and smiled as genuinely as I could. It was not easy to combine real glee at having the tickets with complete disdain for the person who had issued them. Anyway, we were on our way home. What could possibly disrupt our plans now? Well, tanks on the streets of Moscow for one thing. It seemed that this huge, fascinating and frustrating country would keep testing us until the very end.

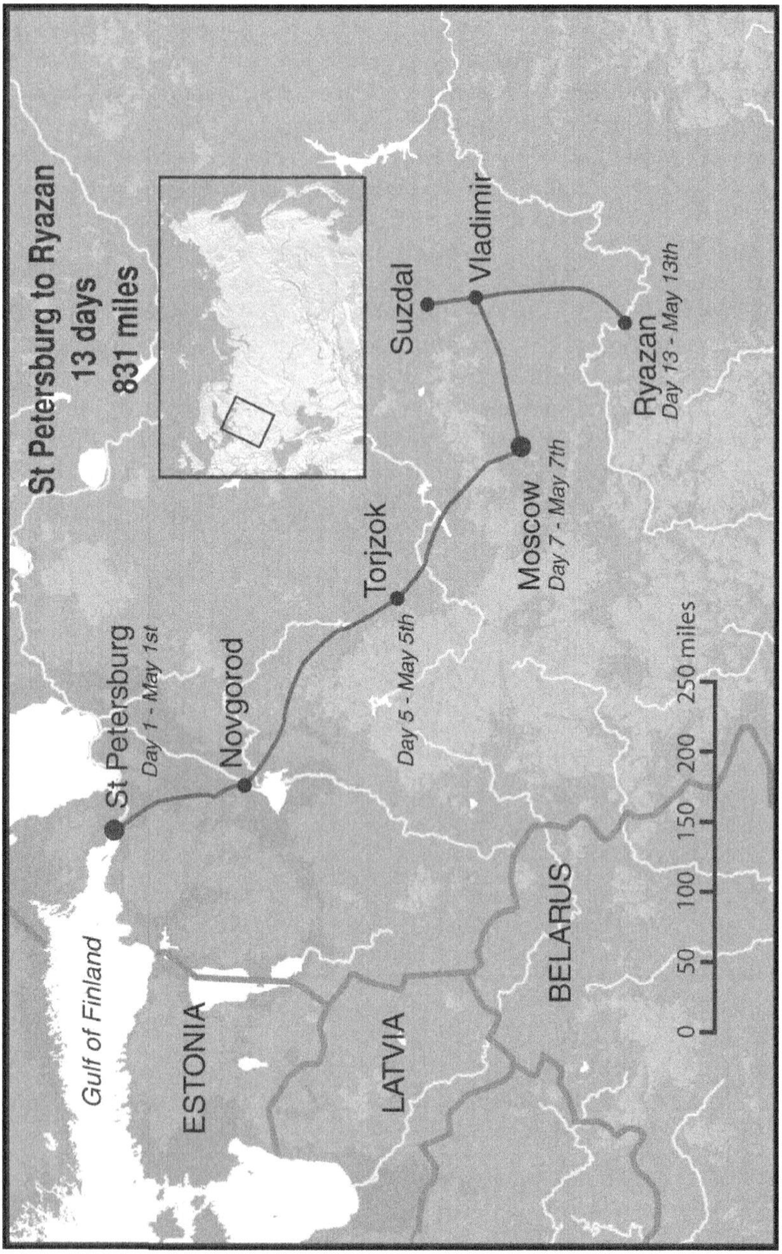
St Petersburg to Ryazan
13 days
831 miles
Gulf of Finland
ESTONIA
LATVIA
BELARUS
St Petersburg
Day 1 - May 1st
Novgorod
Torjzok
Day 5 - May 5th
Moscow
Day 7 - May 7th
Suzdal
Vladimir
Ryazan
Day 13 - May 13th
0
50
100
150
200
250 miles

SECTION 1

~~~

SETTLING IN:
ST. PETERSBURG TO
RYAZAN

~~~

Touching down in St. Petersburg after the short flight east from London via Copenhagen, we stretched our aching limbs and shuffled along to join the immigration queue. If I felt this tired after three hours on a plane, how would I feel after thousands of miles in the saddle? Glancing about, the world seemed somehow to have been refracted or shifted, superficially similar to the one we had left just a few hours before, but strangely different from it. The language and alphabet were well beyond my grasp and I had expected that, but the cultural dislocation was enhanced by everything around us having what can only be described as a 'Russian-ness' that set it apart from its equivalent back home. This was man-made convergent evolution at work. East and West had been separated for such a long time, but had faced the same urban, agricultural and industrial developmental needs that they had independently arrived at the same solution, each giving its version a characteristic form and cultural stamp. Vehicles, bridges, clothes, buildings, monuments – even the people themselves – had an inherent quality that identified them as Russian. Perhaps people arriving in England for the first time have a similar experience, and maybe after six months spent seeing this huge country in extreme close-up everything at home would seem similarly peculiar to me.

For now, despite the rigours of a horribly early start and two flights, the excitement of standing on Russian soil, of actually being in such a mysterious country, surrounded by the strangeness of it all, was more than enough to keep me wide awake. At this stage I was happy not to know that very soon, within a matter of hours, I would be plunged into a deep depression.

Just a few short months before, I would not have imagined being in this situation. I had been about to head out of the front door on the way to work on a chilly February morning when the phone rang. The muddled conversation that followed both confused and excited me: "Hello, my name's Kate. I met your sister at a party." Odd opening line, I thought. I have not got a sister. Kate continued, undaunted. "She said you like cycling and, erm, would you like to come to Vladivostok with me?" As propositions go it was one I thought I would not hear again, and despite the incorrect sibling description the rest of Kate's information was accurate – I did indeed like cycling, and had had the idea of cycling across Russia in my mind for a few years. I had not really done anything to move the idea along beyond buying some books about the country to carry out some research. Kate had done more preparation but needed someone to work with her to make the plan a reality. It did not take me long to answer her question, and one letter of resignation addressed to my boss later I found myself caught up in securing equipment, sponsorship and media exposure.

Back in St. Petersburg, suitcases were beginning to land on the creaking wooden carousel. Some bikes appeared, then some of our bags. The large metal trunk came through unscathed. We had a huge amount of luggage – bicycles and mechanical spares, photographic and video equipment, clothing and some food – all of which would need to be sorted out during our few days in St. Petersburg. With little spare time available in the expedition timetable, if something were to go wrong at this early stage our progress could be affected before we had even thrown a leg over a bike. As the crowd of fellow passengers thinned and the appearance of new bags dwindled and finally came to an end, we realised we were one suitcase short. This was not a good start. The case in question contained one of the tents, film for the cameras, sleeping mats, waterproofs and other clothing. After three months of careful preparation it would be a major setback to lose this equipment before even properly arriving in the country. However, it seemed there was nothing we could do about it now and watching the empty carousel trundle on its way would not make the case suddenly materialise. Flights from Copenhagen arrived daily, and we just had to hope that the suitcase would turn up on the next one. The good news was that all the bikes had made it, so we could at least all ride even if we had to bodge some other equipment together.

I stepped forward and handed my passport to the officer behind the glass screen. Even when I do this on arriving home in England I somehow manage to look shifty; concentrating too hard on looking as though it was perfectly normal to be bringing a mountain of shiny new Western goods into the country definitely did nothing to make me look more relaxed, but somehow I managed not to attract any attention. Without any display of emotion from the officer wielding it, but with a hugely satisfying double clunk from the stamp itself, my passport was marked and handed back to me. I was in!

Eagerly, like a schoolboy excitedly checking the latest addition to his collection that would trump all his friends' combined stamps, I turned to the page containing my new entry permit. Surely this was one of *the* stamps to have in your passport. It showed you were a real traveller, keen, and, more importantly, able to penetrate the Iron Curtain (even if it had recently rusted away – a minor detail) and reach areas that most people just look at in the atlas wondering what life was really like 'over there'. People always compare passport pages when they go on holiday with friends, or even people they do not know. It is an ice-breaker, an opportunity to find out something about their travelling companions. Imagine how impressed they would be, flicking through my own passport and suddenly seeing a large and colourful display of Cyrillic jumping out of the page, probably still resplendent with Soviet images of hammer and sickle, toiling workers and Lenin helpfully pointing the way for the weary traveller. Imagine how let down I felt when I saw the real thing. A small, faint, plain rectangle. No dramatic images of any kind, and the word RUSSIA barely legible in orange Cyrillic letters. Orange! I know they had had a major regime change a couple of years earlier, but surely they used to use revolutionary red as the colour of choice on all official documents, and I could not believe that the wheels of Russian bureaucracy turned any more quickly than the old Soviet ones. The old supplies of red ink could not have been replaced this quickly and efficiently, could they?

But this was a country experiencing its most cataclysmic political event of the last 70 years. Most people were looking forwards, wondering what the future would bring. I could not spend my time imagining I was visiting the USSR – that empire was gone, replaced by a collection of new countries coming to terms with independence. If I had wanted a red stamp, well I was just 15 months too late. The next five months would reveal whether the country and its people were moving forwards, happy to draw a line under Communism, or if they were glancing over their shoulders, wondering why they had turned their backs on the order and security that they had enjoyed as good Comrades.

In the queue ahead of us, a well-armed group of middle-aged Germans was trying to explain its collection of firearms. In a country where military field clothing is something of a fashion, these visitors would fit in rather well – better than us in our brightly coloured new fleece jackets – but the Bavarian hats were a dead giveaway. My concern was over what they had come to hunt, how big it was, and how much of it was living out there in the Siberian forests. Perhaps we could persuade the Germans to travel ahead of us, ensuring us a clear run without the inconvenience of bears and other large mammals pursuing us. For a moment it seemed a reasonable idea, but luckily my environmental instincts won and there would be no bear blood on my conscience.

Once the formalities had been completed we made our way out of the terminal building and into the bright St. Petersburg afternoon. A group of four men formed our welcome party on the steps of the arrivals hall and introductions were made with varying degrees of understanding and remembering of names. George (an easy one to start with) would be cycling with us for the first two weeks, from St. Petersburg to Ryazan, and was the only one among us who had the advantage of cycling home to spur him on. Vladimir, who bore a strong resemblance to Charles Aznavour but sadly never burst into song, was on home ground in St. Petersburg and would join us for the first seven weeks, to Yekaterinburg. Sasha, at 21 the youngest of the group, was here to take a large part of our luggage by train on to Ryazan, where our expedition base would be, before joining us on the bikes for the second half of the expedition from Krasnoyarsk. Last but not least was Ilya – he would not be riding with us beyond the first hour or so of Day 1 but as our host here in St. Petersburg, along with his wife, Luba, and daughter, he played an important role helping us settle in to our adopted country.

With the luggage, minus the suitcase, safely stowed onto a truck, we travelled by bus to the outskirts of the city. On the way, I could feel the excitement of my arrival giving way to despair as I looked out across the greyness of the suburban landscape. Repetitive blocks of flats marched beside the wide roads, and thick layers of dust collected on the kerbs, in the gutters and doorways. Crowds of people in grey and brown clothes made their way home. This did not look like a country embarking on a new and exciting era; it was one that had just crashed out of the last one and was still blinking in the bright light of its new dawn, not quite sure what to do. Then the bus caught fire.

Eventually, after finding some new transport, we made it to Ilya's small flat high in one of these blocks and proceeded to take over his cramped space with all our kit.

Diary: Friday April 30th 1993
The housing area is very bleak - boring high-rise with no greenery at all, and many dogs. There is loads of broken glass, trampled mud, no grass, and nasty skip-like incinerators spewing foul smoke in the middle of the housing blocks. The first bout of depression set in as I stood on the balcony looking at the god-awful view and wondering what we will do if the other suitcase doesn't turn up.

While Kate and I spent the majority of the next two days going through every possible arrangement of packing our panniers and trying to establish the most efficient way to load everything onto the bikes, Ilya kindly went back to the airport to track down the lost suitcase. When he returned home later we were extremely relieved to see that he had the case with him, and we could add the remainder of our equipment to the pannier-packing puzzle. While all this was going on we did find some time for a little sightseeing. A journey to the city centre was just what I needed to restore my faith in the value of having come to Russia. The architecture of Peter the Great's Baltic gem could not have contrasted more dramatically with the blandness of the more recent Soviet additions.

The work of the Italian and French 18th Century designers is obvious in the beautiful buildings and series of canals. St. Isaac's Cathedral, the Peter and Paul fortress and the Church of Our Saviour's

Blood (a mini St. Basil's, but with a minty green and blue colour scheme rather than the reds and oranges of its Moscow version) lifted my spirits as we enjoyed a tour along the banks of the Neva and through the attractive squares and main streets of the former capital with Ilya as our guide.

Having spent many late nights sorting out our equipment at home, the last thing we wanted to do here was more of the same. Early nights and plenty of sleep would have been the best preparation, but somehow we managed to find things to do into the early hours. The Russian cyclists joining us throughout the expedition would be bringing out the appropriate spares for their respective sections, and we needed to divide everything into different bags for them – this sounds a simple task but it is surprising how long it takes. As a result of all this late night activity, plus more than a little anxiety at the thought of striking out across this huge unknown country on a journey the like and scale of which I had never experienced before, I was completely knackered when I finally fell into bed. Tomorrow would show if we had peaked too early.

Setting the pattern for the next five months, my alarm went off well before I was ready to be disturbed. For a few moments I lay in bed enjoying the comfort and warmth, trying not to think about what lay ahead. As the flat woke up around me and the smell of cooking wafted in from the small kitchen, I persuaded myself to get up. The meals Ilya's wife had prepared over the last couple of days had been simple and filling, but not very varied. This morning's breakfast continued the same theme, with spaghetti and fried chicken. It was not easy to force this down so early in the morning, but the pasta contained valuable calories and, setting another pattern that would repeat throughout the expedition, I ate whatever food appeared in front of me.

Suitably fuelled, and with bags definitely packed for the last time, we shuttled ourselves and the equipment down in the cramped and dimly lit lift and assembled on the ground floor. Ilya led the way and Kate and I wobbled cautiously, gradually becoming accustomed to our heavily laden bikes. Did we really need all this stuff? Once in the city centre we headed for our official starting point and our rendezvous with Vladimir and George, who had been staying at Vladimir's flat. We had chosen to start the expedition from the statue of the Bronze Horseman – a triumphant Peter the Great rearing up on a great wave-like granite plinth in the middle of Decembrists' Square. From across the wide and smoothly flowing Neva the noon-day gun rang out, signalling, at last, the start of our journey. Kate and I had only taken a few short months to get everything organised but it was still an enormous relief finally to be on the bikes and on the road. No more endless planning, equipment checking, sponsor chasing, phone calling... If it had not been sorted out by now it was too late – we would just have to deal with it as best we could. At this point I realised that the planning had just enabled us to reach this point – The Start. Ahead of us lay five months, and the only thing we knew with any certainty about our future was the route we were hoping to follow. That, and the fact that if we cycled too slowly the freezing grip of the Siberian winter would close around us and hold us firm. Knowing that vodka remains liquid at sub-zero temperatures would be cold comfort.

Between now and the end of September, our progress and success could be affected by a host of things that we could not plan for – the weather, the state of the roads, illness, accidents, equipment failure, extreme homesickness and depression. Before actually encountering any of these factors there was simply no way of knowing what their effect on us would be, although before setting off there had been endless opportunities to discuss and theorise about them at length and without coming to any conclusions other than that we should take clothes for warm, cold, wet and dry, a first-aid kit and knobbly tyres. As for the homesickness, well we would get home more quickly if we just got on with it.

Suitably prepared, then, for the first hour or so of Day 1, we heaved our bikes upright, settled onto the what we hoped would soon become nicely moulded and broken-in saddles, and pushed the pedals round in earnest for the first time. "Vladivostok here we come!" I thought, for roughly half a second, before realising that the scale of the whole trip was too much to cope with in one go. Vladivostok was over 8000 miles away; I would deal with it nearer the time, but for now Moscow was an easier target – one week away and not too far over the pleasantly flat horizon.

Cobbles, tramlines and potholes tested our concentration as our procession made its way generally south-west through the city street. Just two years since the collapse of the old order and Ilya was confident that things had got worse. If it was this bad here in the country's second city, what would things be like in the far reaches of the countryside, miles (and miles and miles) from sources of funding and organisation? Another subject for endless discussion. Time was certainly something we had plenty of now, but it just seemed a waste of it to spend ages chatting about something that we would find out the answer to soon enough anyway. The here and now became far more important – food, water, shelter, the road, the view. And we had not gone far before encountering our first unforeseen problem.

In the planning stages Kate and I had come up with a simple and brilliant plan to make sure the expedition get off to a smooth start: we would ask a native of St. Petersburg to ride with us. With Vladimir as part of the team everything would be plain sailing as he navigated a quick way out of his hometown, local knowledge proving indispensable. After only a few miles, however, we questioned the effectiveness of our plan. Not far from the city centre we entered the large World War Two memorial roundabout – a local landmark and key point for navigation. We were heading for the capital, and there, on a lone signpost in large and, even at this early stage of the proceedings, easily decipherable Cyrillic, a single word gave us all the information we needed: MOCKBA.

I saw it. Kate saw it. Vladimir, somehow, did not see it. Happily taking another turning he plunged us back in to small streets with no distinguishing features. Thus, within an hour of starting, we were lost. This did not bode well. Looking at the whole map of Russia, there was not exactly an abundance of roads to choose from to get from one side to the other, and here we were on one of the wrong ones already – despite a large signpost handily pointing out where we should have gone, and with a Russian riding with us.

There was another factor that was not helping us at this point. The idea behind finding Russians to join us throughout the trip was to make our journey more enjoyable (they could help us interpret the country and the culture we were experiencing) and easier (they could speak the language, we could not). A key part of the plan was that the Russians would be able to speak English; sadly, with Vladimir, a confirmed monoglot, this had failed spectacularly.

As Vladimir flagged down the occasional pedestrian in a deceptively casual way, looking for all the world as though he was doing nothing more than catching up with friends and explaining what he was doing on a bike with a couple of foreigners, Kate and I were floundering with our attempts to explain that the right way lay 'back there' somewhere. George, whose grasp of English was strong enough to manage straightforward conversations, sensibly realised that more people getting involved would just complicate things and let Vladimir carry on with his route-finding. Eventually, with a look that suggested neither relief, pleasure nor even 'I don't know what you lot were getting so worried about', he led us back to the main road and we resumed our stately progress. It was an important early lesson in Russian navigation skills – ie they were more or less non-existent, and any information and advice given in answer to the question 'Can you tell me the way to X?' was best ignored.

Safely back on our way and having at last left the greyness of St. Petersburg behind, we were now moving steadily through the grey, flat countryside. Travelling to Russia had seemed like a journey back in time in more ways than one. On top of the retrograde social planning, we were also experiencing a shift in the calendar, or so it seemed. Back in England spring was in full flow, with buds bursting, birds singing and sap generally rising; here in Russia the trees were still bare, held in check by the lingering cold and longer nights of the higher latitude. The skies were clear, though, and the low sun warmed us as we rode along the good quality tarmac. The traffic thinned as we left the last straggling suburbs and now occasional Ladas buzzed past, their drivers managing to keep a straight line as they examined the rear-view mirror to confirm what they thought they had just overtaken.

I had come to Russia because it was a country surrounded by mystique and which had to a large extent, through the politics of the Cold War, shaped the world I grew up in. Despite its importance I knew very little about it, and any information I had picked up was generally concerned with Moscow and the goings on within the Kremlin. There must be so much more to a country this big – 60 times larger than the United Kingdom. More than just the politics, and more than the onion-domed churches and propaganda images of happy dancing locals celebrating the latest bumper harvest. To see the whole picture I would have to travel beyond Moscow and get out into the provincial towns and villages, meet people living their normal lives and spend time amongst them. For me, cycling was the best way to do this, travelling cleanly, cheaply and quietly through a country, arriving without making a disturbance or becoming the centre of attention.

Vladimir and George meet Greg and Kate at St. Petersburg airport, minus a suitcase.

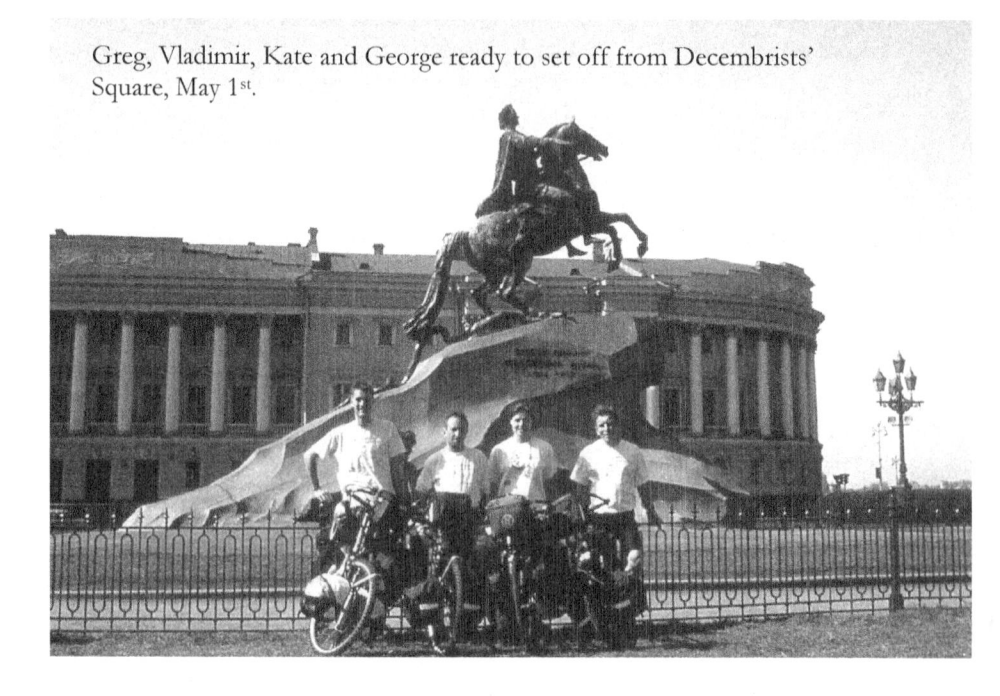

Greg, Vladimir, Kate and George ready to set off from Decembrists' Square, May 1st.

Ilya leading us through the streets of St. Petersburg.

Typical village outside St. Petersburg.

Day 6: Riding into Tvjer.

Day 2: Homecoming icon, Choodova.

Day 9: Crowds in Red Square, Moscow.

Cycling puts up no barriers between you and the people and places you visit, and gives you the real experience – the heat and cold, the dustiness and clarity of the air, the strong smells and pleasant scents, the loud noises and quiet rustlings, the exhaustion and the exhilaration. Plus, Russia is the biggest country in the world. Its size dominates the atlas and draws your attention. To cycle across it would be the ultimate achievement.

Right now we had ticked off the first 50 miles. It felt good to have got going – the cycling felt comfortable and we had suffered no mishaps. Now, as the day was drawing to a close, we had to sort out where we would sleep. Our stops were not carefully planned; each day we knew roughly where we were aiming for, and whether we would probably be camping or staying in a hotel, but the details would be sorted out day by day. For our first night we would be happy with somewhere reasonably comfortable to help us settle in, and as we approached the village of Ryabova the uncomplicated wooden houses with their small gardens given over to vegetables looked welcoming. George took the initiative and chose a house – there was nothing to distinguish it from its neighbours – and knocked on the door.

The owner, Sasha, was a small-framed, unshaven man of indeterminable age. With his lived-in woolly hat and heavy jacket he was well-protected against the cold of the evening. After a short conversation with George he opened the door wide and welcomed us in. This was his summer house – his *dacha*; in the winter he lived and worked in St. Petersburg, but weekends and the majority of the summer would be spent here rearing rabbits and growing vegetables that would be an important supplement to his winter diet. The house was just a simple wooden cabin with two main rooms and a kitchen. A single large metal stove provided all the heating and was incorporated into the wall so it was half in one room and half in the other. Cardboard insulation lined the walls and two very thickly insulated doors led to the outside. In the corner of the deep porch, a large pile of potatoes was stacked to dry.

George busied himself helping Sasha prepare dinner while I checked over the bikes, attaching mileometers to both George's and Vladimir's. Looking across Sasha's fence along the backs of the other houses, they were all similar but each had its own character, built not from a plan but from an idea in its owner's head. His immediate neighbour's house was particularly interesting. A large wooden framework had been built against one side; it may have been the early stages of an extension, but I could not be sure. Perhaps it was an elaborate display of *dacha* one-upmanship, a complicated woodpile constructed in the form of a proto-extension to fool your neighbours into thinking you were enjoying a period of unusual wealth, only to be burned later in the year. It seemed a lot of trouble to go to if it was just about keeping up with the Jonesoviches. But this was only my first day on the road. The niceties of Russian social relationships had yet to reveal themselves to me, so I had no context in which to place this possible manifestation of friendly village rivalry.

George announced dinner. The benefits of Luba's meals over the last few days seemed to have worn off already and a day in the saddle had given me a keen appetite. I am unsure what I was expecting – perhaps some sort of hearty country stew, delicately infused with herbs freshly cut by Sasha while still damp with the morning dew. Maybe one of his rabbits, nicely hung, accompanied by a medley of root vegetables, well-cooked but retaining a delicate and satisfying crunch. This proved nearer the mark – the root vegetable part, that is. I had forgotten about the large pile of tubers in the porch. Clearly they were a particular favourite of Sasha's, and tonight he would share his potato passion with his guests.

There is something about a meal, however simple, taken after a hard day's exercise, particularly when enjoyed in the rude surroundings of a simple wooden *dacha* with a host who clearly was very happy to welcome strangers and share what little he had with them. And so, tucking in eagerly to our plates of mashed potato and gherkins, we felt happy, after only one day on the road, that we were already experiencing the 'real' Russia in a way that 99.9% of other visitors never would.

The road to Moscow took us through two major towns: Novgorod and Torzjok. There is some disagreement over the date of Novgorod's founding. It is mentioned in Nordic sagas dating from the 7th Century but archaeological information and other records suggest that the town came into being in the 10th Century. There is no dispute over the fact that it was a former Viking settlement, and had quickly become an important city-state and major trading point along the route from Scandinavia to Byzantium. Looking around the kremlin ('*kreml*' means castle; it is only the Moscow Kremlin which is synonymous with government) confirmed this country's extremely rich and accomplished artistic history. Mediaeval churches and intricately ornate monuments, such as the extraordinarily detailed 19th Century bronze monument 'Millennium of Russia', displayed the skill of their creators and I wondered how a nation and empire that had grown so huge and ethnically varied could have apparently lost these creative skills.

Our arrival in Torzjok two days later at first seemed uneventful, but as the road led down to the bridge over the river Tvertsa the view across the old town centre spread out to reveal three fantastic Orthodox churches. The complex golden crosses, anchored to the blue domes by golden wires, glinted in the spring sunshine. There was also a ruined monastery in town, which we went to have a look around. The entry fee was three roubles each – about ¼p – so I hoped the restoration costs were being met from another, more lucrative, source of funding.

The outsides of these churches were always very plain, and I had expected quite austere interiors as well, particularly in more remote areas. I am not sure if anything could have prepared me for the concentration of colour, gold leaf and ornate design that is found inside all the Orthodox churches. Not a single square inch of wall is left uncovered by the iconography; the images extend onto the ceilings and are even cleverly painted onto the inside of the domes, making perfect allowance for the curve so that the finished painting appears undistorted. There are no pews, just a large space for the congregation to stand in. The result was a more crowded service, with people moving around, giving a slightly impromptu feel to the proceedings.

Throughout the expedition we saw plenty of churches, ranging in condition from pristine to ruined. Since 1991, religion had been enjoying a resurgence – Ilya had told us the priests were now being invited to preside at events such as the opening of a new swimming pool. In Choodova, on the way to Novgorod, we could hear amplified music drifting across town while we were having lunch. We tracked it down to a large, plain red-brick church. It looked somewhat neglected, but the crowds of people milling around suggested something important was happening. An old lady, hair respectfully covered with a colourful scarf, stood in front of the church, repeatedly crossing herself and quietly intoning scripture in a publicly private moment. The event was the restoration of an important icon to its original church. Clearly, despite the best efforts of the Communists over the previous 70 years, the importance and significance of religion to the people of Russia had not been reduced, and it was now being restored as a focal point in their lives.

We were able to look around, moving in and out of the church with the other people who were coming and going while the patriarch got on with the matter at hand. As I stood near the door it took a few moments to realise that people were talking to me. Unfortunately they were not trying to ask me who I was or where I was from. I had walked onto the red carpet stretching from the doorway and down the steps of the church – apparently a serious breach of etiquette – and was being quietly admonished for my *faux pas*.

The scene was dignified. Although we were to see plenty of support for the old regime, I felt here that people were confidently turning their backs on an unwelcome aspect of it and that the very thing that the Communists had tried, unsuccessfully, to ban had been a source of strength to help the people endure the privations of the last 70 years.

The birch and pine woodland we had been riding through for the first few days opened up, with views across the undulating landscape. All of a sudden, spring happened. One day the countryside was brown and grey, the next the buds were bursting. The vivid green of the fresh leaves contrasted sharply with the flaking white bark of the ubiquitous birch trees. Pink and purple lilac blossoms released their rich scent, which we breathed in deeply. This was Nature making up for lost time, and by the end of the first week the landscape had transformed itself.

Before setting off from home we had found few people to offer us positive advice about our trip. Generally, the response to the statement 'I'm going to cycle across Russia' was a pretty straightforward 'You're mad!' This would then be followed by any or all of the following: the country is falling apart; there's no food; it will be freezing cold; the mafia run everything; you can't speak the language; you'll die. Okay, the last one did not come up that often, but I got the feeling that was what people were building up to. Luckily we were able to deal with each of these objections through careful planning and preparation. There was one thing we could not really plan for, though. Something to which, even if we had managed to do a sensible amount of training (which sadly we had not; once the planning had started there had not been much spare time for cycling at home) we would not have been immune. A friend of mine eloquently summed up the problem shortly before our departure: 'You're going to need a huge tub of Vaseline for your arse.' It was a useful comment, well-meant if potentially a touch ambiguous. The unfortunate truth was that even a liberally applied daily application of a good dollop of petroleum jelly would probably not have saved me from the war of attrition being waged between the lumps and bumps of the road and the sensitive skin of my buttocks. Cleanliness was my best weapon, but it was not always possible to enjoy a decent wash at the end of each day, a situation that got worse as we went along (I'll describe later the fun to be had washing in the wilds while trying to repel a determined attack from the local wildlife).

Even after just the first few days, when we did have some half-decent showers available, the combination of long hours in the saddle, wearing the same shorts each day and a couple of camping nights meant that bottom-ache was setting in. Foolishly, I thought that it would simply be a case of becoming accustomed to the rigours of the trip, that after a period of 'settling in' my behind would no longer complain about the gentle but incessant pummelling. The longest I had ridden up till now had been a two-week trip through Europe – good facilities, no camping, reasonably long days – but I had not suffered anything beyond the usual soreness now and then; nothing different from my legs or shoulders feeling the strain. This time around it was different. My diary entry for the afternoon of Day 6 reads: *The road was okay, but the first hour was a real bum-killer: very uncomfortable.* Day 7 saw no improvement: *Bum ache is not getting any better - I had a very uncomfortable second hour or so. I wanted to stop but just had to grit my teeth and keep going to get the miles done.* The problem recurred for the next few months. There was no perfect way to sort it out. I could try to cycle while keeping my weight off the saddle a bit, which was awkward and tiring; on Day 49 I would resort to two pairs of cycle shorts with a tee-shirt folded between them. Nothing worked particularly well and bum ache, along with the poor food, general fatigue and mind-numbing Russian bureaucracy, became just another aspect of the trip that I had to endure.

The traffic started building up again as we got closer to Moscow. The road was wider, usually three lanes now, and cars raced along at what seemed a frightening speed given the variable road surface and the fact that so many of them had cracked or crazed windscreens. The lorries were huge and often looked like something out of Thunderbirds. Their cargo never seemed to be very securely loaded, and the potholes sometimes got the better of it, with iron bars and pipes bouncing off and crashing to the ground as the driver motored on, either oblivious or indifferent.

After seven days of riding we rolled into Moscow. We had covered 501 miles and were ready for a rest, but we spent a frustrating hour cycling through the monotonous suburbs looking for our destination, George's sister-in-law's flat. The roads did not seem to have any name signs and it was difficult to work out whether we were on a main road or a smaller one. Plain blocks of flats repeated into the distance. Eventually we arrived outside Luba's block and in a final burst of exercise lugged everything up to the fifth floor.

It was a relief to have completed our first week, not just because it meant we would have a rest (although as we quickly learned, our stops every two weeks or so were barely rests; they were just days when we were busy doing things other than cycling) but also because it was the end of the settling in period – of checking the equipment, establishing a workable pattern to the days, getting to know each other's cycling habits. George had assumed the role of expedition cook – in the evenings he just got on with it, assembling the slightly-dangerous-to-use petrol stove and preparing the food. We had camped a few times already in the peaceful, sylvan surroundings of a Russian wood in springtime, or on the banks of the swift and wide Volga, and stretching out on our sleeping mats with a restorative supper bubbling away seemed perfectly natural. The sight of George doing the cooking on the table in our hotel room did not seem quite right, but the hotels we had experienced so far fell somewhat short on the service side of things. Day 3's, near the town of Lubova, had no electricity, so we lit a fire on the verandah to cook. Day 5, in Torzjok – again no electricity, so we walked 15 minutes to a café. It was shut. We made our way back to the hotel, where, at 10.15pm, George began making the soup by candlelight. He would only be with us for another week, so we would have to start paying attention to his recipes and camp cooking methods.

The other disadvantage with the fact that George would be leaving was that Vladimir spoke no English. Fair enough, we were in Russia and it would be polite to assume that Kate and I would make an effort with the language, but having English-speaking Russian cyclists would also be a big help. After Ryazan it would be just me, Kate and Vladimir for five weeks, and while the challenge of communicating would be fun to tackle it would also be very difficult. I had brought a dictionary with me, but the way the Russian language works means you cannot simply look up the words you want and string them together to form a sentence. Conversations would be painfully slow but gradually the furrowed brows and frustrated gesticulations were replaced by a look of mutual understanding and it would all end in smiles as we each realised what the other had been going on about. (Kate, of course, was Australian, but we managed to work around that one, as well.)

Luba's flat was in Moscow's northern suburbs. The view from the balcony was depressingly similar to the view from Ilya's balcony in St. Petersburg, and would be repeated in each of the cities we visited as we cycled a third of the way around the world through one huge country. The blocks of flats were arranged in squares, with what might have been be an attractive garden area in the centre. Instead, it was generally a worn out patch of mud and grass with a bit of basic play equipment for the children, some washing lines, maybe a small fire or two on the ground and some sort of smouldering incinerator which the residents could chuck their rubbish in. The whole scene had an almost post-apocalyptic feel.

Luba lived here with her son, and seemed to have at least three jobs, the main one being in the post office. With two bedrooms and a reasonably large living room the flat was a decent size and fairly typical. They were lucky, though – these flats often had to accommodate more than just two people from two generations. Extra space was often gained by turning the balcony into a room or storage area of sorts by cobbling together makeshift walls.

For our first meal in the capital, Luba produced a daunting quantity of food. Reports of our possible starvation definitely had been exaggerated. The table struggled with vegetable and meat soup; beetroot, garlic and mayonnaise; cucumbers, spring onion and yoghurt; chicken, mashed potato and a preserved vegetable ratatouille-style dish; tea with home-preserved cherries, and biscuits. It was the biggest meal I had eaten all year, and I could not move. Vladimir had left us as we arrived in the city to make his way to a friend's flat – I hoped he was being looked after this well. It would certainly recharge his batteries.

Vladimir's performance had, even in the first week, become something Kate and I spent a lot of time talking about. Not necessarily because of the effect it was having on our progress at the moment, but more importantly because of how it might affect us once George left us at Ryazan.

Day 5: Wednesday May 5th
Vlad. did his odd cycling the hour after lunch. He was a long way behind, and not catching, so we slowed and waited. He caught up and promptly set off at about 17mph, faster than he had been going before when he wasn't catching up. He kept this up for a while, pushing along, and then on the next decent hill ended up as far behind as before! It's a daft way to cycle when covering long distances.

Day 7: Friday May 7th
Vlad. was fifteen minutes behind. We reckon we are losing about an hour each day to him. ... [He] is staying somewhere else, so we parted company just after getting to town. I don't know what he and George were talking about, but it might be that he misses out the next bit and goes straight to Ryazan. Even then, there will be another five weeks until Novosibirsk, so I don't know what he will do. Kate and I don't want to slow down.

We would have to see. There would be plenty of time to sort out any problems once we were back on the road. For now, we were looking forward to exploring Moscow, and we had chosen a very good weekend for it.

Day 9: Sunday May 9th – day off, Moscow
Today is a national day of celebration, marking the end of the 2nd World War. We heard on the radio that the Communists are planning more demos in the town centre, and that they will fight if the police try to stop them. Last weekend (May 1st) 150 were injured in clashes in Red Square. We are going there in a minute!
Went to the local shops. The exchange rate today was $1 = R880. There was lots on offer, in the market and in the shops. You have to pay first, and then present the receipt to obtain your goods. In the market, there were bananas (about £1.10 for a bunch of eight), grapes, oranges, herbs, meat, but all more expensive than in the shops (about the same as UK prices). Kiosks are everywhere (and in St. Petersburg) with cans of drink, alcohol, cigarettes, chocolate, small articles of clothing.
There is broken glass everywhere, and trampled mud. It must be a real mess in the rain or when the snow melts. Have to forget prejudices about people not smartly dressed, as the vast majority are fairly drably/functionally dressed. Saw quite a few tee-shirts with western writing.

Survived Red Square. There were lots of police around, including vans of riot squad waiting. A line of army trucks left just as we arrived. People with Communist flags were singing old songs (not always sure of the words, it seemed), and there were also monarchists and fascists. Animated discussions about politics were going on, but there was no violence. St. Basil's is amazing. Even knowing what it looks like I was stunned when I came around the corner and saw it for the first time - more dramatic as it was uphill from where we were standing. Roamed around Moscow centre, which was pleasant as many of the roads were blocked off to traffic. Sent some letters home. Heard on the evening news that there were 10,000 people in Red Square all demonstrating against Yeltsin. They must have all arrived some time after we left. Went out to see the fireworks at 10.00pm. Easily the loudest I've ever heard, fired from two launchers on the back of a couple of lorries. Huge smoke rings. Very impressive. It all proved too much for one dog, which went running off at great speed into a car. From where we were standing we could see at least four displays.
More food when we came back - I haven't eaten so much for months. Serious liver ache. I've nearly managed to catch up on about a month's sleep, but we're back on the bikes tomorrow, so it will be another early start.

Refreshed and refuelled, and replete with another large breakfast of spaghetti, meat balls, cucumber salad and cherries, we set off to rendezvous with Vladimir. After an hour and a quarter, we finally arrived at the meeting point, 50 minutes late. Luckily, Vladimir was 55 minutes late. He looked well rested and was full of energy as he cycled at the front of the group out of the city. The road was smooth, we had a slight tail-wind and there were few clouds – we looked set for a good day's riding. It was another public holiday, and the countryside was busy with people working on their *dachas*. Potato planting seemed to be the theme for the day.

During the planning stages Kate and I had differed slightly on what the emphasis of the trip should be. To me it seemed that we had so much to do in a limited time that we should concentrate on making as much progress eastwards as quickly as we could, especially in the first half of the expedition as we knew the roads would deteriorate into trackless swamp later on. The main factor, though, was the weather. Having worked out roughly how many miles the trip would cover, and knowing more or less what we could manage each day, we had to match that with the availability of decent cycling conditions. Essentially this meant that we had to allow all of spring, summer and autumn for the journey and make sure that we cycled as far and as fast as possible in the early stages so that if we encountered any serious problems later on we would still have enough time to deal with them and get to Vladivostok before the onset of the Siberian winter. This meant we were putting ourselves under considerable physical and mental pressure to keep going even when what we might really have preferred was some time off. So, my approach was to keep heading east as directly as possible. Kate understood this need to keep to the timetable, but she was also keen to make the most of what would undoubtedly be a once-in-a-lifetime journey, and there were a few sightseeing diversions that she wanted to include along the way.

Leaving Moscow now, Kate wanted to add a diversion to include the town of Suzdal – part of the famous Golden Ring, a route to the north-east of Moscow that passes through some of the country's oldest and most beautiful cities. We had already changed the timetable slightly by delaying our arrival in Ryazan (our next target) by a couple of days to make sure that we met Misha Malakhov, our Russian expedition coordinator, so I was keen not to take any more time at this stage. Adding a day or two here and there might not seem significant, but over the whole period of the expedition it could delay our arrival date in Vladivostok by a couple of weeks or more. That could see us still on our bikes at the end of October, with the mercury falling and winter's first flurries of snow blowing around us. In any event, at this stage we were only one week in; to start fiddling with the timetable this early, when cycling conditions were good and we could make decent progress, felt unnecessary. The Suzdal diversion seemed achievable, though, and as it turned out the tail wind improved during the day; that, combined with Luba's breakfast, meant that we covered the whole 122 miles from Moscow to the town of Vladimir in one go, arriving a day early.

We rode in at about 8pm, tracked down the hotel and checked in for the grand total of 4,500 roubles, or about £3.50.

Day 10: Monday May 10*th* – Moscow to Vladimir
122.8 miles (total 624.0 miles)

Again seemingly huge discussions to secure the rooms. A simple 'Do you have two rooms for one night, please?' 'Yes, I do.' 'Thanks, I'll take

them' would seem adequate. I'd love to know what they talk about. The hotel is okay; the room is bright, but the bathroom is dingy. Couple of cockroaches scurrying about. I really wanted a banya [sauna] after such a long day (I think 122 miles is the longest I've ever done). We got directions from someone and tracked down an unlikely-looking building - indeed, we found that it was already shut. It had, in fact, shut two years previously. So, showers back at the hotel - cold, though. Hot water is provided centrally from the electricity stations, and in May they take the opportunity to clean their pipes, therefore there is no hot water.
I really wanted a good dinner. We'd eaten loads at Luba's, which undoubtedly helped us to make the distance today, but we do need to keep eating. We went to the hotel's restaurant, but apparently arrived too late. Despite admirably persistent attempts by George to get us in, we gave up. I wouldn't really have minded if it had been a grotty stolo, but we could see people eating decent food. It smelled appetising, too. There was a band playing. A more bored collection of musicians I have never seen, and the music was crap. All electronic keyboards just going on and on, with one of them playing an awful solo every now and then. They wouldn't even be given a spot on the QE II. We tried the buffet in the hotel next door, but it was expensive and we didn't like the look of the stuff on offer. So, soup, bread, sausage and rice pudding in the room cooked on the primus. Not bad, really. As George said, "Problems will make us strong."

Our day trip to Suzdal proved to be an interesting and relaxed interlude. Vladimir stayed behind, so George, Kate and I headed off after breakfast, enjoying the feeling of not having any pressure to cover a long distance. The pine, birch and willow forest had been cleared for fields, and the views across the rolling countryside were more the sort of thing I was used to at home. Suzdal itself was unusual in that it seemed to be looked after – the verges were not trampled and worn, the tree trunks were whitewashed, and the streets were being sprayed to keep down the dust. What made it more remarkable, though, was the amazing concentration of churches, big and small. From our vantage point above the river we looked out across the town. The churches poking up as the tallest buildings; the earth rampart around this part of town; the Kamenska river, with its flood plain below ramparts with some small-scale cultivation; the many-legged wooden footbridge over the river; the wooden huts on stilts on the river bank. All these gave a very mediaeval impression to the place – unsurprising, really, since the town dated from 1024, and it did seem that things had not moved on a whole lot since then. It was a very relaxing place to spend the afternoon. As we wandered among the monasteries and churches the sound of bells started to ring out from one of the towers. Looking around we spotted the bell-ringer, and I was surprised to see that the sound we could hear was produced by just one person. The bell tower was quite open, revealing a line of bells each larger than the next as if they had been taken from a nesting set modelled on *matryoshka* dolls and each connected to the resident campanologist by a single string so that he had four in each hand. Somehow he managed to isolate the intended bell, and produced an almost mesmerising display of bell-ringing that rose in complexity from an initial single tolling to a complicated and intricate tune before diminishing again. It was an impressive physical and mental feat, and added another layer of beauty to our experience of the richly decorated Orthodox churches.

After nearly two weeks in the saddle, George was clearly very keen to finish his stint. He was up at 6am and got the porridge on for his last day of cycling that would get him back to his home town of Ryazan. For once we managed a reasonably early start, leaving at 8.15. As always, when we were heading for a place where we would stop for a day or two, we fooled ourselves by saying, 'Oh, it's only a quick 50 miles or so – shouldn't be too bad.' It turned out to be 63 miles along a poor quality tarmac road with a long afternoon slog into a raging headwind. The sticky tar only made things worse and the only way to find a decent strip to ride on was to hog the middle of the three or four lanes – as there were no lines we were not entirely sure – but the cars coped, passing on either side of us.

By a lucky coincidence, when Kate was getting her plans together in London she had found a key contact in Robert Swan, the polar explorer and motivational supremo. We worked closely with Robert throughout the planning stages, and he was able to put us in touch with his Russian expedition partner and Hero of the Soviet Union, Misha Malakhov, who was busy running commercial expeditions to the North Pole. Misha's company, Centre Pole, was based in Ryazan, some 125 miles south-east of Moscow, and would become our HQ during the expedition, holding our spare equipment and acting as a communications hub. The arrangement worked very well, although the distance involved did pose a problem later in the expedition when it had become equivalent to cycling in Europe and having our HQ in

New York. Centre Pole also provided three of the local cyclists who would ride with us: along with George there were Eugene, who would join us in the Sayan mountains in July, and Sasha, who would be our companion from the half-way point of Krasnoyarsk to the end.

From the Centre Pole office a 50-seater coach took Kate and me to Sasha's flat, while Vladimir went with George, who had a spring in his step despite the ride. Luckily we had not needed George's professional skills – he was an orthopaedic surgeon – but we had enjoyed his cooking skills and companionship which had helped us settle in during the first two weeks. When we met up with Sasha again, having met him only briefly in St. Petersburg, it was clear that we would have a very different character in the group, someone operating at a different pace and volume compared with Vladimir and George. He would not be joining us for another couple of months, though (which seemed a strange thought in itself, that in two months' time we would be doing the same thing, in the same country), so for now I would concentrate on relaxing and checking equipment for the next stage.

Sasha's parents, Misha and Iraida, lived in one of the older blocks of flats found in most cities, with better rooms and slightly more space than the newer, pre-fabricated ones like Ilya's in St. Petersburg. They were better looking from the outside, and as they were in the older parts of town the trees had grown up and with the blocks helped give these areas a more appealing character. In the early evening, with swifts screaming overhead, Sasha took us onto the roof of the town's tallest building and it was surprising how green the view across the rooftops was, with lime trees softening the urban landscape. An avenue of chestnut trees stood out; it had been planted by a visiting deputation from Italy shortly after World War Two to honour a local man who had saved many children while fighting for the Italian partisans.

Until recently, Ryazan, with its three military academies, had been a closed town, with tight restrictions in place on the movements of both locals and foreigners. This was a situation repeated across the USSR, but things had changed rapidly since the Soviet empire collapsed in 1991, and as well as resulting in improvements for Russians it also made life much easier for Kate and me. In the past, securing a visa to visit the Soviet Union had meant submitting a detailed itinerary listing where you would be staying and when, an invitation to visit the country was needed, and once within the heavily controlled borders it was necessary to register at the local police station. Suddenly that had all changed (except for the invitation requirement, but had been easy to get through Ilya's cycling contacts), which was a huge relief. It would have been impossible to state where we would be every day over a five-month period, and given the scale of what we were doing and the areas we would have to pass through, such as the strategically sensitive far east of Siberia, we would no doubt have had be assigned an official escort of some sort, which would have changed the whole character of the expedition. As it was, we were able to apply for a straightforward visa that allowed us to visit the whole country with no restrictions. The Russian world was our sturgeon, you might say.

For now, we were in Ryazan enjoying not only the freedom to roam but also an abundance that we had not anticipated. Misha Malakhov had just returned from the North Pole with his group of paying clients, and we were being treated to a sumptuous and waistline-enlarging dinner washed down with Pepsi, champagne, brandy, beer and vodka. Too much of this kind of diversion and our eastward progress would come to an abrupt halt.

We spent three days in the city, relaxing with Sasha's family and the North Pole group, and working on preparations for the next stage. A trip out to a local lake was a good opportunity to chat to the polar adventurers. They were an international mix; for some this was just the latest in a string of adventures, for others it had been a one-off impulse. Among the group was Miloslav, who had previously lost most of his toes to frostbite in the Andes and who took a vacuum cleaner to the Pole to satisfy his sponsors. (Fortunately we had not been supported on our expedition by any manufacturers of large and unwieldy household appliances; heaving a chest-freezer across the swamps would have proved logistically awkward, although it might have allowed us a more varied diet as we could have stocked it with favourites from home. Thinking about it, I might have chosen a washing machine and tumble dryer combination over a freezer – I almost got used to Russian food, but turning up on strangers' doorsteps in the same pair of cycling shorts that I had been wearing, without underpants, for the past four months probably cost us a few offers of accommodation.)

Along with Miloslav there was Ivan the Mexican (actually half-Russian), getting in some preparation for his planned first all-Mexican assault on the Pole; Richard, a Brit based in Hong Kong, and Anthony, based in Tokyo where he ran an outward-bound management training school called 'I Will Not Complain International', which sounded like a good approach for us to adopt. Ken (Japan), Gerry (USA) and Nobu (China) completed the party.

Some went swimming in the lake – a sensible way to avoid the mosquitoes, which were now out in force every day – while the rest of us relaxed around the barbecue listening to Miloslav on the guitar (the polar credentials of which remained unconfirmed, and for the playing of which he still enjoyed a full complement of fingers). It was a fine example of the unself-conscious and unbothered way in which Russians and in fact all Eastern Europeans are able to entertain themselves in the outdoors and feel completely at ease with their natural surroundings. In Britain, it would be almost impossible to find people behaving like this – unless of course they were in a designated area bristling with signs and instructions, mostly describing the things they are not allowed to do. To step outside the boundary and take your own initiative would risk having some goon in a fluorescent waistcoat come down on you like a ton of bricks. What a contrast with Russia, a land of totalitarian control, where people can swim, light fires, gather in small groups to sing and drink, or roam through the forests gathering berries and mushrooms, without first asking permission or having someone provide guidelines, and without attracting the interfering attention of an over-enthusiastic official.

Back in town we finally managed to sort all our gear into separate piles and pack it into bags that would be brought out to Novosibirsk and Krasnoyarsk by the riders from Centre Pole. I also dumped some clothes that I had not used, to make space for food. There would only be three of us for the majority of the expedition now, so one less set of panniers to hold all our equipment.

Misha spoke to Vladimir about the time ahead. For the next five weeks there would be just Kate, Vladimir and me, and Misha stressed to Vladimir that the purpose of the expedition was for Kate and me to reach Vladivostok by a certain time. Vladimir knew that he could not cycle as quickly as we could, and that over five weeks losing an hour or more each day could have a significant effect on our timetable. Misha said that it was not important for Vladimir to cover every mile by bike and he could hitch a ride if necessary; that his main role was to help us by interpreting and sorting out some logistics. It was almost impossible for Kate and me to discuss all this with Vladimir, pointing to words one at a time in the dictionary, although clearly it would have been better if we could. We did not want him to think we had been complaining about him behind his back and had got Misha to do our dirty work for us. Fortunately Vladimir took it all in good spirit and seemed a bit relieved – I think he was genuinely finding the pace of the trip quite tough. We were relieved, as well. We had been concerned about Vladimir's cycling for a while, and had worried what would happen once George left the group. With no-one he could easily chat to about the cycling, where we were going next, how long the day would be and how he, and we, were feeling about it all, we worried that Vladimir might lose interest and become an unwilling participant. Once he and Misha had had a chat the pressure was off him to keep up with us all the time and we could all relax. How it would work in practice, though, we could only find out over the next 2,400 miles to Novosibirsk.

I had been feeling homesick over the last few days. It seemed to be worse when we were not cycling, when there was more time in the day to dwell on things – which seemed odd, as there was plenty of time available for thinking when I was on my bike. I think I just cycled along enjoying the view and trying to ignore my aching legs and bum. Once we stopped somewhere for a couple of days and had more time on our hands, my mind would start wandering back to people at home, which made me feel a bit low. I had only been away two and a half weeks, but it felt a lot longer. It was still less time than most of my summer holidays. It must have been the daunting prospect of the trip – the whole experience of Russia – stretching well into the distance that was having such a strong effect.

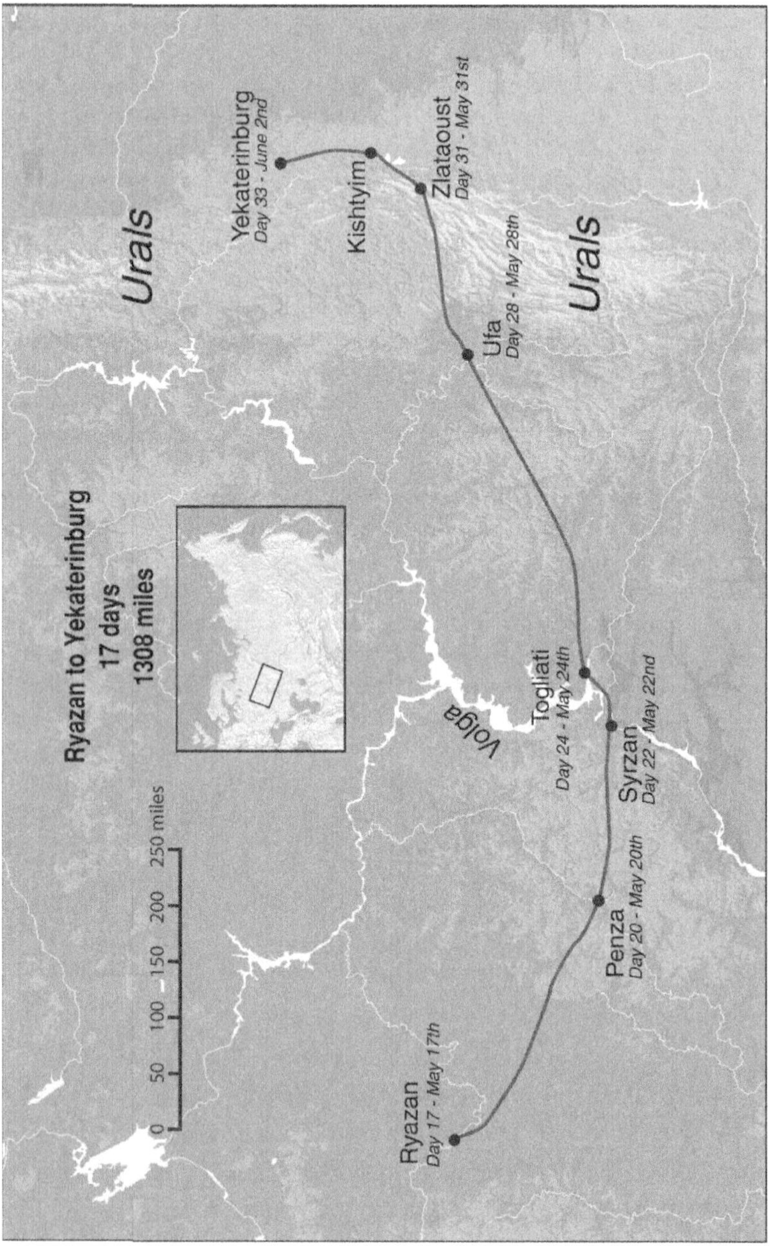
Ryazan to Yekaterinburg
17 days
1308 miles
0 50 100 150 200 250 miles
Urals
Yekaterinburg
Day 33 - June 2nd
Kishtyim
Zlataoust
Day 31 - May 31st
Day 28 - May 28th
Ufa
Urals
Togliati
Day 24 - May 24th
Volga
Syrzan
Day 22 - May 22nd
Penza
Day 20 - May 20th
Ryazan
Day 17 - May 17th

SECTION 2

~~~

RYAZAN TO THE URALS

~~~

Our next target was the Urals, the boundary between European Russia and Siberia. They lay 1,300 miles over the horizon but would be the first major physical barrier we would have to cross, so there was much discussion about what they might, or might not, be like. As before, this served no other purpose than to pass the time. We had to cross the mountains, and did not have enough time to come up with large-scale detours, so we would just have to deal with them whatever they were like. In the meantime we had 1,300 miles to cover.

Day 17: Monday May 17th – Ryazan to Ryazsk
74.8 miles (total 906.2 miles)
Went to Centre Pole's office for an interview with the local TV, which was going well until the bloke said, "Just one more question. What do you think about religion?" Fortunately it was directed at Kate, who parried it okay. But then the bloke went on, "If you are in trouble, do you ask God for help?" What?! 'Please, God, send some more puncture repair patches,' or 'Send me a sign - a road sign.' Misha will try to get us a tape of when we are on.
Rode off out of Ryazan okay - the morning and early afternoon were sunny, with a slight tailwind. The landscape was very open and agricultural. Rolling hills. We had lunch next to a small lake,

accompanied by goats and lots of noisy frogs. In the afternoon there was a big thunderstorm, but fortunately just ahead of us. Very windy - lots of large twigs on the road. Stopping to get petrol, we discovered the worst cock-up so far - we had actually been on the wrong road since Ryazan (I had thought it was a bit small and quiet!) There was nobody in particular we could blame. We decided to stop where we were (Ryazsk) as it was 7.30, and set off early tomorrow to get to the correct road. Fortunately it was not too far, although we lied to Vlad and told him we were going to do a bit less than we actually want to. Found the hotel okay (R1640) and cooked in the room.

Day 18: Tuesday May 18th – Ryazsk to Shatsk
91.0 miles (total 997.4 miles)

Managed to start by 8.00am! Things were okay until lunch, except for some extra distance not shown on the map. Also, Kate's map has a road we wanted to take (shorter than going straight back up to the main road) which isn't on Vlad's (Russian) map. I reckon it's because there was something very like a nuclear reactor nearby. We had lunch in the stolo at Seraie. Okay soup (bit oily) with meat in, risotto, sok (juice). Tried some 'kvas' (bread water). Not very nice.

The afternoon was awful - two hours on the road from hell, with a monstrous crosswind. We decided to go straight back to the main road because of the weather, and the road was on both maps. The surface was really bumpy and broken, with piles of gravel in the middle of the road for future repairs. We just had to get on with it - had to concentrate. The last hour or so was okay, and we stopped at Shatsk in a very cheap hotel, but only about 120 miles from Ryazan. We should have been here early in the morning if we had gone the right way.

No electricity in the room; stinking loos again; only cold water and a basin to wash in; drunken blokes - pretty standard.

After our wiggle through Vladimir and Suzdal, our route was now following a reasonably straight line eastwards. The quietness of the countryside, with no aeroplane noise and only the rare intrusion of music, enhanced the scale of our surroundings. Lilac blooms were everywhere, and their scent floated to us on the breeze. For the local people, this sudden profusion of sweet greenery after the long, dark, cold winter was obviously a welcome change, and we often saw them with clumps of blossoms in their hands. On one occasion, a lorry rumbled past with its cab full of lilac flowers, and as he came by us the driver called out and threw us a bunch.

The only wildlife we had seen so far was birds. In the more open areas, harriers hunted low over the fields and meadows. They travelled at the same speed as we did so we could get a good look at them. Holding their wings in a characteristic V-shape, the agile birds glided along, their sharp eyes scanning for small mammals and their yellow talons ready to close around their next meal. We still had a while to go before reaching the truly wild landscapes of Siberia and the taiga – the coniferous forest that defines the wildernesses of Russia, northern Europe and Canada, and home to all manner of large beasts that might find a curious-looking cyclist too interesting to ignore. For now, I was satisfied seeing the harriers as they quartered their territory on the lookout for lunch.

The miles rolled past under our wheels. Day 17 – 74.8 miles; day 18 – 91 miles; day 19 – 115.3 miles; day 20 – 66.3 miles. On the way to Nijzny Lomov, we stopped at the roadside for a picnic lunch. For some reason, it was not possible to say simply 'Shall we stop for a bit?' 'Okay. Here?' 'Why not.' There was always a short discussion about just where we should stop, and given that we were usually in the countryside, where one stretch of road was much like the next, I often wondered if this was motivated by the need for Kate and me to have a bit of a chat more than really trying to establish the relative merits of one potential rest spot over another. Given that we would not know which spot was best anyway, since we would only stop at one, it did seem rather pointless. Occasionally a bus shelter might loom into view, or a mile-post of some sort, and these would become obvious targets, satisfying some primitive need to reach a defined point rather than just a space.

On the day in question, the object we had spotted by the roadside as our reason for stopping in one hundred yards' time rather than right here turned out to be a small memorial to the victim of a car crash. We had seen a number of these so far; as we moved into the quieter eastern reaches of the country they would become less frequent. Generally, they were made to a plain design with a photo and a few words. Sometime there would be a steering wheel attached, to make sure passers-by got the message. Kate and I had arrived ahead of Vladimir and were just getting organised when he rolled up. Seeing where we had chosen to stop he gestured that we should move a short distance further along the verge.

Again it was frustrating not being able to communicate easily with Vladimir about things like this, but it was clear he had a sensitive side. During a quiet moment in the hotel in Vladimir, he had taken out his wallet and proudly shown me the small black and white photo of his mother that he kept there; she had died ten years earlier, and he was clearly still very attached to her. His father had died in Leningrad during World War Two, when Vladimir was only eight months old, and there had been no brothers or sisters to dilute his mother's affections. His behaviour on other occasions showed he was a gentle, considerate chap – has was always careful to clean up the hotel room after we had cooked in it, and he did not want to leave the key at an unattended desk when we checked out. From a practical point of view, he was indispensable when it came to changing money. An all-round good egg. If only he could cycle a bit faster!

People would always come and chat to us. Sometimes the attention was not particularly welcome; sometimes the conversation turned out to be extremely productive. Once we had settled in at the hotel in Nijzny Lomov (having negotiated the typically cavernous and dimly-lit lobby and presented ourselves to the terminally-bored-looking ladies behind the desk, who were struggling to tear themselves away from the trashy American soap opera on the television) we were befriended by Mikhail who bought us a beer and invited us to the sauna. It was late, so we declined (which meant another wash with cold water in the sink), but then he turned up at the room with a bottle of vodka and a strong urge to talk about life, particularly with Kate. We both really wanted to go to sleep and eventually persuaded Mikhail to leave. Another encounter with a drunk Russian – generally harmless, and I could understand their curiosity about us, but faced with the prospect of having to consume a bottle of questionable quality vodka, it was always better to resist their advances.

Vladimir had had more success. Earlier the same day we had stopped at a petrol station to fill up on fuel for our stove and he had fallen into conversation with a man on the forecourt. We would be reaching the city of Penza the next day; this man happened to know a cyclist who lived there, and he gave Vladimir his phone number.

After a very windy day's riding we pulled in to Penza in the mid-afternoon, and rang the number hoping to find somewhere to stay the night. Nikolai answered, and was apparently more than happy to have three unknown cyclists and all their dirty kit descend on his flat at absolutely no notice. This was just the latest example of the unconditional hospitality that was extended to us, and which for Kate and me would become the real highlight of our expedition. It was also a great example of Russian friendliness and friendships – while we were at Nikolai's, his friend Helena joined us to interpret, and two Eugenes came round to meet us and took us for a tour of the town. Again, people were probably curious to meet us, but the feeling I had was that in England there would be a whole lot more inertia towards the whole thing, with people happily staying at home on the sofa rather than getting out for an impromptu evening with strangers.

Before leaving England, Kate had sent a letter to the Orion cycling club in Russia describing our plans and inviting Russian cyclists to join us (which is how we found Vladimir and, later, Yuri). The club had published the letter in its magazine and Nikolai happened to see it, so he already knew something of what we were up to. He was a keen cyclist and had recently accompanied two Belgians across the Karakom Desert in Kazakhstan; last year he and his friend had cycled around the Black Sea.

Helena's English was very good, and she gave private lessons, but at 1000 roubles an hour (90 pence) she was not making a living from it. Despite her high standard, we still had a few problems. I was trying to explain where I was from, but for some reason the simple phrase 'near Windsor' was getting hopelessly lost in translation. Attempts to tell Helena about the Queen and Windsor castle just drew blank looks, so eventually I looked up 'castle' in the dictionary. At last, the kopek dropped: '*Ah, Windsorski zamok!*' Easy, really.

Penza was founded in about 1660 and stands in the green and hilly landscape beside the Sura river. Heroic monuments decorate the city: Marx (Russia's first statue of him), proletariat revolutionaries, the city's founder. The local population are Tartars and Muslim. The nearby Republic of Tartarstan was originally established in 1920 but cleverly managed to avoid including the majority of Tartars within its borders. The mosque in Penza had recently been re-opened and as elsewhere in the country religions of all sorts were re-establishing themselves.

After spending a sociable evening discussing past and future cycling journeys, we set out the next morning escorted by Nikolai and Valery, another of his cycling buddies. We had not gone far when a passing car flagged us down. The driver, Victor (one of Nikolai's friends, obviously) was a reporter in the newly set up television news department of Penza TV and Radio State Company. There followed another interview on camera, fortunately this time without any questions about our religious leanings. The director called 'Cut!' and we were on our way. The wind had become stronger overnight and the hills were steeper but not very long, and in the afternoon the road turned south-east moving the wind onto our backs for a few hours. Setting up camp near Kushnetsk to the accompaniment of the large local frog population, I became aware that my belly was not quite feeling as it should. Nothing to get concerned about, I hoped. It was more a case of becoming aware of my belly, rather than of anything specific that might have been happening within it. There may have been the occasional over-active gurgle, but it was lost among the general cacophony of amorous amphibian croaking. Nonetheless, the combined pressures of consuming large quantities of stodgy and pickled food, drinking questionable well water and forcing my body to cycle an average of about 80 miles each day may well have been starting to have an effect. Unfortunately there was no opportunity to change the regime.

The weather was not helping. Until Penza, temperatures had been comfortable and rainfall uncommon. Suddenly things changed. I did have my tee shirt on when I rode out of the campsite the next morning, but I was also wearing my long sleeved top, cycling jacket and a fleece, with winter gloves on. Flurries of icy snow blew around us and dark rain clouds scudded along low in the sky. I did not warm up all day, a situation not helped by our typically poor lunch of lukewarm spaghetti in a local *stolovaya* (workers' caff). The weather remained wet and windy until the end of May.

We were not using a very detailed map. We had one which covered the entire country on one page, and some US Air Force charts for the more remote areas later on. The one-country-to-a-page one was admittedly printed on a fairly large sheet of paper, but it did not have much on it beyond the main roads. It seemed to take a long time to be making our way across it, and turning over a fold marked major progress. In a land where it is possible to travel from Europe to the Pacific without any change in language, currency, building design or basic personal demeanour, it was easy to spend all our time moving but with no obvious indications of progress. Turning a fold on the map to move onto the next section was therefore a major event, confirming that we were indeed heading in the right direction.

Crossing into a new time zone served a similar purpose, although the arrival of a new one usually took us by surprise since the boundary marked on the map rarely matched the actual reality on the ground. From St. Petersburg to Vladivostok we would ease our watches forward a total of six hours (finishing in the same time zone as Adelaide in Australia), and two days out of Penza we completed our first bit of time travel. I did not feel any different; it just meant we effectively set off an hour late the next morning.

Following the Volga, we had thought our route here would be reasonably flat, but the road was much higher than the river and included plenty of ups and downs. A roadside market looked like a good place to stop for lunch; there was plenty of fish from the river for sale, smoked and dried, along with small jars of caviar (5000 roubles, about £4.50), soft drinks, Snickers bars, dried fruit and apples. After a two-and-a-half hour stint in the afternoon, we enjoyed a long descent into the town of Togliati, crossing the huge river via a hydro-electric barrage. The water was surging through the turbines in an impressive display of noise and power.

The town centre was still quite a long ride further on, and when we reached it all the hotels were very expensive and seemed unwilling to take us (the Hotel Volga did not accept English guests, but it did have a bureau de change – happy to take their money but not to let the nasty foreign devils stay there). So we returned to the edge of town where we found a new hotel among the more-of-the-same blocks of flats and unfinished roads that made it indistinguishable from Moscow, St. Petersburg, Penza … Not only was the hotel fairly cheap (at 7200 roubles for two nights, or £8) but there was hot water (joy of joys), electricity and a toilet clean enough to make you happy to sit on it. It was a rare combination and something of a hospitality triumph. I immediately decided that I like Togliati.

We took a rest day here and actually managed to relax. We were not staying with anyone, and although meeting Russians in their homes was always a pleasure it made a welcome change just to have some time to ourselves, and for once there were not too many chores to sort out. After a decent lunch of chicken and potatoes, radish salad and cranberry juice we lounged around in the public park, watching children play on the small funfair equipment of a Ferris wheel, roundabout and slides. Also watching them were the usual old ladies in headscarves and dull clothes. Actually, what they were doing was more 'keeping an eye on' than simply watching. These ladies were the 'keepers of the small-scale play equipment', in the same way there would be the 'keeper of the hotel corridor' or the 'keeper of the area in front of the block of flats'. Some were more overt than others, and although their roles had reduced recently since the fall of Communism, where they did crop up they would be quite formidable and it was a sensible person who encouraged their favour. (One that we would do well to introduce at home was the 'keeper of the doorway out of the baggage reclaim area', who would make sure that the tag on the suitcases you were trying to remove from the airport actually matched the tag on your ticket.) Fortunately, on this occasion the Ferris wheel was something we could never hope to have the pleasure of, given its diminutive size, so we left its guardian unexercised. Frankly, I think they should have been more concerned about the possible collapse of the equipment rather than who may or may not have been using it. Whenever we saw this sort of funfair it always seemed rather run down.

We were now three and a half weeks into the expedition, and the reality of it all was really sinking in. The novelty of being in a very different country, one which no-one I knew had ever visited, was wearing off fast. What replaced it was not a simple dread of the scale of what we had taken on and what we now knew to be the conditions under which we would have to carry it out. It was more complicated than that, and my feelings about where I was and what I was doing varied from day to day. Sore neck, shoulder and backside; being wrenched from sleep at 6.30 every morning; initial rumblings of revolt from my body; pedalling seven hours a day – no wonder I was having occasional negative patches.

Day 24: Monday May 24th – day off, Togliati
I had a couple of crises yesterday morning, ie 'Why am I here?!' and 'I'm never going to do anything like this again!' If I were on my own I would definitely grind to a halt in places, but being in a group keeps me going - a varying mix of will-power and muscle-power is needed. A sore bum doesn't help as it makes it difficult to relax properly, so my legs support my weight a bit as well as pushing the pedals round. I just have to tell myself that I'm here because I chose to be - at least Kate is having the same thoughts!

Generally these feelings did not last too long – definitely a benefit of travelling with other people, even if I could not talk to one of them very easily. When I was feeling fine, which I was a lot of the time, things could not be better. Here I was, travelling through Russia! Biggest country in the world, international bogeyman and all-round place of mystery. And I was seeing all of it, independently, not as part of some carefully choreographed escorted tour. Not only that; I was doing it by bike. How many people could make that boast? Actually not very many at all; we were the first cyclists to ride across post-Communist Russia, and as far as I knew I was the first British person to cycle across the Russian Federation (ie not straying across into any of the former Soviet satellites). So things were not all bad. We were, after all, here for five months, and it would be unusual for my mood to remain unchanged over that length of time whether I was struggling through trackless swamp or leading a regular nine-to-five life back at home.

Togliati had been such a welcome break, even if only for one day, that I decided to buy a pack of postcards as a keepsake. Postcards are a wonderful invention, a simple way to send a quick message to friends and family showing the delights of where you are and inviting them to join you. But if I had ever received a card, with the message 'Wish you were here' on the back and resembling any one of those I had just bought, I would have questioned the depth of my friendship with the sender. Usually a card will show people frolicking in the surf or enjoying the local uplifting scenery, or a splendid old building glowing burnished gold in the sunset. The Togliati set bravely bucked this established and proven formula. They did show real views of the city, but they were deathly dull and no doubt contributed to the absence of thronging tourists. Typical images were the expanse of a road junction, the plain façade of a public building, or the glorious local factory. For Kate and me, though, the cards did make a good souvenir; at first we thought of buying a pack to share, but seeing they only cost one rouble we decided to splash out and buy a set each. What the hell!

From Togliati we had three days of riding to reach Ufa, 230 miles distant. The countryside alternated between large expanses of agricultural land, and wood and grassland. There were no fences – something I had not experienced before – which gave the impression of wild, unclaimed land, and areas seemed to be chosen at random to

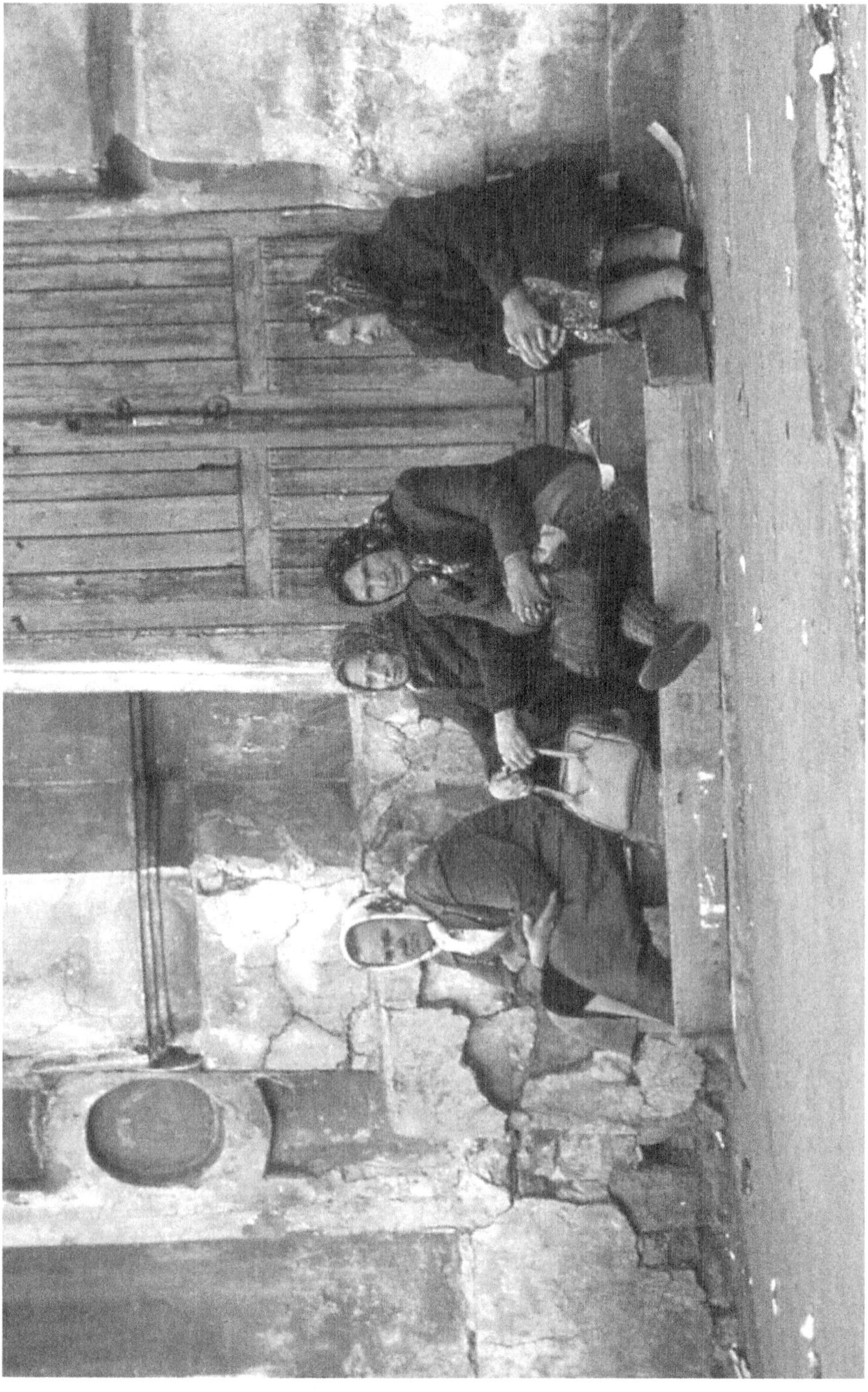

Day 27: Maria's *stolovaya* on the edge of the Urals near Ufa.

Opposite: Day 22: Ladies watching the world go by in Syrzan.

Day 29: Dodging the traffic in Ufa.

Day 31: Getting directions – generally not a very reliable way to navigate.

Day 32: Wasteland around Carabash, with girl playing.

be ploughed by the characteristic stocky caterpillar-tracked tractors. The geology had changed; the pine trees had disappeared, replaced by birch and lime, and occasional oak trees. In the woodland glades and in the sward wild strawberries flourished, the bright white flowers hinting of luscious summer pleasures for human and animal foragers alike. Violets of all shades from purple to white nodded in the breeze, and cowslips raised their pale yellow flowers for pollination. Cuckoos called but remained unseen; house martins chattered, scooping the air with their open beaks and feasting on the abundant mosquitoes.

Day 27: Thursday May 27th – Oktabrskii to Kob-Potrovka 76.1 miles (total 1708.7 miles)
Porridge and apple and raisins for breakfast. Filtered some water from the river to drink - this is only the second time the filter has been used. Generally we have been using Puritabs or nothing. Well water seems okay. Started the day with a long climb (about thirty minutes), and the morning was generally quite hard with fairly steep (1:10) gradients. At the first stop, Vlad asked if he was slowing us down. Every day, Kate and I moan to each other, as we wait for about fifteen minutes at each stop, that we cannot keep losing time this way - we get the distance covered, but tend to arrive quite late, so there is not much time to relax. However, we told Vlad that it was okay most of the time - we would just have to see what happens in the mountains. After Yekaterinburg it should be all downhill and fairly flat to Novosibirsk. The conversation was tricky and slow, using the dictionary - one word at a time. Vlad said he wasn't tired, but that he was just not as strong as us - he was not keen on my idea that he cycle with us in the morning and then put his bike on a truck in the afternoon. I said that we needed him to speak Russian to the police, hotels etc. He agreed to cycle for two hours at a time to save stops, as this is where we lose time. Picnic lunch, plagued by loads of small flies, so we sat in the wind. Very windy again.
Short afternoon to Kob-Potrovko on river Karmacan. The police (GAI) pointed out an unlikely-looking stolo up the hill, where we went for supper. It was run by a lady called Maria, and was the best and cleanest stolo so far. Freshly made meat dumplings, tasty apple and cherry juice, cakes, good bread. We decided to camp here with only 45 miles into Ufa tomorrow, and bought some more cakes for evening tea and some eggs for breakfast. Camped just outside the village of Khlebodarova.

Infuriating insects tonight, apparently oblivious to our repellent. Quite a relaxed evening, as we didn't have to cook. Lost an hour, though, moving into a new time zone.

On the first day out of Togliati we had had another lucky conversation by the roadside with a couple of blokes who looked like they were from the local militia, in their camouflage gear with rifles over their shoulders. While Vladimir was talking to them he looked to be just having a general chat and I had been getting impatient because I wanted to get on with the cycling. The conversation I had with him about what he had been discussing proved very difficult, so I had not really grasped what was going on. Clearly I still had to learn the full value of Vladimir and his contribution to the expedition – it turned out that one of the men, Robert, had also read Kate's letter in the Russian magazine and was actually offering us the use of his own flat in Ufa. It was exciting to know that the brief contact Kate had had by post with the Orion Club had been so successful and that we were getting to meet local cyclists who knew what we were up to and who could share our enthusiasm and help us along the way.

When we crossed the White River and arrived in Ufa Vladimir rang Robert, who cycled out to meet us and led us back to his flat just behind October Square in the city centre. We moved in wholesale, taking over the small space with our filthy wet kit. Typically, Robert and his wife Diane did not seem bothered by this intrusion and went out of their way to make us feel at home. They were Tartars, but we were now in Bashkortostan, another of the 14 semi-autonomous republics that all lie within the boundaries of Russia and which, along with the host country, go to make up the Russian Federation. Bashkirs are not ethnic Russians; they have their own language (the street signs in Ufa were bi-lingual) and flag. Their national hero, a warrior and poet from the 18th Century called Salavat Yulaev, sits astride his horse high above the White River, his carved eastern features clearly marking him as being from non-Slavic stock. On the road working as a security guard Robert had a tough, paramilitary image – a modern Tartar warrior – but there was nothing macho about his home, with its Bach and Beethoven CDs and collection of beautiful Russian stamps.

Soon after our arrival, the table was spread with a very generous amount of food and, except for the vile lurid green kiwi fruit liqueur, we enjoyed our dinner. The general expedition rule is to accept whatever food is offered as you never know when the next opportunity will come along, and we had done well by it. Tonight, though, would almost prove to be our undoing. For what we had not realised, perhaps understandably given the quantity of food Diane had prepared, was that this was not meant to be the supper at all, but just some sort of early evening snack. Replete and ready to relax, we were told to get ready to go to Robert's mother's flat for dinner! Fortunately it was a twenty-minute walk away, so the first course had a brief chance to settle, but all too soon we found ourselves staring down the barrel of another huge spread. (Our friends back home who had been concerned about our possibly inadequate daily calorific intake clearly were speaking from a position of such unsubstantiated ignorance that I could only wonder what other surprises Russia had in store. While we had been kept in the Cold War dark by our conniving Western governments, the Red Devil had in fact developed an efficient and popular centrally controlled political system, perhaps. Or maybe a free market where entrepreneurially minded individuals could indulge their zeal for business unconcerned by the spectre of visitations by the local heavy mob had in fact become a reality? Sadly, no evidence seemed forthcoming to support these ideas. Nor was I convinced, for that matter, that the average citizen could run to such mealtime generosity as we had been lucky enough to experience on a few occasions so far.)

In addition to the very welcome fresh salad we were treated to an array of cheese, jams and honey, these last two added by the spoonful to cups of steaming tea. The centrepiece of the meal was a dish known as *manti*, a traditional Bashkiri meat dumpling. We ate far more than our fill, convincing ourselves that despite the level of discomfort we had not only acknowledged our host's hospitality but had also refilled our own fuel tanks and some spare ones as well.

The following morning dawned very wet and we were unenthusiastic about heading off. Luckily, we spent so long chatting to Robert and Diane and visiting the office of Sasha, a cycling friend of theirs, that we did not leave town until the afternoon, by which time the sun had come out. The roads were busy with people heading out to their *dachas* for the weekend on their Ural motorbike and sidecar combos, leaving us coughing on the vapour trails of blue fumes. Sasha rode out with us the short distance to our campsite on the edge of some lime woodland near Baltika. He was full of interesting information about edible and medicinal plants – I hoped we would not have to resort to foraging in the undergrowth to sustain ourselves, but the richness of the landscape was undeniable.

The Ural mountains were not quite living up to their name. The road certainly climbed a lot, but it also descended a lot, and we were not surrounded by traditional mountain landscapes of high rocky peaks. We were riding across the central section of the range where the elevation is only about 400m and the scenery more like a range of large hills. The high peaks lay some 750 miles away in the northern reaches nudging the Arctic Circle, but even there they do not reach the impressive stature of other mountain chains. Narodnaya, the highest, only attains 1894m, well below many Alpine peaks. The reason for their relatively small size (vertically, at least; lengthwise they stretch an impressive 1300 miles from the tundra in the north, south to the borders of the central Asian desert in Kazakhstan) is that these are some of the oldest mountains in the world, formed between 250 to 300 million years ago, and time has worn them down. The orogenic activity resulting from the collision of Siberia and Europe, though, created a startling array of mineral deposits including gold, silver, platinum, iron, aluminium, lead, copper, asbestos and many others – a fact that would contribute to the mountains' rapid and unregulated exploitation.

So far we had been following major roads through this region, sharing them with the many filthy trucks that rumbled between the cities. For the next few days, though, we turned onto smaller roads to make our way to Yekaterinburg, Boris Yeltsin's hometown and scene of one of the 20th Century's most notorious events.

We were moving along well, with days of 98, 67, 97 and 93 miles from the Baltika camp to Yekaterinburg. Our first evening was spent in an uninspiring looking motel/truck stop in Yooryazan. The town itself was not the best we had been to; snaking around the verges, up and over entrance ways and into buildings there was the usual network of hot water pipes supplying homes and businesses from a central source, but here the insulation on them, so critical during the severe winters, was even worse than usual. I was not sure if it was asbestos or some sort of glass fibre or mineral wool, and did not want to get any closer to find out. Whatever it was, it was falling off in chunks, exposing the pipes to the air and the population to the dangerous fibres.

Having checked into our room, which was more like a portacabin in a car park, Vladimir displayed a Russian trait that was perhaps understandable but was also very frustrating for us, namely the resignation that settles on Russians' shoulders after they have had years of living in a badly run country. The electricity in our cabin was not working, and Vladimir's initial reaction was simply to shrug his shoulders and say 'That's motels for you.' I corrected him, saying 'No, that's Russia.' Fortunately, the lady in charge happened to call round and she found someone to fix it. If that had not happened, Vladimir would have been happy not to make a fuss and just accept the situation.

Despite the dreary surroundings and problems with our room, the motel came up trumps with food (buckwheat, fried eggs and cutlets – twice) and a *banya*. This was only the second of the trip, but I was already growing to like them. Imagine a cross between a sauna and a steam room, with large quantities of very hot water literally thrown in. *Banyas* come in various sizes – municipal ones might accommodate a hundred people or more, private ones built onto the back of a *dacha* are more intimate, with space for six or seven people. Whatever the scale, the idea is always the same – to sweat, scrape and sloosh away the grime. Men and women have their own rooms, so at the first one we visited Kate had to fend for herself. Going to bed with bits of the road still stuck to me was a fairly unpleasant experience, and washing in rivers when we camped was not very satisfactory. *Banyas* were not only excellent for achieving a level of glowing cleanliness I rarely experienced even at home, they were incredibly relaxing as well. Best of all, though, was the childish enjoyment I had of throwing hot water around.

Next morning the rain was really coming down. Vladimir was concerned – he said he had spotted a tick on him in the *banya* and wanted to go to the doctor. Kate and I were happy not to have to ride out in the filthy weather, but we shared Vladimir's concerns. Ticks carry all sorts of nasty diseases, the worst of which can prove fatal. Kate and I had had vaccinations against tick-borne diseases before leaving home (among many other things; my arm felt like a tea-bag it was so perforated from the needles) but I did not know if Vladimir had been as cautious. Fortunately, on his return he had been given the all-clear. Later in the day, having encountered a number of individuals along the road who had been behaving strangely, we found out that there was an asylum nearby and that these people were inmates suffering from encephalitis. No matter what the doctor might have said, if I had been Vladimir I would have gone back to being very concerned.

The rain stopped but it stayed cold all day and I never found a comfortable cycling rhythm. My energy levels rose and fell with the hills, and the snack stops were welcome opportunities to rest and refuel. At 7.15 in the evening we reached a junction – straight on would have taken us to the monument marking the boundary between Europe and Asia, but we wanted the other road. It would only have been a 10-mile detour, but it would have added over an hour by the time we had got there, photographed, filmed and returned, so unfortunately we had to forego marking this symbolic moment on our journey. Instead we would slip into Asia quietly the following day, unannounced.

We turned off and bumped our way downhill for five miles to the attractive lakeside town of Zlataoust. By now we were getting used to wildly different rates being applied to Russians and foreigners, and here the hotel wanted to charge Kate and me each three times as much as for Vladimir. We had run out of roubles, and despite his spending two hours trying to negotiate rooms and exchange money with the hotel it was more than we could afford and a night in the tents seemed the only solution. Just then Vladimir struck up a conversation with Tatiana, a lady who worked at the hotel. After hearing about who we were and what we were up to she kindly invited us to her flat over the road, and we stayed there. It was a very satisfactory end to our first month. The next day was June 1st; a new month and a new continent, with 1948 miles completed.

Day 32: Tuesday June 1st – Zlataoust – Kishtyim
96.9 miles (total 2045.8 miles)

We left quite late (about 10am) after a hearty breakfast at Tatiana's. Vlad is not the quickest person in the morning, and we have tried on a number of occasions to explain that the earlier we start the earlier we finish, and therefore have more time to relax, have a banya, find a hotel/camp site, get a decent percentage of the day done before lunch etc etc. It seems to fall on deaf ears. Also, he makes the most of any opportunity to speak Russian, so he was having a chat with Ivan this morning.

I thought we had to go back up the 5 miles of downhill we did last night, but we went the other way. Then Vlad directed us back into town, then he stopped to get directions again, which always involves a long conversation. I was pretty angry as we had wasted enough time already. Kate and I established the route and set off for Miass. The map was fairly inaccurate today and didn't actually have the road which we followed (a concrete jointed road, so it was fairly bumpy.) We had actually wanted to follow a different road (more scenic) but everyone we spoke to advised the one we actually took: it started off hilly but after Miass was pretty flat.

Arrived in Karabash for lunch after some unsuccessful attempts to find some stuff for a picnic. We did manage to buy a couple of loaves in a village after Andreyevska, a village similar to those we went through before Moscow. Karabash is a disaster area. The town is dominated by a large copper smelting works producing loads of slag which has covered a huge area now devoid of trees, with pools of blood-red chemical-stained water. It put me in mind of industrial revolution England. Clearly there are no controls over these industrial practices. Kate took a photo of a girl happily playing near the slag heap. The average life expectancy in these cities around Ufa and the Urals is only 55 years. The children seem to be pale and generally not as healthy as they should be - a combination of the effects of diet and pollution.

Lunch in the stolo was crap - good cakes, though, which we bought for afternoon snacks. We set off down the hill past another huge heap of either slag or coal at least fifty feet high. It would have been an excellent photo - jet black, with bright green birch trees growing at the bottom, and Kate zooming off in her bright red jacket with red panniers. However, she was zooming too fast so the picture is in my head.

A very hot afternoon after a hazy start. Huge cock-up after lunch. After three-quarters of an hour we came to a diversion. Vlad was behind us, so we followed the diversion expecting him to follow, as he is a law-abiding sort of chap. Kate and I speeded up to cover the extra distance, so Vlad had no chance of catching - if he was indeed coming the same way. Eventually we arrived at Kishtyim at 8.45pm - we usually stop no later than 8.00, and we wanted really to have gone further today. We cycled to the edge of town, back to the junction with the original road, where we had said we would have our first stop after lunch. We sat there and waited, not really knowing what else to do. We hadn't seen Vlad for about four hours.

Suddenly, a police car arrived with about five officers in it who leapt out explaining that Vlad was back at the station and that they would bring him over to us. Huge relief when he arrived - he had actually been in town for ages, having ignored the diversion!

We camped next to the lake at the junction, watching the sun dip below the Urals with a capercaillie's booming call coming over the water from the pine woods. A beautiful calm evening - no wind. (Fortunately there had been no rain today - I'd have been very pissed off if we'd had to make a two-hour diversion in the wet). Cooked large amounts of bolognese. Late night: 12.30.

We were pleased not to have mislaid Vladimir, and it seemed we had found a pleasant spot beside the lake to pitch the tents. If we had known a bit more about the surrounding area we might not have been quite as happy. Across the Volga and into the Urals we had noticed that the children looked young for their age. The industrial plant we had seen around Togliati looked in poor condition and spewed foul smoke and fumes. In Ufa, Diane had explained that there were a large number of hospitals to deal with respiratory problems. Residents of Omsk, east of the Urals, are occasionally warned not to drink the water because the purification systems have failed, and, incredibly, a broadcast will sometimes advise them not to breathe the air. The environmental devastation around Karabash was the worst I had seen anywhere. The industrialisation of this region had begun in earnest during World War Two, when Stalin had moved production eastwards beyond the reach of the Nazis. The results of the country's drive for self-sufficiency and lack of regard for the environmental consequences were clear for all to see, and feel. Technological developments in the 1950s and 1960s, though, produced a legacy far longer-lasting and damaging than dirty factories, and this is what it would have been good for us to know about before settling down for the night on the outskirts of Kishtym.

A study of Cold War maps of the region will reveal many examples of towns that exist on the ground but not on the cartography. They were known simply by their postcode; during our tour of Penza with Helena and Eugene, for example, we had seen in the distance the lights of the closed military town Penza-19, where components for nuclear warheads were produced. The town relevant to where we were now was Chelyabinsk-40. It was built very quickly immediately after World War Two as part of the Ural's secretive *Mayak* (Beacon) complex and came on-stream in 1948 as one of Russia's plants producing plutonium for nuclear weapons. It was situated just 15km to the east of Kishtym. Chelyabinsk-65 and Chelyabinsk-70, two further nuclear and military cities, were also located in the *oblast* (region). Three key incidents at the *Mayak* complex between 1949 and 1967, together with other accidental spillages, have left this region with the unenviable title of 'the most contaminated area in the world' (for completeness, we would pass through the challenger for the title, Krasnoyarsk (site of one of the country's three major underground waste storage facilities throughout the Cold War), just over one month later).

From 1949 to 1956, the Techa river was used as a convenient sink into which to pour thousands of gallons of high level radioactive waste that had been used to cool the reactors. This had a direct effect on the population living downstream, and as the Techa flowed into the Ob and on towards Russia's north coast it took its pollution with it. Just two years after the practice had begun, radiation was detected 1000 miles away in the Arctic Ocean. The Techa river provided the local villages with their drinking and cooking water, as well as a regular supply of fish. A barbed wire fence was eventually installed, putting the river and its surrounding hay meadows off limits to the 124,000 inhabitants, and some but not all of the villages were evacuated.

Once it had been realised that discharging waste into the river was a bad idea, the tactics were changed. From 1951, Lake Karachay was used as a dumping ground and over the next 16 years it accumulated a quantity of potent radionucleides of caesium and strontium equivalent to nearly 100 times what was released in the Chernobyl accident in 1986. As the radioactive waste seeped into the groundwater and moved beyond the confines of the lake to contaminate the surroundings, the real disaster happened in 1967. Sustained dry weather caused the water level of the lake to drop, exposing the muddy bed. Dried out by the sun and wind, the mud turned to dust and was blown far from its source, spreading the contamination over an area equivalent in size to Belgium and irradiating up to 400,000 people.

The most serious single incident had occurred a few years earlier in 1957. Storage tanks that had been built to receive the waste that would previously have been pumped into the Techa river were brought into operation in 1953. A fault with the cooling system in one of the tanks resulted in its exploding with a force of approximately 75 tons of TNT, spreading a cloud of contamination over 8,800 square miles and 270,000 people. After Chernobyl, this rates as Russia's second most serious nuclear accident. Again, evacuation of the local villages was slow and incomplete. As with the other two incidents at *Mayak*, staff at the local hospitals were not allowed to explain the real reasons why their facilities were seeing such a large increase in admissions. The central authorities were certainly not releasing any information, making sure it was contained far more effectively than the pollution itself, the result being that the local population still has little knowledge and understanding of the significance of what happened. It was not until 1992 that Russia officially acknowledged the 1957 explosion.

The new *glasnost* (openness) of the Gorbachev era did at least mean that reports of incidents came out more quickly, although the information released would do nothing to reassure people around the world of the condition of Russia's creaking nuclear infrastructure. On April 6th 1993, just two and a half weeks before Kate and I flew to St. Petersburg at the start of our journey, a familiar scenario took place at the Tomsk-7 reprocessing plant when a cooling tank exploded. This incident was reported in New Scientist on April 17th, and although the details of exactly what had happened varied according to which local reports were being read, at least the fact that the explosion had indeed happened had quickly been admitted.

Ignorant of all the Chelyabinsk information we enjoyed the sunset across the lake and talked about the day's events before crawling into our sleeping bags. It never took long to fall asleep – for Kate, she wanted to beat me to it to avoid having to listen to my snoring; for me, I was just worn out.

Five-and-a-half hours later the alarm shattered my peaceful slumber. With a head full of cold, I climbed back onto my bike for the final 93 miles to Yekaterinburg. Although he was still slower than us, we were becoming more relaxed about Vladimir's progress. Without George, I was talking more with him, however slowly, so I had more of an idea of what he wanted and what he was capable of. He asked if he was slowing us down, and was clearly taking Misha's words in Ryazan seriously – that he was on the expedition to help Kate and me complete it successfully rather than to satisfy any personal aims he might have. We were sticking to a tough timetable, much more demanding than anything Vladimir (and I, frankly) had done before, but he was doing alright, and although Kate and I did still get frustrated with waiting for him it was more important to keep the team spirit up and motivate each other rather than highlight each other's perceived shortcomings.

I mused on all this while kicking my heels by the roadside for an hour the next day, waiting for our diminutive Russian co-rider to come into view. His delay this time was down to a puncture and the strong head wind, so I said nothing and got on with the picnic. After yesterday's efforts I let Kate set the pace for most of the day, and with energy reserves running low we made it to our hosts' flat as the skies darkened and a thunderstorm broke over our heads.

We were staying with Ilya's brother-in-law and his family. Sasha, a flight engineer at the local airport, his wife Irina and their two young daughters seemed to be the most well-off family we had met so far, at least if judged by the standard Capitalist measure of the number of material goods. In their spacious flat were two televisions, a video, a large freezer and a piano. Rather than Russian folk music, Sasha's record collection was made up mainly of Beatles LPs. Whether all this stuff made them a more attractive target for local criminals or not, security was clearly a major concern – the entrance to the flat was guarded not just by one or even two, but by three heavy front doors. (In St. Petersburg Ilya had explained that one of the iron front doors that were proving popular cost twice his monthly salary.)

The plan was to have three days off here, catching up with some official business and doing some sightseeing. We had been on the road for 33 days and had covered 2139 miles; taking our rest days into account, that was an average of 79 miles per day, so as well as seeing the attractions of Yekaterinburg I was also keen to catch up on some sleep and generally relax. I ought to have realised that this was a wildly optimistic wish.

The purpose of our expedition was two-fold. Not only were we aiming to cycle across Russia from the Baltic to the Pacific, we were also raising money for Children's Aid International (CAI). Personal and corporate sponsors had provided us with equipment we needed to succeed and also with money for the charity in recognition of our efforts. The funds we raised would go specifically to CAI's Children of Chernobyl project, which provided children from areas affected by the explosion at the Chernobyl nuclear plant in Ukraine in 1986 with recuperative holidays. Unlike many other schemes, which took the children thousands of miles away to places such as the USA for a little R and R, thus exposing them to extreme and potentially damaging culture shock, CAI's project operated holidays in other eastern European countries, allowing the children to relax in reasonably familiar surroundings while their immune systems had a chance to recover.

Because of our link with CAI Kate and I had been contacting organisations in the medical world, asking if they would like to support the expedition. One of these, via Amersham International, was the British Healthcare Consortium, and their Russian office was in Yekaterinburg. The lady in charge there was Helena Vassina and we arranged to meet her; by a large stroke of luck her office was only one block from where we were staying. Having sent faxes back home to update everyone of our progress, we chatted to Helena about the work of the BHCC. Boris Yeltsin, Russian President at the time, had initiated a link between the Moscow Narodny Bank and Amersham International with the aim of improving healthcare provision in Yekaterinburg. Two years later, and with a group of British pharmaceutical and medical companies on board, BHCC's office was formally opened. Areas of work included the training of managers for the medical industry, mother and child-care, and the design and construction of a new oncological unit. The work seemed to be progressing well, but expanding the programme to other cities in the region, such as Ufa, were proving difficult, apparently due to resistance to outside influences. Given our own experience over the last ten days or so in this area, there was a great deal of progress to be made on the healthcare front.

As far as supporting our expedition was concerned, a BHCC delegation was visiting from the UK and we were invited to join them for dinner that evening. Another free meal was fine with us, and we never knew what connections we might make at these events, so it was always worth going along. The venue for the evening was the government *dacha* on the outskirts of town. Although called a *dacha*, the building we found ourselves in front of bore no relation to the rough and ready wooden cabins that we had become used to. This was a country home situated in light woodland, no more connected to the *dachas* of the masses than Marie Antoinette's Petit Trianon was connected to the lives of the French peasants. Built by German POWs, the grand house had been used by all visiting dignitaries, local and foreign. Kruschev, Nixon, Yeltsin, Gorbachov, Virginia Bottomley – they had all stayed here during their world-changing political careers, and now Kate and I could add ourselves to the list of international movers and shakers.

Dinner was huge and varied, and the company lively. There were 12 of us around the table and the mood was very happy as everyone enjoyed the hospitality and success of BHCC's programme. One member of the group, Jane Penn, proved to be the evening's useful connection. She had just returned from Irkutsk, near the shores of Lake Baikal, where she had played an important part in helping to set up Raleigh International's Siberian project. We were planning a week-long break there and any leads for potential accommodation were very welcome – especially if they included staying with a large group of young British people. I enjoyed Kate's company, but the idea of having new people to talk to, easily and in my own language, was very appealing. Plus, there would be a very satisfying irony in being put up by the organisation that had rejected my application to join one of their projects seven years earlier.

Very full and feeling very satisfied, Kate and I returned to the flat at 11.30pm. Irina had been hard at work, and ushered us into the kitchen for supper! Communications had seriously broken down. This was in fact our third dinner of the day (Irina had given us a large tea before we set off to the *dacha*). It really began to look as though we would be killed by excessive hospitality rather than anything sinister. A key Russian word I learned during my stay in Yekaterinburg was *dastachana*, meaning 'enough'.

BHCC had also organised a guide to show us around. Olga was a very pleasant and enthusiastic lady keen to show off her city. Seven years earlier she had swapped her job as an engineer in one of the local military factories for one as a tour guide, and when Yekaterinburg became an open city five years later (1990) she had decided to learn English in preparation for the arrival of overseas tourists. She had made very good progress, and through her and her 12-year-old daughter Karia, whose English was excellent, we learned a lot about the city.

Like a number of other cities around the country, Yekaterinburg had reverted to its pre-Revolution name after 1991. During Communist times it had been known as Sverdlovsk, after Yakov Sverdlov, the first Secretary of the USSR. Its original name was chosen in 1723 by the city's founder, a Mr Tatichev, who was a friend of Peter the Great's and who honoured the Tsar's wife by naming the town after her. The city centre consisted of grand town houses, well-preserved and painted in mint green, white and pale blue. Older wooden houses of significant citizens has also been preserved, such as those of Pavel Bajov and Mamin-Siberiak, local authors who wrote of life in the Urals in the late 19th and early 20th Centuries. The local wealth had come from the rich mineral deposits in the region (gold, copper and semi-precious stones) and Russia's first mint had been located here.

Apart from Yeltsin and the coin factory, Yekaterinburg's main claim to fame, or notoriety, comes from a darker period of the country's past. Walking out onto an empty plot on a slope near the edge of the city centre, we arrived at a single white cross in the distinctive Orthodox style with its three cross-spars. Flowers had been placed at the base, and some photos had been attached to it. While we were there, a young man approached the cross, crossed himself and bowed. This was clearly a place of some significance, and given the symbols and photographs it represented something the Communists had tried unsuccessfully to remove from the country's cultural past. A smaller, plain wooden cross gave a clue. It marked the position of the first foundation stone, already laid, of what was to be a grand new church, commemorating the last Tsar of Russia, Nicholas II, and his family. For it was here on this very spot in April 1918 that the Imperial family was assassinated in a gloomy cellar by the Bolsheviks. The building was demolished in 1977, but the dream of restoring a monarchy was still very real for many people. Photos of the Tsar pinned to the white cross were a tangible connection to a more glorious period of Russia's history for these people, and the promise of a church on this symbolic site must have represented a first step towards the full rehabilitation of the Tsar to what they believed was his rightful place in the nation's history.

Back at the flat we worked on the bikes. No spare parts had come out to us here from Ryazan, although Misha had rung to say he had received all the spares that had been posted from the UK and that he would send them with Eugene to Novosibirsk. That was reassuring but it did mean we would have to wait another three weeks and 1,100 miles before we saw them. Fortunately we had not had to put up with too much poor quality road, and the bikes were handling the terrain well. Nothing was particularly worn out, we had only had a few punctures and few slow motion tumbles without any other vehicles involved. The small collection of spares we had with us would keep us on the road unless we suffered some major mishap. A potential problem that was a concern was Kate's headset (which secures the steering column into the bikes' frame); something was definitely wrong with it and it kept working loose. In the meantime, Kate would just have to bodge it and keep a close eye on it. As long as the condition of the roads did not deteriorate too much it ought to be okay…

Some letters from home had also arrived in Ryazan. The news would be very out of date by the time we got to read it, but we were looking forward to receiving it all nonetheless. Kate and I had both managed long phone calls home over the last couple of days. I seemed to have got over the homesickness of earlier in the trip, and although it was great to be able to chat with my family and friends I did not end the conversation feeling down. I had clearly settled into the rigours and routine of the expedition.

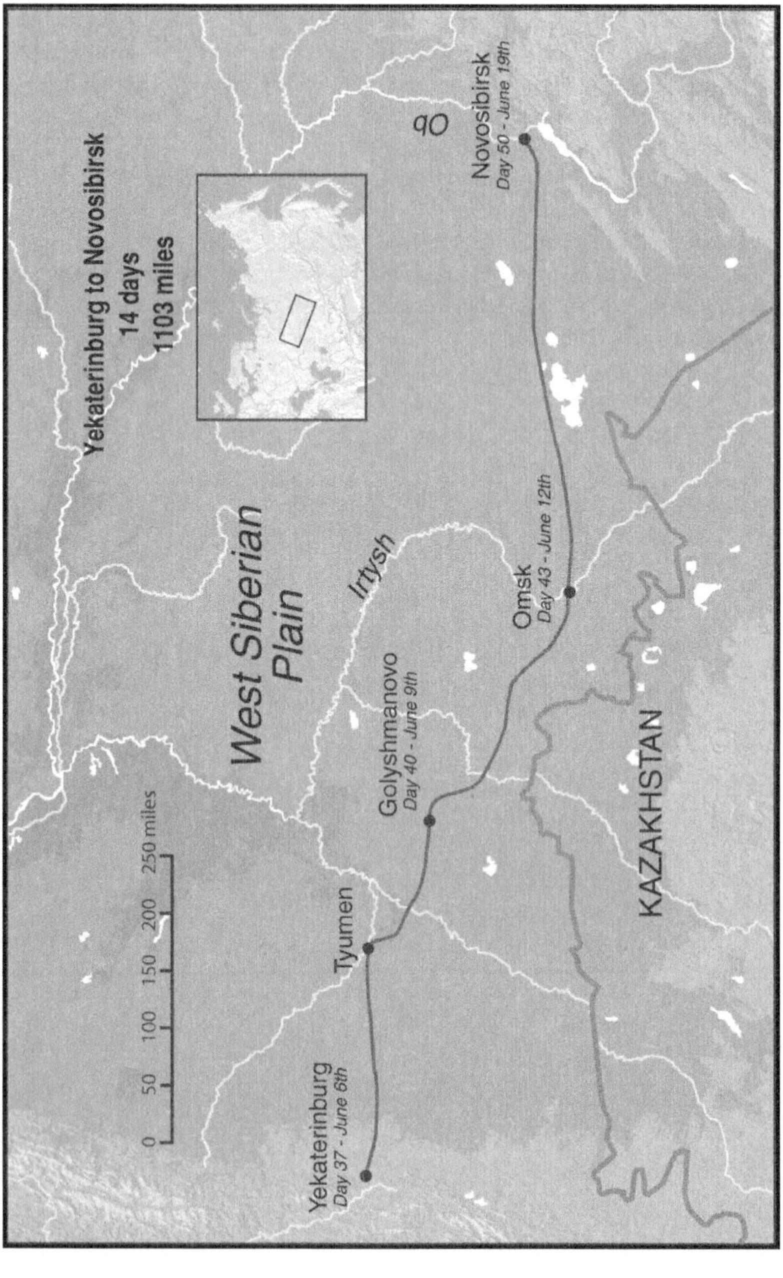
Yekaterinburg to Novosibirsk
14 days
1103 miles
West Siberian Plain
Irtysh
Ob
0 50 100 150 200 250 miles
Yekaterinburg
Day 37 - June 6th
Tyumen
Golyshmanovo
Day 40 - June 9th
Omsk
Day 43 - June 12th
Novosibirsk
Day 50 - June 19th
KAZAKHSTAN

SECTION 3

~~~

ACROSS THE STEPPE

~~~

Sasha and Irina had been perfect hosts, plying us with delicious meals and making us feel completely at home. We were eager to continue our journey east, though, and after three days off we somehow managed to pack what appeared to be an entire room-full of clothes and equipment back into our panniers. I never seemed to change my cycling kit, pulling on the same, gradually deteriorating, tee-shirt and shorts every day, so I did sometimes wonder what all the other stuff was for. As the expedition wore on, though, I would be pleased that I had carried it all this way.

It was early June and we were entering the steppe. I had imagined Yekaterinburg as some sort of Tolkienesque fortress city situated prominently on the flanks of the Urals, with featureless plains stretching away towards the hazy horizon. The reality was far less romantic.

Day 37: Sunday June 6th – Yekaterinburg to Kamislov
90.9 miles (total 2229.9 miles)
The morning rain had stopped before we left at about 11.30, after a big breakfast - curds and jam, porridge, fish and potatoes. We managed to find our way out of town no problem - a first, I think. Rolling along okay, with Vlad in front for first 1½ hours, then about 15 minutes behind.

The town of Asbest was signposted - that is the one where the roads are mended with asbestos. Very muggy. A thunderstorm rumbled over in late afternoon when we stopped for petrol at Bogdanovich; Vladimir from Kamchatka kept a clean station with many plants and flowers inside, and gave us tea.
After a short break we set off, and I slipped over on the wet road, tearing a pannier. Vlad had fallen earlier, and had then ridden on the mud at the edge of the tarmac, which was why we had to wait ages at the garage. Stopped briefly for halva, then went to Kamislov. The ground was too wet for camping, and the hotel wanted about R2000 and R450 for the bikes. Another piece of luck - a bloke who walked past mentioned the town's cycle club, so Vlad asked if there was any possibility of somewhere to stay. The bloke went and got Alexei, who took us to the club's underground HQ, and eventually we went to Vassily's, his friend. Hearty meal - fried eggs and potatoes (twice), meat and egg pancakes, pancakes and jam, tea, biscuits. Again, lots to eat, but high fat and high sugar. I haven't seen fresh fruit in people's houses yet.
Vassily spoke very, very quickly and despite all attempts to get him to slow down and to explain that we didn't understand, he kept babbling on. He's more-or-less the first Russian I've seen smoking, and was a down to earth bloke, burping and hacking, a bit of a lad with his feet-wide-apart stance. He and his wife Lisa had their 40th birthday medals. Huge stereo (reel-to-reel) - big but crap; tacky ornaments. Good view into town - the old church is being restored. Iron Maiden on TV. Late night. Had to share a bed with Vlad. The cat kept attacking me, so I kicked it out, and apparently it went and kept attacking Kate.

Our journey across the steppe to Novosibirsk would take two weeks, with a break half-way in Omsk. The landscape was not as pancake flat as we had expected, but there was still nothing resembling a hill. Fence-less fields, spinneys and thickets of birch, and stretches of water formed the elements of the undulating and undemanding countryside. Dominating everything was the broad vault of the sky, reaching uninterrupted from horizon to horizon. At some point each day, usually in the afternoon once the clouds had developed, either Kate or I (and sometimes both, if we forgot that it had already been mentioned, or did not realise that the other one had actually said something) would exclaim with some sort of child-like awe, 'Wow, look at that sky!', as if we had never seen clouds and blueness before.

But the combination of the scale of it, the clarity of the air and the blueness of the water against the bright green fields did give the scene an amazing quality – one that we clearly felt deserved comment. Even if what we said was hardly poetic.

For most of this section the road was good quality tarmac. When I am talking to people about this expedition they generally assume that this was an easy section, following smooth roads across an undemanding landscape. In reality, it was no different from any other section. Ultimately, we had to complete a full day's ride each day, and while there may have been fewer obstacles to our progress here it just meant that we could ride further – our average for the seven days to Omsk was 90.5 miles per day. On top of this, because the road was mostly flat there was no variation in how we rode each day – we did not have to change gear, or move position on the bikes. There were very few descents where we could enjoy a relaxing freewheel.

The smallest thought would trigger a song, or, more annoyingly, just a line or two of a song, which would then lodge in my brain for the day like a fish bone. Kate passed the time by performing mental calculations to work out how many pedal revolutions it would take to travel from one side of Russia to the other. (4,056,000, since you ask, although I am sure you will be quick to appreciate the variety of assumptions that Kate made, such as a continuous ping-pong-ball-smooth surface, constant cadence and accurate estimation of the total distance. Anyway, the figure she arrived at after her mental gymnastics was large enough to make her want to forget it straight away, and there was no way we were going to keep a tally so we could see how close she had been to the correct final figure once we leaped off in Vladivostok.) Thank heavens for the fluffy clouds to drag our minds off these intrusive things.

Although we had met quite a few local adventurous cyclists we had not seen any serious roadies, those brightly-clad lean figures frequently spotted in countries like France and Italy zooming about on racing bikes. We were surprised near the town of Pishma, then, when a peleton shot past in the opposite direction, a blur of spinning legs and Lycra. 'Peleton' is perhaps overdoing it; there were four of them. Maybe they liked to think of themselves more as a permanent breakaway from the main field. They must have been as surprised as us – as we trundled past on our carthorses they reined in their thoroughbreds, turned around and came over to say hello. The group consisted of Yuri and his three young charges, who were being put through their paces with a tough training regime, on the smooth empty roads.

We had a long way to go but ended up spending three hours with Yuri, being treated to a free lunch at the local *stolovaya* and swapping cycling stories. The bikes he and his boys were riding looked enviably light, but with a welcome tail-wind blowing us along in the afternoon we made up the time and reached the village of Tyoogoolim. Here we pitched our tents on a spot of dry ground near some log buildings, bought some fresh raw milk and set about dealing with the mosquitoes.

The first week of the ride had been okay from the point of view of very small yet massively irritating insects. That had all changed abruptly as we left Moscow, and we had been besieged by mosquitoes ever since. It is difficult to get across in words the effect of this onslaught. Fortunately we were not harassed by them much during the day, but in the mornings and evenings, particularly when we were camping, they became unbearable. On more than one occasion I woke to what I thought was the sound of rain falling on the tent, but in fact it was the local mosquito population bouncing about between the fly-sheet and inner.

It is always a good idea to see what the local people wear when you visit new parts of the world, as it usually shows the best way to cope with the local conditions. Thus, the sensible and astute traveller is always to be seen sporting bird of paradise feathers and a penis-sheath in Papua New Guinea, or modelling a fetching cagoule in Wales. However, we did need to be practical as well. Kate may have been well-advised to adopt the garb of your average rural Russian lady, the thick woolly tights, heavy jumper and headscarf ensemble no doubt having proved its worth against the marauding bloodsuckers for many generations. However, it would not have helped her cycling, and we might easily have lost her in a crowd. The men seemed to adopt a slightly different approach, fumigating themselves by smoking nasty cigarettes. I did not think this was the time to take up smoking, in the middle of a demanding sporting endeavour.

But rather than ignore the local practices completely, Kate and I just adapted them. Apparently a favourite method of Stalin's for dealing with awkward gulag inmates was to have them tied to a tree, naked. The poor individuals would not die from bears or wolves, but from loss of blood as the local mosquitoes enjoyed this unexpected feast. Forest animals are not immune, either. Tundra reindeer can lose a pint of blood a day to biting flies. We did not want to suffer in the same way so rather than thick woollies, we would slip on our waterproof trousers and jackets once the cycling was over for the day. This was hardly a comfortable option since we would be hot, sweaty and dirty, but we were happy to put up with a bit of discomfort from our clothes as they were the only things the mosquitoes could not bite us through. That still left our faces, necks and hands exposed. A liberal smearing of maxi-strength insect repellent did the trick there, and once all our defences were in place we could relax and derive some vindictive pleasure from stirring into our evening soup any mosquito daft enough to have mistaken it for a warm-blooded snack of their own.

We might have thought we had dealt with the insect problem, but there were two important things we needed to do regularly that opened us up to attack again: washing and going to the toilet. It is important to keep clean on a bike trip like this. Saddle sores can creep up on you from behind if the sweat and grime is not washed off, and feet can slowly rot in the same damp socks day after day. It just makes sense to keep your body in the best condition possible to give yourself the best chance of success. Maintaining this condition involved something akin to the hokey-kokey. With water and soap close to hand, I would take my first leg out of my waterproofs, lather it up quickly and relax for a moment. The mosquitoes, it seemed, did not like the soap. I would then quickly rinse off the lather, dry my leg and put it back into my trousers. I then got my other leg out, repeated the process, and put it in. Arm out; arm in. Other arm out; other arm in. Other bits of my body followed in a similar way. It was necessary, and almost amusing. The important thing, though, was that I had some control over how long I was exposing myself. When it came to going to the toilet, it was more a case of having to let nature takes its course while hoping that I had not left any areas of buttock and other nearby naked flesh untreated by repellent. Squatting in the undergrowth was hard enough work on my tired thighs without having to jig about trying to swat insects aiming for my beacon-bottom, so I had to trust the chemicals to do their job so I could maintain some sort of balance and emerge from the whole exercise with dignity intact and unassailed. Apart from that, the prospect of my saddle pummelling a constellation of mossie bites on my bum for the next few months was one I did not want to contemplate.

We made excellent progress over the next few days. Vladimir had a few slow moments, but he did now seem happy to hitch a ride on a passing truck in the afternoon, which meant Kate and I could keep up the tempo throughout the day. My appetite continued to grow – on Day 40 I consumed three helpings of porridge, followed by goulash and potato for breakfast; at lunch, after my seconds of *pelmeni*, I spotted that the person on the next table had left without finishing theirs, so I polished that off as well. I was not developing a paunch, so I must have been burning all the calories. My concern was how quickly my appetite would return to normal once the cycling came to a sudden end.

The hotels were not improving as we made our way eastwards, but they were still absurdly cheap so it was difficult to complain. In Yalutarovsk our room cost R720 – approximately 45p – and the shower was glacial. The following day, in Golyshmanova, we were originally told the hotel was closed for renovations but there seemed to be people staying in it. We negotiated our stay and while the bikes spent the night at the local police station we made the best we could of the as-yet-unrefurbished water system (cold and intermittent) and lack of electricity. There was no point complaining as there was no alternative. In the smaller towns there would only be one hotel so we had to accept what we were given.

Wherever we slept – in a hotel, our tent or an accommodating sofa in somebody's flat – I never had any problem falling into a deep and satisfying sleep. The only irritating thing about it was that it never lasted long enough. On a camping morning my alarm would go off at six o'clock to give us enough time to cook breakfast, pack up and get going within a reasonable time. In a hotel we allowed ourselves the luxury of an extra half an hour – a little morale-boosting treat!

Crossing the wide and marshy Ishim river by ferry at Abatski we advanced another hour. There were still differences between Kate and Vladimir's maps, with Kate's underestimating distances, but we were still keeping up with the timetable. Arriving in Tyookalinsk we checked into the hotel and decided to take a room each. I had not been feeling a need to have my own space but being able to spread out and relax by myself was very welcome. Not wishing to appear antisocial I invited Kate and Vladimir round to my place for supper. My diary sums up the event: *"Excellent supper - soup, then rice pudding with raisins, plum jam and sweetened condensed milk. Follows cucumber and mayonnaise sandwiches at lunch - not a bad day's food."* We were six weeks in to the trip and my expectations had adjusted well! Gradually as the months passed I found myself being satisfied with less. It was not a conscious thing; it was more a case of simply accepting what was available. 'TIR' as we used to say – This Is Russia. We still grumbled about plenty of things, though. Vladimir displayed a general acceptance of the situation, but our grumbling about it might have stirred something in him. On the morning of our ride to Abatski we had gone to the local *stolovaya* for breakfast (why restrict ourselves to *pelmeni* only at lunchtime, we thought, when we can have it for breakfast as well?) The sign on the door said 'Open at 8am' but we had to wait until 9am before there were any signs of life inside. In a notable departure from character, Vladimir actually expressed some frustration at this. He had to mime it – pointing at his watch, then the sign, and turning his hands palms upwards, that sort of thing – so he might not have succeeded in conveying all the raw emotion he was feeling, but since his reaction was off the scale compared with what would have been his usual shrug of acceptance Kate and I got the message.

For me personally, I think the closest I came to becoming an adopted Russian in terms of achieving the nadir of my level of expectation of what I would call basic services came much later in the trip, on Day 113 towards the end of August. We had cycled to Nerchinsk, a decent-sized town just east of Chita. The hotel looked promising, but as we were checking in the lady behind the desk explained in a very matter of fact way that there were no washing facilities in the building. Asked where we might be able to find an alternative she pointed helpfully along the street. We thought she was indicating the way to the local *banya*, where we would be able to enjoy a hearty steam and scrub. But no. She was in fact showing us the way to the river! There was no expression on her face to suggest that what she was inviting us to do was in any way peculiar, and we all accepted the situation. It had now become perfectly reasonable for me to accept that being offered a river to wash in rather than the snug confines of an en-suite was totally normal. If I tried hard I could almost convince myself that this arrangement represented some sort of upgrade: fresh running water permanently available, wonderful views from the bath and an opportunity to meet the locals and discuss our different national approaches to personal hygiene.

Day 43: Saturday June 12*th* – Tyonkalinsk to Omsk
88.5 miles (total 2778.0 miles)

For once, not a hearty breakfast to start the day. The stolo only had cakes and hard-boiled eggs - no porridge or goulash etc. Vlad wanted to go and try another stolo in town but we would never have got going until late - we didn't set off until about 9.30 anyway. Vlad doesn't seem to like the oat porridge we make.

A very windy day. The very strong head/cross-head made it hard going until about 5.30. It was very sunny, too, at first (hazy), then dark clouds, then rain. The wind died down once the rain had been and gone, but it stayed gloomy. Vlad managed only 2½ hours today. We stayed in a group of three for a while, Kate and I doing 10-minute bits, but Vlad dropped back and couldn't cope with the wind. He decided to take a truck to Omsk, so we said 'See you in 7 hours,' which didn't give us much opportunity for relaxation. We could only cycle at about 9mph most of the time.

Sending Vlad ahead is actually very efficient, as he can sort out our accommodation etc so we don't have to hang around once we have arrived. This worked very well today. As Kate and I approached Omsk, a car pulled up and out leaped Sasha, Sasha, Valery and Alla, with Vlad. They offered to whisk us off to the banya in the car while Sasha and Sasha rode our bikes round to the flat. It sounded like an attractive idea, but Kate and I decided that it would be cheating if we didn't cover every mile ourselves. There followed a high-speed chase through the streets of Omsk as they showed us the way to the flat. This wasn't really what we needed after 7½ hours of hard cycling, and surprisingly we managed to keep up a decent speed (16-17mph, even hitting 20mph briefly). But it couldn't last - the legs went eventually and it took a large chunk of Kendal mint cake to get me the last little distance.

My first view of Omsk was a gas flare and lots of tall chimneys lurking in the mist and drizzle. In the distance it looked like a cross between a fantasy castle and a 'satanic mill'. The outskirts were the same as in every town - new blocks of flats, crap roads, unfinished appearance, made worse by the muddy and oily puddles everywhere, apparently poor drainage, and loads of potholes. It was the same in the centre. Kate and I got dirtier in the last half hour of the day than in the first 7½! We were filthy, and got drenched by a number of cars ploughing through the puddles.

We had ridden hard for seven days to reach Omsk. It was still quite early in the expedition and we had to make sure we stayed up with the timetable. We knew that conditions would get much worse later on, so if we fell behind now we would be putting ourselves under more pressure in the wilder sections of Siberia. While the terrain was undemanding it made sense to push on, and we only allowed ourselves one day off.

The city was founded in 1714 during a gold-seeking expedition. Its industrial base has progressed through tank production to oil refining and although there were still plenty of beautiful old buildings in the centre, the city was dominated by the physical presence of the chemical plants and their effect on the air and water. We took a boat ride on the river Irtish through the city – a more relaxing form of sightseeing – to see things from a different angle. The waterway was busy with barges hauling their loads of timber up and downstream, and huge cranes lined the wharfs. The river is clearly a very important means of moving goods around, but at the same time it is also an important place for Omsk citizens to come and relax. After the previous day's heavy rains, the warm sunshine had enticed crowds of people to the river's beaches, where they lounged about and swam in the busy waters.

We had found Sasha, our host, in the usual friend of a friend roundabout sort of way. Over dinner in his flat we got to know the other Sasha (our original contact here), Alla (who knows both of them and who secured our stay) and Verida (a Kazak born in Omsk). They were a good cross-section of young Russians involved in various emerging aspects of the new country. Host Sasha was one of Russia's new private farmers, owning 6 hectares of wheat-producing land. It was cheap to buy but distribution problems and lack of equipment and capital were not making life easy. Kate grew up on a farm in Western Australia's wheat belt so they had plenty to talk about; I am afraid that after four or five vodkas and a walking tour after our boat trip, the finer points of grain sampling could not hold my attention. I chatted to Verida, another of the self-employed English teachers who were springing up. As well as an enthusiasm for learning new languages, it seemed that Russians had also developed a keen interest in themselves. Self-development courses were proving very popular, Verida explained.

Day 46 – before the rain. Vladimir enjoying hard, flat mud.

Day 47 – after the rain. Kate unclogging her bike, before falling off.

Day 49: Kate frying up some bread for dinner in Gina's house, to accompany the potatoes and garlic leaves.

Day 49: Signs of the old times, Chulin town centre.

Day 50: Yuri and Kate navigating the blocks of flats, Novosibirsk.

Previously everything had been done by the State; people had not thought of themselves as individuals and had not considered their own identity and what they wanted. Now, though, they realised that they could act for themselves and address their own feelings. In the interests of not pricking the entrepreneurial bubble of the country's burgeoning self-help departure lounge book industry, I decided against advising Verida that such courses and publications were put about by snake oil pedlars dressing up common sense as extraordinary revelation. I felt she would not appreciate my input. Indeed, as I turn to face the sun each morning my affirmation of 'I will not trip up others as they follow their chosen path' rings out clear and strong. And I feel better for it.

Alla and the other Sasha worked for the Central Property Fund, a government body helping to organise the privatisation of businesses. The jobs each of our new friends had were symptomatic of the new Russian regime. They were not without their problems, but the Sashas, Alla and Verida were all keen to make them succeed.

Having only partly recovered from the previous week's exertions during our short stay in Omsk, we pushed off again. Our next target was Omsk's friendly Siberian rival, the city of Novosibirsk. This had been my main goal after Yekaterinburg, and would be the end of Vladimir's seven-week ride. We had contacted our new cyclist, Yuri, to tell him when we expected to arrive, allowing five days to cover the 464 miles. Up to now things had been going well for us. The roads had been pretty good and we had not had any particularly bad weather; we had each suffered fatigue at various points, but no-one had had more than a cold. With three-and-a-half months still to go I did not want to tempt fate by wondering how long our good fortune would carry on. As it turned out, it would be about twenty-four hours.

Towards the end of our first day out of Omsk an unfamiliar noise was coming from the back of my bike. The sound only occurred while I was riding, so it was difficult to work out where it was coming from. After much tapping and prodding I tracked down the source: one of my rear pannier rack's lower attachments had sheared through and the free end of the strut was tapping against the bike frame. Vladimir had suffered the same problem a few weeks before, so I knew how to fix it with wire, but the prospect of our equipment beginning to suffer was not a welcome one.

The following day, as we made our way along the main road connecting western Siberia's two major cities, the tarmac ran out. 90%

of the day was spent on mud, with some sections of loose stones resembling railway ballast. The stones were awful to ride on and quite deep in places, making it difficult to keep going in a straight line and tough to get going again when we ground to a halt. So far the mud was dry, and was in fact as good as tarmac in this condition. I did wonder what rain would do to it and glanced at the skies. They had provided some interest for us recently but would they now bring a change in our fortunes? All seemed well – no ominous clouds in sight. As the afternoon wore on, my concentration was interrupted by a now familiar tapping sound. The attachment on the other side of my pannier rack had broken. If my equipment carried on like this I would become the first person to unicycle across Russia balancing a carrier bag on his head. (Now there's an idea...)

We arrived in Vengerova for the night. Old Communist emblems and new Russian flags vied for prominence on the public buildings. The country was still very much in a change-over phase. We saw the same thing a couple of days later in Chulin: the new Russian flag was flying as Lenin looked down from a poster. If Communism had been rejected why were these old symbols still in place two years on? Maybe the people in the smaller provincial towns were less bothered by the whole process; and we were, after all, in Russia, the ruling power of the USSR, where people were proud of the strength of their former leaders. No doubt in the girdle of occupied buffer states such as Latvia, Hungary, Uzbekistan and the others the populations had been quicker to remove traces of their bolshy neighbour. With these thoughts running through my mind we wheeled our bikes into the hotel pleased with the day's progress over the awkward terrain. As the receptionist handed us the registration cards to fill in, the first drops of rain began to fall.

Day 47: Wednesday June 16th – Vengerova to Kubichev 74.9 miles (total 3022.7 miles)

The road out of town was very bad due to overnight rain - we had to use the meadow next to the road. Kate changed to a knobbly back tyre. The main road was variable, with some very muddy bits. Lots of concentration was required, but it was quite a giggle, really. We had our tea-break at Tooroonovka, on a bridge over the river - an unexpected engineering structure. Kate fell here. There was some more ballast road for a while - it's okay riding in the truck ruts - then it got disastrously muddy. The cars

were having real problems. We used the meadow again, but that just put us among the thousands of mosquitoes.
Basically, it was awful from here to lunch at Pokronka. It rained, making the mud very slippery. One large lorry had slipped off the road into the ditch. The scenery was beautiful, though. In the morning it was fairly thick birch forest, and then more open. We had to walk some bits, and made slow progress - 25 miles by 1.30pm. Kate fell a couple more times, managing to land on the same ribs each time. She was close to tears at one point. Cracked ribs?
For lunch we had a picnic, sheltering from the rain in the shop where we bought a jar of pickled vegetables for variety. We had a long way to go after lunch. Nicholai, a lorry driver, flagged us down. He wanted to chat, and insisted we ate bread, eggs and cream. We didn't fancy his vodka, though. I suppose all truckers have a bottle in the cab. He was an emotional chap, giving me a hug and Kate a kiss. She isn't very keen on those, though.
The road was much better in the afternoon. Big skies again. The landscape was very flat, but the trees kept it from being boring. We arrived quite late (about 9pm) in Kubichev, and checked into the hotel after having dinner in the hotel (I had two main courses, as it had been a tough day). We had to clean the bikes as there was no oil at all on the chains - they were squeaking badly. A late night, after a cold shower.

With Kate's accident and the tough conditions it would have been easy to cut the day short but we would only have had to cover the miles the next day. The timetable would have started to slip. It looked as though we would need a bit more than the five days we had allowed to reach Novosibirsk anyway, and who could say that the conditions would not get worse? We could not just keep chopping the daily mileage. On Day 47 we cycled 75 miles, with Kate in a lot of discomfort. Day 48 dawned sunny. The road was still mud, but it dried out quickly. We wasted an hour or so while I changed a spoke – the first of my cycling career, and I had no instruction manual. Once that was out of the way we had another long but more pleasant day and managed 95 miles. There really was no opportunity to slow down.

Viewed from a broad perspective the landscape we were passing through might not have appeared very interesting – wide areas of grass, some trees, and often very soggy. As is often the case, though, a closer look will reveal plenty of interest, and one of the pleasures of travelling by bike is that these details can be appreciated. Fields of buttercups, rich purple vetches and wild irises spread a beautiful palette of colour through the vibrant green grassland. Pochard, waders and ducks dabbled and probed in the many pools and marshes. Pretty yellow and pied wagtails skittered around the margins, while harriers and other birds of prey soared in the clear air scanning the ground for their next meal. Hooded crows called coarsely from the trees. Far from being a bland agricultural scene, the steppe was varied and alive.

Our two weeks across the steppe had been very hard work leaving us tired and in Kate's case with an injured rib that would take another month to mend. Our last night before arriving in Novosibirsk was spent in a typical small wooden house in the village of Lesnaya Polyana, about three hours' riding short of the city. After a steaming pot of barley porridge for breakfast I certainly had enough energy to make it, but the bumpy roads over the last week had left me with a sore back and an aching backside – at one point I had had to stuff a spare tee-shirt between two pairs of cycling shorts to try and make the whole experience more comfortable.

In Novosibirsk there would be a change of personnel with two new Russian cyclists, Yuri and Eugene, taking over from Vladimir. In what turned out to be a typical display of enthusiasm, Yuri had ridden out from his home city for two hours to meet us. There were no other groups of cycle tourists heading east that season, so we were easy to identify and he flagged us down for introductions over a flask of tea by the roadside before completing the last twenty miles or so with us. With Yuri proudly leading us into his city we were heading for his parents' flat, located somewhere in the sprawling suburbs of repetitive blocks that could have been anywhere in Russia. Eventually he put the brakes on and called out over his shoulder, 'Here we are!' I was happy to hear these words and was looking forward to unpacking and relaxing at the end of a long seven weeks of riding. We got off the bikes and Yuri led the way in, pushing his machine through the front door. (Having just seen his bike in action I was relieved that we had supplied new mountain bikes from home for our Russian team members to use. As we soon discovered, however, good planning does not always translate into hard reality...) In the lobby, the single 40-watt bulb was losing its struggle to illuminate the concrete and incomplete tiling, and it was taking a few seconds for my eyes to adjust to the dimness. As I blundered blindly after Yuri I bumped into something and found that not only was my way blocked but that I was also being pushed back towards the door. As I could not see what this obstacle was I thought it would be sensible not to push against it, at least not until I (and it) was back out in the daylight. As I crossed the threshold once more, the object resolved itself into a now-familiar figure – it was Yuri, reversing out of the building, and calling over his shoulder again (slightly less triumphantly this time) 'Oh no! Wrong block!' We had exposed a major flaw in the centralised approach to town planning - although thinking about it, if all the blocks were the same maybe it would not matter if people turned up at a random flat each day under some sort of city-wide hot-bunking arrangement. When we did ultimately reach their flat, Yuri's parents were not there, not, we were reassured to hear, because they were roaming the streets trying to find their way home, but because they had in fact moved into Yuri's flat for a few days to give us a bit more room. Having unpacked, any thoughts I had had of putting my feet up were shelved as we hit the streets again, this time heading for Yuri's flat – it may have been smaller but it had the hot shower, so I was happy to endure the bus journey across town, and since it was his own place I felt confident that Yuri would be able to lead us there with a display of assured navigation. The effort of all this urban wandering, plus all the cycling, proved too much and I fell asleep on the bus and again while waiting for Kate to finish washing. I clearly needed a few days off.

We had a busy three days, working on admin and equipment and recovering from the last seven weeks. Our first day had been quite inactive, writing diaries and faxes, which was not the best way to allow our legs to unwind. When on our second day we visited Yuri's laboratory at the Institute of Cytology and Genetics, part of the vast *Akademgorodok* or Academic Town, where he worked as a plant geneticist, Kate had a severe attack of very painful cramps in her legs. The spasms were so bad she could not walk, and she made her way gingerly back to the flat with Vladimir. Kate had more than demonstrated her toughness on the expedition and to see her close to tears because of the pain in her legs convinced me that it must be serious. She had experienced similar cramps on a previous ride through Norway, though, and was confident that they would pass after a day or so if she kept moving and massaged her legs.

A bigger concern for us was what Yuri was planning to ride.

Day 50: Saturday June 19th – Lesnaya Polyana to Novosibirsk
42.2 miles (total 3242.1 miles)

Kate and I had a bit of a shock in the afternoon. Yuri plans to cycle with us on his own bike, and Eugene (from Centre Pole) will not bring out the spare bike. He will use Vlad's. That's fine, except that Yuri's is a heap and doesn't have sufficient luggage capacity. We will have to improvise! Not only that - Eugene (who arrived tomorrow morning; I'm getting ahead of myself!) did not bring the fourth sleeping bag or the fourth set of waterproofs. Yuri apparently has a goatskin he has used in the past(!) and a couple of rucsacs he can jiggle with. This is a bit of a cock-up, especially after finding and buying all the equipment in England. And Yuri isn't even a cycle tourist, as we had believed, although he has been on scientific expeditions to tundra regions (bird surveys), and goes skiing and hiking. Eugene isn't a cycle tourist, either, and nor was George, so I think we will be okay. Kate spoke to Misha and asked him to send the other bike with Eugene, but he said 'Not possible' (too late).

Day 52: Monday June 21st – day off, Novosibirsk

Yuri and I went in to town to try and find a bike shop. After a 70 minute bus ride and tube journey (on the new line, about three years old), we discovered that the bike shop now only sells things for cars. At this point I was feeling more than a little frustrated about Yuri's bicycle situation - who was it exactly who had decided not to send the fourth bike out from Ryazan? Unless Yuri finds some new components he will not be able to join us, which isn't a problem in itself as Eugene is with us (although if he weren't here, as Kate and I had originally planned, we wouldn't have this problem). I'd rather he didn't come than attempt the trip on a semi-adequate bike. The second shop we visited was shut. There are plenty of people with bikes in this town - they must buy them somewhere. So, Yuri has a busy day lined up tomorrow trying to arrange all his equipment.

It felt as though we had spent half the day on the buses and the underground. I kept nodding off and was less than happy that our plans for supplying good equipment, which Misha had insisted upon when Kate met him before we set off from the UK, were being scuppered. There was nothing we could do about it until the next day; the only thing for it was to go and visit something worse off than I was, so Yuri and I went to the zoo. The range of big cat species housed there was impressive, and included lions, leopards, ocelots and Siberian tigers. The old-fashioned cages they were kept in, though, were woefully inadequate, with hard floors, iron bars and no real attempt made to recreate the cats' wild environment. A polar bear lay with its chin on its paws staring at the tiny plunge pool – a ludicrously poor imitation of its natural habitat. In the end, it did not make me feel any better at all.

The following day, while Kate and I tried valiantly to get in touch with Vladivostok, Yuri hit the streets again. We had given him $16 (approximately half his monthly salary) to buy a brand new bike, which he eventually managed to do, and the rest of the day was spent cannibalising it to fix up his original bike properly and converting his two canvas rucsacs into far-from-lightweight panniers. It all seemed less than perfect to me, but Yuri's complete refusal to be fazed by any of the apparent shortcomings of his equipment, plus his obvious mechanical competence, helped me feel that we would have no problems.

Yuri's fellow Russian for the next stage was Eugene from the Centre Pole office. He seemed perfectly happy with the equipment we were supplying, which was a relief. He brought with him the letters from home we had been waiting for since Yekaterinburg – friends had thoughtfully provided a copy of Viz and a selection of newspaper crosswords to keep me alternately amused and challenged – and Kate's new headset.

After seven weeks and 3242 miles, Vladimir's journey had come to an end. Despite the language barrier we had managed to communicate pretty well if slowly, and although the riding was more strenuous than what he was used to he had managed brilliantly. It was not easy to tell – emotionally speaking Vladimir did not give much away – but I think he was relieved it was over. It was a shame to see him head off to the railway station to catch his train back to St. Petersburg, and through our goodbyes in broken Russian we managed to convey how helpful he had been to Kate and me and to the expedition's success so far. But we could not dwell on what we had already achieved. There was a long way to go and two new team members to get to know. Always with an eye on our timetable we had to push on from Novosibirsk. I enjoyed the breaks from the cycling, but the opportunities to relax were few as we had to shop for supplies and maintain the bikes. The cycling days, although physically tough, were straightforward – we got up, we cycled, we went to bed. I was always happy to set off again after a couple of days off. It meant we were making progress, heading east towards our ultimate target, and every day completed was a day less to do.

Our next immediate goal was Krasnoyarsk, but we would not be taking the direct route. South of the main road, down towards the border with Mongolia, lay the Sayan Mountains. Kate had been keen to include these in our itinerary, purely from the point of view of wanting to visit a scenically impressive area, but I was not really convinced. The detour would add about 750 very energetic and mountainous miles, and would do nothing to help our easterly progress. It seemed to be an unnecessary addition. The main purpose of the journey was to cycle across Russia, and inserting a two-week sightseeing section just added two weeks of wear and tear and potential problems. On top of that, it would mean we were moving through the unpredictable far eastern area of Siberia two weeks later than necessary – two weeks closer to winter. However, I had to agree that it was unlikely that I would be passing this way again and that we had a perfect opportunity to visit the Sayan region. So, romantic traveller notions overcame the practical expedition planning approach, and a large loop was drawn on our route map.

SECTION 4

~~~

AROUND THE SAYAN RING

~~~

To reach the Sayan Mountains, we first had to complete a six-day cycle to Achinsk, from where we caught an overnight train south to Abakan. The roads out of Novosibirsk were good quality tarmac; thankfully we had left the mud a long way behind and Yuri and Eugene could settle into the cycling on easy surfaces. Kate's legs were still cramping up on the first day, but the renewed exercise, plus a few painkillers, seemed to sort them out.

Day 55: Thursday June 24th – Oyash – Novoromanova
77.0 miles (total 3384.5 miles)

One of the best days so far. Up at 6.00 to confront the mossies. Off by 8.00. Good conditions - tail wind, cloudy, cool. Eugene was teaching me some vital Russian phrases, eg 'It is cloudy today.' It takes ages for new words to sink in, and then I suddenly remember them two weeks later.

Eugene and Yuri don't seem to eat much at the moment. I'm sure that will change! We had a very good stolo lunch - there was even a choice of what to have on the spaghetti, and hot vegetables (cabbage/carrot mix), and fresh tomato. Heavenly! The air in town (Yurga) was thick with poplar seeds - it looked almost like snow-drifts in place. The seeds are very small and surrounded by fluff. Novosibirsk was full of it, too.

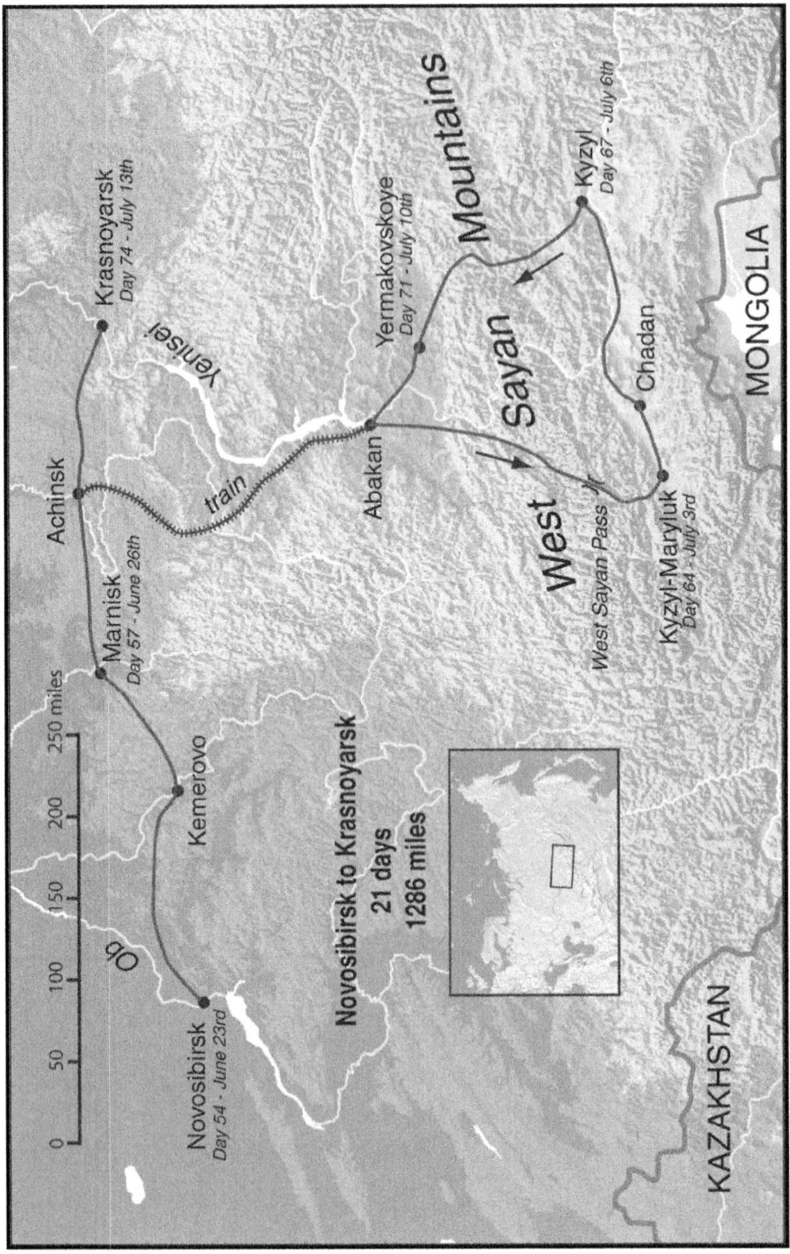

0
50
100
150
200
250 miles
Novosibirsk
Day 54 - June 23rd
Ob
Kemerovo
Marnisk
Day 57 - June 26th
Achinsk
Krasnoyarsk
Day 74 - July 13th
Yenisei
train
Abakan
Yermakovskoye
Day 71 - July 10th
Kyzyl
Day 67 - July 6th
Chadan
Kyzyl-Maryluk
Day 64 - July 3rd
West Sayan Pass
West Sayan Mountains
Novosibirsk to Krasnoyarsk
21 days
1286 miles
MONGOLIA
KAZAKHSTAN

In the afternoon, there were even more white butterflies than yesterday. Quite amazing numbers of them - it's like flying through a blizzard sometimes (bit of hyperbole, but there were hundreds of them!) I've never seen anything like it. The grassland is beautiful - patches of purple vetches, plantain flowers, cinquefoils and others I don't know.

After lunch, we followed the river Tomj, which has some unexpected and quite large cliffs. We had wanted to go a different way, but were advised that the road was very bad, and so decided to follow the river - it adds about 56 miles but I don't mind. It's not a main road, so there wasn't much traffic. The scenery is wonderful - lush pine/birch forests. Sunny afternoon - again the thunderstorm went through before us. Very lucky.

We found a good camp site on the river Tomj at Novoromanova, and arrived at a decent time for once (no hanging around!) - about 5.45 - so we had time to relax. Everyone went for a swim - the water was cold to begin with, but got better. It is a very wide river, and must get much more water in winter by the look of the beach (40-50 yards wide). I'm a bit concerned about ticks because of the wood nearby, but I think we're okay. There are loads of local kids hanging around. I'd prefer it if they went away as it means we have to keep watching the bikes etc. I'm sure they're okay really, but we have to keep an eye on them. And there is actually time to write this before supper and sunset - normally I do it by torchlight while wanting to go to sleep. I was in a good mood all day today. Bum feeling better, no back ache, good scenery. Up and down with some steep but only short climbs.

Eugene and Yuri keep up well. They did well today considering it's only their second day. I hope we didn't go too fast - they will feel tired in a day or two. It takes a while to catch up with you at first.

It was good to have a very relaxing evening around the campfire, which we cooked the rice and soup on. The mossies didn't arrive until after supper, which made things more enjoyable. Cloudless evening, wind died away; toast and honey (we finished the 2lb of jam which we started only last night). Yuri and Eugene laugh and smile a lot, in contrast to Vlad, who would only shrug his shoulders. We watched the fishermen and eagles flying along the river. Yuri's English gets confused at times: 'Only heaven under the mind' means 'Nothing but clear skies above our heads'.

Eugene and Yuri were good expedition companions. They just got on with things, were ready in the mornings without any prompting and they rode well. I felt more relaxed than I had with Vladimir and did not waste time wondering how we would fare each day. As long as we picked a realistic target we could be confident to reach it within a reasonable time. It also meant that we all rode as a group, which was more enjoyable.

Road surfaces came and went with the hills; some of the descents on gravel were a bit hairy and Yuri came off at one point after failing to spot a bump. Considering he only had four gears compared to our twenty-one he managed very well on the uphills, although he was spotted hanging on to the back of a truck and enjoying a tow on more than one occasion.

In this wide and uncluttered landscape, we could often spot our next town a long way in the distance because of the tall factory chimneys painted in their distinctive red hoops. In Kemerevo these materialised into a collection of very run-down-looking factories. From their general condition it was difficult to guess if they were still in use or not, but the chimneys gave the game away, belching out evil-smelling exhaust. The town was located on the banks of the river Tomj, and I was slightly alarmed to realise that it was upstream of where we had been swimming the day before. From what I had seen and heard of the local industrial practices it was a fairly safe bet that as well as chucking out filth into the air the factories would be using the local rivers as a handy waste disposal route.

As we crossed into another time zone, the midsummer evenings held on to the daylight. At 10.30pm the sun was still well above the horizon and I could write my diary outside without a torch. Camping close to Krasnoy Jar we cooked, ate and wrote on the tarmac as this seemed to be a good way to avoid the worst of the mosquitoes. With the pot of soup and rice bubbling away on the stove, we could relax and listen to the cuckoos calling across the wooded hillsides.

With 50 miles to go to Achinsk, we pulled in to Bogotol and made for the hotel. As the price of the room went up and up each time the flame-haired ladies at the reception desk found out something new about us ('Ah, you have bicycles.' Ker-ching! 'Ah, you are not Russian.' Double ker-ching!) Kate and I resisted the temptation to try and negotiate. We gave our address as Park Lane, which was duly recorded as Park Lenin, and headed up with our equipment. A couple of minutes later we headed down again, collected the linen that the chambermaid had neglected to leave on the beds during her rounds earlier in the day, and returned upstairs. The hotel was actually next to the railway station, so Eugene and Yuri checked out the timetables. They estimated that we had until about 1.30pm to reach Achinsk station the following day, which was plenty of time – enough even to accommodate the idiosyncrasies of Yuri's bike, the freewheel of which broke for the third time, and the vagaries of his riding style, as he fell off again and needed some first aid to his elbow. When we arrived in front of the station we were confused to see the clock over the entrance showing 8.15am. I knew we had been cycling quickly, but even with two months' expedition fitness in our legs we would not have been able to attain the near light-speed necessary to slow down time and allow us to cover the 50 miles in just 15 minutes. So there must have been some other explanation.

Faced with the problem of having to regularise an extended transport system covering such a wide area but all within one country, the Russians had adopted a straightforward centralised policy whereby the entire railway network operated on Moscow time. This was certainly done for practical reasons, but tampering with time had a bit of 1984 about it, where "It was a bright cold day in April, and the clocks were striking thirteen." China has gone further, extending this approach not just to the transport network but to the entire country; from the Taklamakan to the Pacific, rather than the four time zones you would expect the whole country is covered by just one and everybody is on Beijing time. If the governments can tamper with nature and change time itself, surely that is a sign of ultimate power. In 19th Century Britain a similar thing happened, but in typically reserved fashion designed not to upset people too much. Again, it was because of the railways; the introduction of fast travel around the country revealed local time differences that had to be standardised so the timetables were meaningful (something that many would argue has, even now, not been properly achieved). But I do not think that the introduction of London time country-wide could be seen as the work of a megalomaniac, not when the correction needed to the difference between London and Reading, for instance, was a mere five minutes.

When Eugene and Yuri had checked the timetable they had not spotted this detail in the timekeeping, and as a result we arrived four hours ahead of schedule. Buying the tickets, though, did take a long time and it was good not being in a rush. The open-plan carriage was stuffy and crowded. The wide gauge track allowed larger trains than I was used to at home, and as well as the usual bunks running crossways there was also an extra set running along the windows of the open corridor. The lack of individual compartments and the ready friendliness of most Russians made the whole experience quite sociable, although we did not get off to a good start with the two women who had already settled in in my bay. Lifting the bikes to stow them on the rack over the bunks, water came out of one of my bottles and dribbled onto the lower bunk. The women paused in their conversation, looked at me, looked at the bikes, looked at the water. Russians are friendly, but their openness also extends to being happy to let you know their feelings very plainly, so I was unsure what reaction this incident would provoke. I need not have worried; clearly water spillage in a crowded area did not register on the scale of events to take offence at, and the ladies settled back to their snack of instant coffee and hard boiled eggs while carrying on their conversation in a confiding whisper.

It was strange to see the landscape go by with no effort on my part. I could get used to this, I thought, sitting back and enjoying the view and the banks of wild yellow lilies growing beside the railway as I tucked into a picnic supper with the others. Tasty fresh bread and salami, sponge biscuits and lemonade; I was happy with the menu, but Kate and I found ourselves fantasising more and more about good (ie familiar) food. At the moment we were fixating on crunchy juicy apples, but throughout the trip it could be anything from a good cheese and pickle sandwich to a fine pint of ale; a warming Bolognese to a chilled and refreshing sorbet. Anything, in fact, that we were unlikely to encounter on our journey. We were not going hungry, but we were not enjoying a particularly varied diet. Breakfast was generally porridge with dried apples, lunch would be either *pelmeni* in a *stolovaya* or a picnic of some sort, and for supper we would cook packet soup with either rice or spaghetti added. It did not change much from day to day. Fresh fruit was a very rare treat, and fresh vegetables were something of a novelty. What we were getting was plenty of sugar. Russians definitely seemed to have a sweet tooth, consuming large amounts of jam (mostly spooned into their tea, as far as I could tell), honey and sweets. Eugene certainly enjoyed his *confjet* and was quite insistent every day that we had *chai* when we had set up camp or unpacked in a hotel, even if it was very late and we really just wanted to get on with cooking the soup and rice. It seemed to be a mark in the day for him, the point at which relaxation could begin. Frankly, it became rather annoying, but there was nothing Kate or I could say that would convince him to break his habit.

Something that I looked forward to as a sweet treat were the tins of condensed milk that we were now buying at every opportunity. Porridge and rice pudding became Michelin-starred delights once the thick, almost sickly-sweet ambrosia was stirred in. Often my enthusiasm for the milk became almost a craving. Rather than wait to add it to my pudding I would just drink it straight from the can, gulping down the sweetness with an almost insatiable eagerness. All this, together with the jam, honey and sweets, not to mention my broken toothbrush, was giving my teeth a real hammering. If I stayed here too long I could see myself developing a splendid glinting smile like so many of the locals, as my teeth rotted away to be replaced by a fine set of more valuable gold ones. If ever there was a country that could claim to put its money where its mouth was, this was it.

Day 60: Tuesday June 29th – day off, Abakan

After a decent night's sleep on the train, we arrived in a wet and cool Abakan. It must be an important town, as there are two hotels. The second one was okay (ie cheaper) - Yuri and Eugene checked in, but the receptionist said Kate and I needed a special stamp, so off to the police station we went. They seemed uninterested, and gave us a phone number to ring after 9am. Back to the hotel for breakfast (jam roll, bread, tin of fish, tea, apple and grape juice), and then off shopping etc. Eventually, we found the right room in the police station, where a woman just wrote a note saying 'Please give these people a room'. We thought it was going to take all morning.

I bought some glue for my shoe, changed $50 (@R1215), and went to the market hall - fruit, vegetables, flowers, meat. Loads of stuff available - wonderful smells, especially of dill (very common), and spring onion. Also radishes, cucumbers, carrots, turnips, apricots, oranges, bananas, a spice stall, roses, peonies (the lady gave me a small bunch (currently in the thermos) after I said how beautiful they were), eggs. We buy some vegetables usually to take with us for picnic lunches. There were no fridges or ice in the meat section, and today was very warm and humid (there was a thunderstorm in the afternoon, and rain all evening).

As we were roaming around one shop, a bloke called Sergei started chatting to me. He was very interesting and knowledgeable, from the Xhakas people, with a look similar to Eskimos rather than Mongols.

The Xhakas language is in the Turkish family. Sergei works in the north Russian oil fields, but lives here at the moment, working with his brother in the theatre - he also paints as a hobby, using this to fund his trips abroad, eg to Scandanavia. He told us a lot about the region and its history, explaining the exhibits in the local museum. Originally, there were Caucasian people here, then came Mongol invasions, then Russians. Xhakas traded silks from China to make their beautiful traditional dress, cowries from the Indian Ocean for shaman costumes, and metal from Russia.

On July 3rd in a village before Abazar, a traditional Xhakas ceremony will be taking place for the first time for 70 years. It's infuriating, but we can't really stay in this immediate area for five days - we'd love to see it. Sergei told us about lots of other interesting places to visit, though, and he has a friend in a town two days along the road, so we hope to be able to stay there. He warned us that Ak-Dovurak is an unhealthy place due to the molybdenum and asbestos - we will speed up for that bit.

All along the river out of Abakan (our route tomorrow) there are lots of burial mounds, dating from one large battle hundreds of years ago (before 13th Century). A Turkish khanate army came from the south and caught a Xhakas man - they wanted him as a guide through the mountains to the Abakan valley. He deliberately took them the wrong way and half the soldiers died in the harsh winter. A bloody battle with the Xhakas followed, which neither side won (Sergei digresses about the ancient Battle of Asculum at this point!) All the dead soldiers were buried by the river.

Some cultural similarities exist between northern Mongolia (which used to be Xhakas) and the Abakan area, eg the burial mounds, and the way animals are killed to eat, ie by slitting their belly and reaching in to grab the heart.

Sergei is very anti-Communist. He dislikes them for repressing his culture, language and heritage. At school he was a bit of a rebel, and taught himself the history of Xhakas and read loads of books eg the Iliad. He speaks excellent English (self-taught), and also Xhakasian - his parents speak only this. His village, Troyakov, was destroyed by the Russians. Of about 17 original Xhakas tribes in the area, only about two remain. The others have been killed off over the last 300 years. They were originally a feared people, with brutal laws. For instance, someone caught stealing would be decapitated, and their head hung around the neck of a relative for ever!

Tomorrow Sergei will introduce us to two Tuvan people (Tuva is the region south of Xhakasia) - students with a wealthy father, apparently, who lives two thirds of the way around the ring, so we hope we can stay there, too. And I was just saying to Kate yesterday how we hadn't had any lucky breaks for a while. Sergei presented us with some traditional carvings he had made - a llama for Kate and a pot-bellied king for me.
It was very humid this evening. I hope the weather clears - after not seeing half of the Pyrenees and all the Picos from my bike because of clouds and rain, I will be very pissed off if the same happens here. Plus it will make any unsurfaced roads a nightmare (Sergei says the main ring is okay, though).
Kate changed a tyre, since it was splitting. Looking at a map of the whole of Russia is tremendously satisfying - there are only three time zones to go. Except we will make no forward progress for the next two weeks. Our hotel is very good - clean, with loads of potted plants everywhere, and hot water! R1100 for Yuri and Eugene, and about R2100 for Kate and me. I spoke to Ala in Omsk to get the phone numbers of possible contacts in Krasnoyarsk and Ulan Ude.

We left town following the road along the wide and flat valley of the Abakan river and came to Troyakov, Sergei's native village. There was not much of it to see, as only twelve of the wooden houses were still occupied. The others were in various states of ruin and decay, their timber frames bleached in the sun. In the well-tended garden of one of the twelve, with cabbages, potatoes and tomatoes growing healthily in the rich soil, an old lady with her tanned and weather-beaten face moved among the vegetables. Yuri approached the gate while the rest of us waited a few yards back. The sight of four strange people on bizarre-looking bikes would be quite a shock, and we did not want to scare her. Yuri chatted quietly to the old lady, and she opened the gate to allow us into her garden.

She was called Galina and was about 80 years old. She had lived in the village since 1948 and yes, she knew Sergei's family. Kate was taking photos and I was filming with the video camera – the whole situation must have been rather disconcerting. Galina was reluctant to tell us any more; when Yuri asked her what she grew she denied everything except wheat and potatoes, even though we could see other things in the garden. She said she had forgotten the old stories, although she must have seen so much over the years. There were so

Yuri settling into camp life.

Eugene unwinding after a day in the saddle.

Opposite. Day 61: Galina reflects on the old days in Troyakov, south of Abakan.

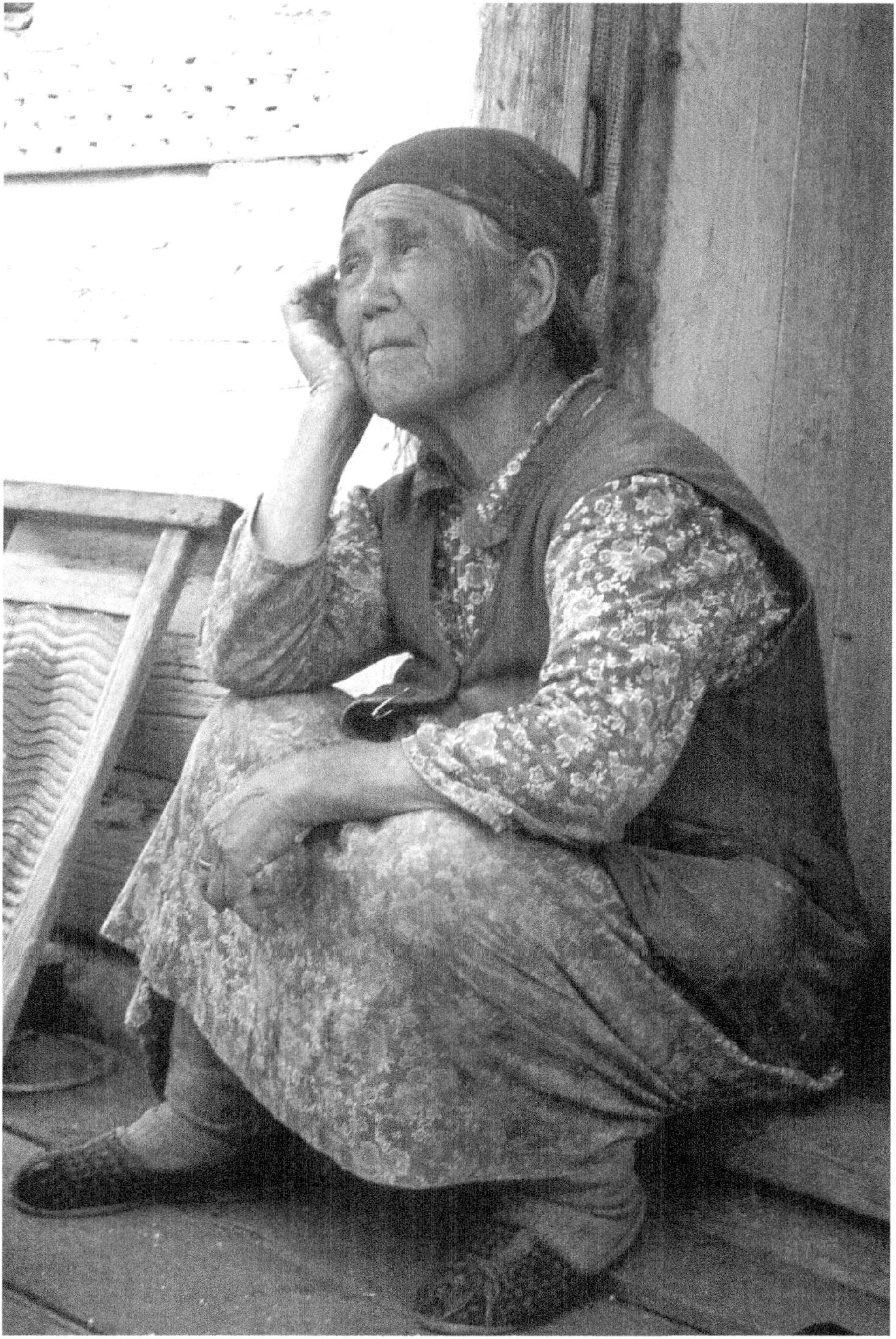

Day 60: In the meat market, Abakan. If only the cow head had fitted in my pannier.

Day 64: Traditional Tuvan family south of the West Sayan Pass, father and son wearing Mongolian-style hats.

many possible reasons why she did not want to talk to us – uncertainty over our real intentions, indifference about the whole thing, unwillingness to remember the old days, genuine memory loss. Maybe she was just tired and did not feel like entertaining us. Whatever it was, we were not here to make people feel uncomfortable, so we thanked her and pedalled away. It was an interesting encounter. The people we had met so far had all been happy and eager to talk about their lives and situations; Galina had been our first reticent Russian, but her quiet tolerance of us and the way she maintained her dignity while her village fell apart around her made an impression.

From Troyakov we could see what lay ahead of us. In the distance across the wide grass plains the mountains rose up, suggesting some tough days over the next couple of weeks. How Yuri's bike would cope was something of an unknown quantity; five spokes broke at once on this day, which gave me an opportunity to practise my crossword skills while he knitted his back wheel together. We pitched the tents in a field near the railway at Anxhakova having bought a few buns and the last two loaves in the shop in the previous village. Mosquitoes persuaded us to keep away from the river, but they could not diminish the evocativeness of the landscape, as the many standing stones wet from the recent rain glistened in the evening sun under a glorious double rainbow.

Over the next two days we made our way up towards the West Sayan Pass. These were some of the longest mountain days I had experienced, and the weather swung between heavy rain and very hot sunshine. On July 1st we had three passes to cross, each taking about an hour; unfortunately I failed to pace myself properly and paid the price towards the end of the day. The first two went by without any problems – we had lunch after the first one in Abaza in an excellent *stolovaya* attached to the local iron ore mine (just 35p for all of us, and good food including *okroshka* (a cold soup of bread-water (*kvas*) with eggs, spring onions, *smetana* (sour cream) and potato) and paused at the top of the second to savour the view across the wild forested ridges to snow-capped peaks in the distance. There was time, too, for a local lorry driver to share his dried fish with us (*xharios*, a local speciality). On the third pass, though, the morning's over-enthusiastic cycling caught up with me. As my energy drained away with every metre gained in altitude I felt annoyed that I had taken too short-term a view of the day. Instead of pacing myself I had attacked the hills – I had felt strong on the first two climbs and I enjoyed cycling that way, but it was important to remember that each day was just one small part of the overall journey. If I wore myself out here I could jeopardise my ability to continue through to the end. My legs needed a boost to make it up the third climb, and reluctantly I broke into my valuable reserve snacks.

Kate's steady approach was better and she arrived at the top looking fresh. The 40-plus miles per hour descent made it all worthwhile and took us to our overnight stop in the village of Kubaika, a collection of wooden log buildings along mud streets on the banks of the milky-turquoise Ahna river. Sergie from Abakan had a contact here, Raman, who worked for the local forestry management group, and he turned his office over to us for accommodation. He and his crew were responsible for the Tashtiypski region, a wild area covering 600,000 hectares. Each year 250ha would be cut for timber and Raman's group, which looked a motley selection of unshaven and dishevelled frontiersmen, monitored the logging, planted new trees and acted as firemen. Later in the trip we would appreciate the importance of this last role.

The grassland of the Abakan valley had disappeared as soon as the road started to climb. Lush pine and birch forest covered the lower flanks of the mountains and the ground was dense with vetches, buttercups, columbines and wild lupins. The variety and abundance of plants and flowers in the landscape appealed to my ecological side and provided a regular distraction to take my mind off other aspects of the trip. I was pleased to have Yuri along, a fellow botanist with whom I could have conversations that would probably have made Kate and Sasha's eyes glaze over. Despite his undoubted appreciation of the natural world, his work centred on investigating and developing more productive varieties of peas and pineapples (I am not sure if he was working his way through the fruit and vegetable alphabet or not, with pomegranates and quinces next in line for scientific scrutiny on the way to agriculture's holy grail, the elusive high yield zucchini) and this lab-based approach where plants can be cloned and cultured might explain his apparently cavalier approach to the real world of plants outside. On one occasion during a tea break Yuri went roaming off into the undergrowth looking for interesting specimens as usual. A few minutes later he reappeared with a big grin and, holding aloft a pretty purple flower at the end of its just-plucked stem, announced confidently, "This very rare plant!" I could only agree.

The views we had had from the passes showed forest stretching away to the horizon – real wilderness and sure to quicken the pulse of any logger as he surveyed the arboreal expanse, axe in hand. As with many of Russia's natural resources it would be easy to think of this abundance as a limitless supply hardly dented by Man's harvest. But there were plenty of reports of irresponsible and mismanaged use of these resources, with little thought given to the consequences of how the harvests were taken and what state the land and its inhabitants (animals, plants and people) would be in afterwards. Oil and gas exploration in the far north, nickel mining near the Norwegian border, profligate use of water resources for cotton production in the south of the former USSR – not to mention the whole Soviet nuclear industry; each of these industries had directly devastated huge areas and the effects could be felt farther afield as wind and water transported waste materials and by-products. The country's environmental movement was still in its infancy as we explored Russia, and the relatively new Government agency whose job it was to regulate industry and help protect the natural richness and diversity here faced an uphill struggle in the face of corruption and a deep-seated desire for self-sufficiency in raw materials. The work of Raman and his team was therefore very important, keeping track of the activity in the surrounding forests and maintaining the balance of removal and renewal.

For most of the following morning it rained. At lunchtime, cold and wet, we arrived at a hamlet and knocked on the door of the hotel. A lady appeared but explained that the hotel was closed as there was no electricity. None of us expressed any great surprise. We managed to talk our way in anyway so that we could prepare lunch ourselves under cover. Soup, bread, cheese and cucumbers went some way to warm us up but did not prepare us fully for the rigours of the afternoon.

For the next 30 miles, the road climbed. It was not particularly steep, but it made up for any shortcomings in gradient with its relentless ascent. Yuri and Eugene seemed to have found new reserves and moved ahead while Kate and I paused for some bread and dried fruit. The rain had stopped farther down, but the sky was still a menacing gloomy grey with ragged clouds scudding by. I was unclear about exactly where we were heading for the night. The pass itself still lay about 10 miles distant, and with the afternoon merging into early evening and the continuing threat of bad weather I was keen to set up camp and sort out the cooking. The trees thinned as we approached their upper limit; the birch had already disappeared and now the pines were fewer. Patches of snow lay in hollows; house martins flew overhead. About six miles from the summit the tarmac ended and the road became gritty and stony, levelling out for a while across a wide, high valley. Yuri and Eugene had carried on, so we had to keep going until we caught them up. The track rose again and I was feeling very tired by now. Being in front is always better as you can choose when to stop, knowing that you will not get left farther behind. At the back there is always pressure to carry on, even though you would like a rest.

Two miles from the top we spotted a small low building – a workers' hut for road maintenance teams. The lady in the hotel at lunch might have told Yuri and Eugene about it or she might not; either way, I was extremely pleased to see their bikes leaning against the wall as we pedalled up. There was no maintenance team in residence and the door was open, so we had the place to ourselves and quickly settled in as the rain started to fall again. It would have been a bleak, if dramatic, spot to pitch the tent.

It looked as though there had not been anybody in the hut for a while, but once we had tidied it up, made some space and lit the fire in the stove it turned out to be a cosy refuge. With a line rigged up across the room we hung up our wet kit, and Yuri managed to start a generator which gave us two hours of electricity. With light, and hot water from the stove to wash in, we passed a comfortable evening, marred only by Kate and Eugene disagreeing about what constituted an adequate portion of pasta. Hardly an especially divisive issue, but coming at the end of 30 miles of climbing, something like that can take on a significance greater than it deserves, especially when coupled with demands for *chai*. There were no hotheads in the group, though, and a major rift was avoided. Even if it is not quite enough to fully satisfy your hunger a meal can work wonders in these situations, as sugar levels and emotions return to normal. It had been a tiring three days from Abakan to here – 223 miles, of which it felt the majority had been uphill. In the morning we would reach the pass, at 2206m the highest point of the expedition. I tried to convince myself it would be all downhill to the ocean at Vladivostok , but there is never such a thing.

Day 64: Saturday July 3rd – West Sayan Pass camp to Kyzyl Maryluk
66.2 miles (total 3956.9 miles)

A beautiful clear morning about 2000m up in the mountains. A half-hour climb took us to the top of the pass, for spectacular views. We walked to the very top, where there were beautiful alpine flowers - gentians, bergenias, Myosotis and others, with thick lichen underfoot. Superb treeless valleys and a clear view to the snow-capped mountains in the distance. Lots of photos were taken, and we set off just before the clouds came over the top.

The first five miles of the descent were non-asphalt, but pretty good. We met Vladimir (a geologist) and Daniel (his son), doing the Sayan ring in the opposite direction. It had taken them 13 days to do the first 600 miles, on their one-geared bikes. Why did we spend so much on all this fancy equipment?!

The mountain meadows are beautiful, full of flowers and wonderful smells - open pinewoods. The downhill lasted about 20 miles, then flattened out along the river valley, with some short, sharp climbs. There was a headwind, but it was very sunny. During our picnic lunch, Kate went chasing yaks (just like home on the farm), and a Tuvan family came past on their horses. The father was wearing a beautifully embroidered hat, four-sided with a small point in the middle.

The valley widened, and the pinewood followed the river. We could see yurts here and there. At the top of a big climb into the next valley, marked by prayer flags, there was the most spectacular view along the river, with its wood, then the dry valley floor and steep sides stretching away. Mountains everywhere. The strata are all up on end, so there has been some serious movement in the past. Where we had lunch, the rocks were very glacial.

The next valley was drier still - semi-arid. A short, steep descent took us down to follow a new river. We came to a GAI post in the middle of nowhere (Gosudarstvennaya Avtomobil'naya Inspektsiya – traffic police), and actually had to show our passports (the 'Stop' barrier came down, and Eugene tried to go around but the policeman caught him.) Our panniers were given a quick feel for guns.

We thought we had done the last climb, but there were two more. The first came out on the edge of a huge flat grassland ringed by mountains - mini Mongolia. Yurts in the distance look like models - it's difficult to judge the scale. The road ran ahead dead straight, across the dry tussocky grassland.

As we went down slightly the ground became wetter. We could see a large asbestos mine on the left hand side.
The last climb was fairly short. Kate's energy was low again. The final descent towards Kyzyl-Marjalyk was fairly difficult due to a head wind. We bought biscuits, jam (puree), bread, then the GAI we'd asked for directions came and advised us not to camp, and went to the hotel to explain that we needed to stay there. A drunken policeman invited himself in while we were cooking. Risotto tonight, with roasted peanuts. Very tasty. The room was very warm and stuffy as the windows wouldn't open properly. The policeman said two people in town had been murdered recently - that could be why the passports were being checked. The people seem very friendly, though, and are more inclined to wave to us on the bikes. Lots of curious faces poked around our hotel room door - Yuri and Eugene are as much foreigners as we. There are hardly any Caucasians around. Everyone looks Mongol, but they are actually Tuvan.

Tuva had in fact experienced a recent sudden decline in its ethnic Russian population in the early 1990s, encouraged by attacks which had left nearly 90 Russians dead. We were clearly entering a remote part of the old Soviet empire. The northern limit of Tuva runs along the ridge crossed by the West Sayan Pass. The territory of mountains, steppe and forests covers an area slightly larger than Tunisia, extending south to Mongolia, west to the Altai and east to Buryatya, and the Tuvans have cultural and linguistic links with each of their neighbours. One of the most well-known features of Tuvan culture is throat-singing, where individual performers produce rich multi-layered harmonies by carefully controlling the resonances in their throat. This style is believed to have developed in association with the region's animist religion, where the spirituality of the environment is contained not just in the physical objects but in the sounds of the natural world as well.

The Sayan ring was more of a triangle and cycling along the bottom strut, parallel with the Mongolian border, we were at least heading east again, if only briefly. My mood was good. In the planning stage Kate and I had not been able to agree on the value of including this section, but now that I was here I was extremely pleased she had managed to persuade me. The mountain and meadow landscapes were some of the best I had seen anywhere, and for once in our journey we were seeing some variation in the people and culture. We all felt relaxed; the riding was hard, but we were finishing each day at a reasonable time and could spend the evenings chatting and writing.

We found one of the best campsites of the whole journey a couple of days after the West Sayan Pass, after an 80-mile day through grassy plains, forest and scrubby valleys. The sound of larks filled the skies and eagles soared high on thermals. Near Cha-Hoy we turned off the road and bumped across to the river. The setting was perfect. Scented chamomile-like plants soft enough to walk on barefoot carpeted the ground, their gentle fragrance carried on the warm breeze. Washing in the bracingly cold river was a short-lived experience but the invigorating and tingling afterglow was the reward for a brief dip. Best of all, there were no mosquitoes! We could eat supper without constantly swatting, and after my wash, as a large full moon climbed high in the sky, I stretched out on the sweet-smelling sward to write my diary in the unmolested warmth of the Siberian evening.

Earlier, while we had been cooking, we were joined by Aleig, a local Tuvan farmer. He wandered over on his horse to find out who we were and stopped for a chat. We might have thought our journey was impressive, but having fought in World War Two Aleig set off from Germany and walked home to Tuva. Yuri settled for having a short ride on his horse.

People had shown a reasonable amount of interest in us so far, but the usual reaction was quite muted. We could arrive in a town or village without causing much of a stir, and more often than not a friendly wave to a passing driver or potato planter went unacknowledged. In the villages of Tuva, though, we were definitely the centre of attention, four white faces among the predominant Asians. Sometimes the attention was welcome and felt quite benign. In Aryg-Uzyu we stopped to buy some lunch, eating our assorted items on the grass outside the shop. An excited crowd of youngsters gathered, curious about this small band of strangers, and we were quite happy to be watched and talked about behind hands. When we had finished our lunch and set off again, the boys escorted us for a mile so along the road in a lively gaggle on their bikes, weaving, overtaking and shrieking. On rare other occasions, the atmosphere felt different – not particularly dangerous or threatening, maybe just claustrophobic. Usually this was with an older crowd, probably a bit worse for wear after some rough vodka. Rather than watch us animatedly as the boys had done, they would just gather and watch. I felt more self-conscious and it was harder to gauge just what they were thinking. Despite the increased exposure I felt better on a bicycle in these situations as we were not showing off our wealth in a big four-wheel drive. It was just us, filthy, and our dusty bikes. People could see what we had, and it was not much. In Ust-Elegest a crowd built up, the biggest so far. Kate and Eugene were in the shop and Yuri and I were outside, watching the equipment and the over-curious. Once the shopping was done we carried on for a short distance out of town, happy to escape the attention before stopping for a snack.

Half way around the Sayan ring we took a rest day at Kyzyl. I had enjoyed the riding over the last week despite all the effort in the mountains. My energy levels were good and I was ready for the next stage back up to Abakan. How quickly things can change. Having followed the Yenisey river on a short day's ride into Kyzil we checked into the hotel and headed for the *stolovaya* for lunch. It was a pretty good meal of barley, green tomatoes, sausages, corned beef soup, sweet pastries and *smetana*. I left the restaurant feeling fine, but on the walk back to the hotel things started to feel odd. Over the next few hours I got worse until extreme stomach cramps took over and I experienced some extraordinarily thorough bouts of diarrhoea and vomiting as my body expelled whatever bug I had picked up. It left me totally exhausted and aching. There was no recurrence during the night and by the next morning I did not feel too bad, but my appetite had disappeared and although this was a rest day I would need to force something down so I had the energy to carry on the next day.

While the others went shopping I stayed in bed, welcome for the chance to have a very lazy day if not for the way it had come about. The shopping trip was not a great success – milk, bread, jam, biscuits and a couple of wrinkly cucumbers. This was a decent-sized town; how could things be so hard to come by? We needed to stock up for the next four days, and two cucumbers would not fill the fuel tanks. A second sortie later in the day produced a more varied haul of eggs, radishes, dates and bottled tomatoes. We were not going to be winning any awards for menu planning, but as long as we were getting enough calories one way or another I was not fussed about the combination of food items on my plate.

The day was hot and listless. Following my sickness and the hanging around I was feeling very fed up and my enthusiasm for the next stretch had waned. We were now more or less half way through the whole expedition and mid-trip blues had definitely settled in. Although we would soon be able to start counting down the days to Vladivostok it seemed that we had done so much already and there was the same to do again, although we knew that the second half would be tougher, more remote and less predictable. The next few days back to Abakan and on to Krasnoyarsk suddenly seemed very fragmented and felt like an inconvenient bit that I needed to do so I could get back on with the main journey.

Even when I was not feeling ill, one day off was not enough to have a proper rest, and we were all feeling the effect of the previous week's riding as we set off from Kyzyl. Having had a disturbed night with more diarrhoea I was keen to stay in bed, and the alarm had taken a long time to wake me. On the edge of town, crossing the bridge over the Yenisey River, we saw two cyclists coming the other way. Mikhail and Nikolai were coming to the end of their own expedition from Vilnius to Kyzyl, a 'goodwill tour' to spread the message of world peace to the local people. They had chosen to end in Kyzyl as they had calculated it to be the centre of Asia, and that reminded me of how I had got interested in expedition cycling in the first place. In 1987 I had read a book by Richard and Nicholas Crane called 'Journey to the Centre of the Earth' which described their extraordinary ride from the coast of Bengal to the point which *they* had calculated to be the most remote from any sea (somewhere in the remote far western reaches of China). Taking the idea of lightweight cycle touring to almost dangerous extremes (despite the fact that they cycled over the Himalayas, the Tibetan plateau and through the Taklamakan Desert they carried no tent, no food and the tiniest tool kit imaginable) they completed their expedition with the help, generosity and hospitality of the people the met along the way, and experienced great adventures and a couple of arrests.

It all sounded a fantastic way to explore the world; admittedly I was doing it with a ton of luggage, but I do appreciate a few comforts. Mikhail and Nikolai were not carrying much and had been eating up the miles, but I think they should have found space in the panniers for at least a small tube of sun-cream. Their smiles beamed from their red faces and chapped lips – it was almost an early 19th Century polar explorer look – but they had reached their goal and could relax in the shade now. They told us about the new road from here to Turan, which we would pass through later in the day. It was impossible to avoid the mountains completely (the ridges ran east-west and we were going north-south) but the new road did follow a slightly more forgiving line. A new road and hot sun did mean plenty of sticky tarmac, though, and it seemed impossible to build up any momentum. Half the point of cycling is that if you stop pedalling you keep moving – if you had enough time you could compete a journey with very little effort. Today, when we stopped pedalling, we just stopped. The big flock of sheep in the road did not help, either.

The weather seemed to have settled into hot and sunny during the day, ferocious thunderstorms and heavy rain during the evening. It was an incentive to finish each day in good time, especially as we would be spending the next few nights under canvas.

Day 70: Friday July 9th – camp 20km after Turan to camp after Aradan
61.9 miles (total 4278.2 miles)

8.35pm - the most amazing and violent thunder and hail storm is raging right above us, echoing off the mountains. Unfortunately the tent has no window, so I can't watch it! Luckily we have been very organised tonight - we stopped at 6pm and had eaten, washed and put away by 8pm, so everything is dry, unlike yesterday.

We have left the Tuva region, and there is a sudden change back to Russian faces. The scenery has also changed back to taiga. A tiring day. I don't think I'm recovering fully, and still feel tired after being ill. Generally a bit fatigued. Fortunately we don't have to do too much each day, but the mountains obviously don't help, or the soft tar. There were two long (40-45 minutes) climbs this morning, both hard work, and we had only expected one. The road is not as on the map, so we got to Aradan quickly, missing out Idzim. Lunch at Aradan, where we bought a litre of milk, and filled our bottles with water drawn from 9m down. Bread is only delivered once a week - today, luckily. Our road followed the river Boyba (?) in the afternoon, although the river wasn't marked on the map. Steadily up but fairly easy, although I was knackered, of course. Camped in an Alchemilla meadow. Bracing wash in river. Pasta with fish and peanuts for tea, with bread and sweetened chocolate milk. Enjoyed the storm!

The following day it was more than the faces that changed. The morning started cool and misty but after the first climb we had warmed

A tale of two campsites. Above – idyllic in Oleig's fragrant meadow, Day 65.
Below – tempestuous under leaden skies, Day 70.

Day 71: Slavik (left), brigadier of the milk farm. A lovely setting for my Giardia-disturbed night.

Day 74: Roadside watermelons proved tempting on the long, hot ride to Krasnoyask.

Day 75:
Accommodation in Krasnoyask. The view outside, (above) – scythe-sharpening and laundry; the view inside (right) once we had tidied up.

up and the mist had cleared to reveal spectacular views through clear air across the taiga-covered eastern Sayan. The mountains on the skyline were far more jagged than those we had seen earlier; dramatic shifts in the character of the landscape seemed to typify the region. A very long descent brought us out of the mountains, through broad-leaved woodland and back to the open landscapes of two weeks earlier. People were out with scythes cutting hay and sitting by the roadside selling strawberries. Pelmeni was back on the menu, and I was quite pleased to tuck into a large bowl of it, although the novelty wore off in a day or two. Well – a day. My health was about to take a nasty turn.

Day 71: Saturday July 10th – camp after Aradan to near Yermakovskoye
74.0 miles (total 4352.0 miles)

We had wanted to carry on past Yermakovskoye (where we bought some milk to have with bread and chocolate) and camp near the river, but we didn't get very far. Something odd had been happening in my guts all day, producing foul hydrogen sulphide burps, and now I suddenly had an excruciating pain in my belly. I had no idea what it was, and was quite worried. It was too painful to continue cycling, so Kate and Yuri set off down a track to check campsite suitability.

By complete luck (!) there was a big dairy farm. Slavik, the bloke in charge ('brigadier') was very friendly, giving me still-warm raw milk to sort me out, and indicating that we camp right there. There were 8 milkmaids, 150 cows, about 3 cowhands (two of them Slavik's sons), and two three-hour milking sessions a day producing about 3000 litres of very tasty milk.

One of the blokes caught two pike and a perch (?) in the river Oya, which were made into soup with dill and spring onions. I stripped off to have a wash in the river, and wasn't put off by the fisherman who turned up - I certainly wouldn't have taken my clothes off 2½ months ago.

The evening was very warm. I felt crap, so had an early night. My belly pains are now much less - I think it was just a huge amount of wind. It is a beautiful setting for Slavik's farm - flat river valley with hills in the distance. Almost an English scene - true of the whole area, really. Very green, rolling landscape.

Somehow, I had contracted giardia, an intestinal parasitic infection. I could not diagnose it at the time but the foul burps are very characteristic. Luckily we were cycling rather than driving; nobody would want to be caught in the confines of a car or bus with such an obnoxious pong wafting about. Cycling proved very uncomfortable for me, though, as leaning forwards on the handlebars caused the large volume of wind trapped in my gut to press against my liver and diaphragm. Every bump and ripple in the road resulted in a sharp pain, as if I had eaten a blade. We had nothing in the first aid kit that could treat it, and anyway I did not know what the problem was. Various people suggested local remedies but gradually the problem fizzled out on its own for now, although it would flare up again sporadically over the next few years.

Day 72: Sunday July 11th – near Yermakovskoye to Abakan 58.3 miles (total 4410.5 miles)

Crap night's sleep. Four visits to the loo with diarrhoea - I didn't feel sick, though. Pleasant moonlit night. The cowhands were up at 4.30, too! Misty morning. I had my bergenia root and Fillipendula tea. Everybody has a remedy for me! I didn't feel too bad, just a bit lethargic.

Very hot, and some long climbs on horrendously sticky roads. Lunch was at a cafe in Minusinsk, the town where Peter the Great's relatives were exiled, apparently. Roast chicken and swiss roll. Revolting loos in the bus station.

We got to Abakan at 4.40pm and went to the railway station and bought train tickets to Achinsk for tomorrow. Quite a relief to arrive and look forward to a day off. Just as we were working out how to contact Sergei's brother (Eugene didn't seem convinced that it was worth the effort) he turned up with his friend Galina and took us to his office (fortunately close by), where his wife was already cooking something for us.

The brother is Alexei, director of a local theatre. He seems to be a key person in local Xhakas affairs. Gave us each a poster of the old Xhakas alphabet. Knows his lineage for 21 generations, and cannot kill eagles, lynx or xharios (fish) as these are his star signs in various horoscopes. He asked Kate what she thought of cosmic energy (she gets all the tricky questions) and was there a course available at her university. Like Sergei, Alexei has almost South American indian features, but his wife looks vaguely Chinese. They all left us to sleep in the office, and will return tomorrow for work, which will be too early.

Alexei helped organise the July 3rd celebrations near the village of Matkechik on the Xhan Obaazi mountain. The event was named Ada Xhooraii ('Remember our ancestors').

Muggy weather and fatigue produced a very inactive morning the following day, with Eugene, Yuri and me flaked out on the sofa in Alexei's office for a few hours. It was a welcome opportunity to do nothing, but we were clearly wiped out and had been riding hard despite sickness and tough terrain. Now it caught up with us. It was less 'Ooh, I think I'll sit down for a bit, put my feet up and have a relaxing cup of tea,' and more 'Ooh, I think I'll ...zzzzzzzz' as my body just shut down for a while in mutiny.

When we did rouse ourselves Alexei drove us to the *stolovaya* for lunch (the novelty of being back in *pelmeni*-world had firmly worn off by now; a note in my diary for this day reads "*Why do Russians tolerate this unimaginative, overcooked, grey, almost hot, every-day-and-every-town-the-same rubbish? Kate and I have to stop ourselves when we start talking about delicious and plentiful food.*") then on to the station to board the train back to Achinsk. Yuri was very unlucky. Apart from breaking loads of spokes, falling off a few times and messing up his elbow, suffering a temperamental free-wheel and having a broken pedal over the last couple of weeks, when unloading his bike to board the train his pannier containing the three litre jar of juice fell to the ground with a great crash, filling the bag with glass and juice! Having cleared that up, his way onto the train was barred by a very large woman official straight from about thirty years ago, saying that bikes were only allowed on if the front wheels were taken off. Normally very relaxed and happy, Yuri began to get annoyed at this point and started muttering things under his breath. In the meantime, Eugene walked on with his bike in one piece, as did I, calling 'Sorry, I don't speak Russian' over my shoulder as the fat woman protested.

The carriage was even stuffier than before, and we were all perspiring gently as we sat quietly wondering why we had bought what turned out to be a very smelly selection of food for the journey. It was Eugene's turn to feel unwell; he said he had a temperature and would probably stay on the train all the way to Krasnoyarsk. At least he would only miss one day of his planned ride. I could not afford to catch anything more debilitating – I did not want to miss out on any of the expedition.

The train rattled its way north through the night. At 5.45 the next morning I woke feeling well rested – just as well considering what lay in store. We waved Eugene off and at 7.30 we were on the bikes. It was already hot – we were in shorts and tee-shirts from the start – and the air was heavy with a sulphurous smell. Fortunately on this occasion it was nothing to do with my burps; they had cleared up and I had now settled back to my normal background level of gentle effervescence. Fortunately, too, we did not hang about and spend any more time in the unpleasant air than we needed to. A short distance out of Achinsk we looked back; all we could see were three columns of chimney smoke rising from the fug concealing the town.

It turned out to be the hottest day of the expedition, and the second longest. 117.7 miles, which took nine-and-a-half hours and about five litres of water each. If you have been suffering from diarrhoea for four days, why not ride 117 miles in 30-plus degrees? Eugene, no doubt, was having a comfortable snooze. Just to add to the day's efforts, my rear pannier rack broke again. Somehow there always seemed to be some wire by the roadside just when we needed it.

Given the distance we had to cover we stopped only to feed and fill our bottles. While tucking into some fresh water melon at a petrol station we were told about a Polish cyclist who had passed through earlier in the day. He was doing the full world tour by himself. These solo travellers always impressed me. It was one thing to embark upon a major journey in a group, where there would always be other people to spur you on, to motivate and encourage; people to talk to when you were in strange lands with strange languages; and very importantly, people to share the experience with and reminisce with once it was all over. Quite another to tackle these things on your own, where, apart from the human interaction elements, there were also practical aspects to consider. A solo cyclist must carry everything himself, two or three travelling together do not need twice or three times the equipment, so each will carry less than the singleton. In a group, while someone goes shopping the others watch the bikes, or shopping can be done at the same time as bike maintenance. These are small but important aspects to think about when putting an expedition together.

The miles passed in a sweaty heat haze, and at 9.15pm we arrived in Krasnoyarsk. A relieved and refreshed-looking Eugene was waiting for us at the station. Unfortunately he had had no luck sorting out a hotel. Most of them had no vacancies and those that did would not take foreigners. The Kolos Hotel was no exception, apparently being exclusively for Russians. By now it was getting very late and the last thing we needed was a lot of aggravation about finding a bed for the night. In the end Yuri went to the police station to see if anyone there could help out. Russians like and respond to an authoritarian approach. I cannot imagine a policeman phoning a hotel in the UK and having any effect whatsoever on its admission policy. Luckily we were not in the UK, and once the reception desk at the Kolos had been instructed to let us stay we were allowed in. Unfortunately, the policeman's instructions had not included the line "And don't rip them off!" so the bill for all of us came to a hefty 14,000 roubles (about 3,000 for Eugene and Yuri and the bikes, and the rest for Kate and me. How they had a special price for foreigners when they were not really supposed to let them in in the first place remained a mystery).

It was 11.30 before we were in the room, at which point we had to get cleaned up and cook dinner. We had all become slightly hysterical and delirious by this point and seriously needed some food to restore our sugar levels and bring some degree of sanity to the conversation. Eventually, at about 2am, we switched the light off. It had been a very long day.

We had two days in Krasnoyarsk, and did not want to blow the budget on an expensive hotel room. We did have a contact here, someone who worked at the Private Property Fund whose name we were given by Sasha and Ala in Omsk, but our attempts to get in touch with them had been unsuccessful. It pays to persevere, though, and on the morning of our first day off somebody eventually answered the phone. This turned out to be possibly the most tenuous connection for an offer of accommodation throughout the whole trip. Oksana, the lady who had picked up the phone, listened to our story and without any apparent need to be persuaded quickly said 'Okay', met us at the hotel and showed us to an empty flat just around the corner. It turned out that she was nothing to do with the Private Property Fund but had an office in the same building and just happened to share the same phone line. Oksana was one of the new breed of estate agents, and this was one of the flats on her books; it had in fact been recently sold for between four and five million roubles and was being redecorated – hence the fact that it was a complete mess. We said we were very happy with it – it was just the sort of property we had been looking for, the location was perfect and we could move in straight away. The only problem was the new owner Vitali, his girlfriend, their friend Sergei and his girlfriend. They called in, which seemed natural since it was Vitali's flat, but like so many other people we had met they were drunk and had brought some vodka for us. It was a friendly thing to do, but it is awkward communicating with a drunk in English, and painfully so in halting Russian.

Oksana was also keen to chat. She came round later in the day with some cucumbers and peppers from her *dacha*, so we had a snack. It was about 8pm and Kate and I wanted to write faxes and cook supper. Oksana suggested going for a walk around town. It was all very generous and hospitable, but I was much keener on the idea of relaxing in the flat; Kate and I politely declined the offer but Eugene and Yuri agreed to go. They were not seen again for another two-and-a-half hours. In the meantime, Kate and I produced another culinary masterpiece (spaghetti and tomato puree) and enjoyed not having frantic activity and constant requests for *chai* going on around us.

The following day Sasha flew in from Ryazan on the early plane. We were expecting him to bring out various bits of equipment that we had temporarily sent back from Novosibirsk, but there had been a breakdown in communications somewhere along the line. There were only a few realistic opportunities beyond here to get things out to us before we reached the worst section of the trip, so we could not afford mistakes like this. Apparently Sasha could not bring some of the things we wanted because the spare bike in Ryazan was being used by someone and was not around, which rather defeated the point of having it in the first place.

Day 76: Thursday July 15th – day off, Krasnoyarsk

I am annoyed about the cock-up with the equipment. Not only was some not brought out, but some Mars and Marathon bars and Kendal mint cake was missing out of the bag which had been left at Centre Pole. Eugene offered the explanation that some of the staff's kids had probably been into the bag and taken the things, and seemed happy that this was a reasonable explanation. I was not at all happy, and told them that I didn't think Malakhov would be very happy if some of his expedition supplies were taken from their bags and they were to discover this half way to the North Pole. Centre Pole is supposed to be a professional expedition-organising office, and we are paying them $1500 to sort out our trip at this end, so I expect a first class job. I felt like saying something about the fact that the bike wasn't in Ryazan for the bags to be taken off, but kept it to myself. Might mention it on the phone, or in October.

Once I had got over the equipment situation as much as I was going to, we all went into town for a final lunch with Eugene and Yuri. I do not think we were asking too much to find a *stolovaya* operating in the middle of the day. British people get very frustrated when they visit the post office at lunch time and there are only two desks open because the staff have, in a shocking display of customer dis-service, gone for lunch. The customers tut-tut and mumble loudly, and may even be sufficiently moved to talk to each other in the queue about it. But at least the post office is still open, if slightly understaffed. The *stolovayas* in Krasnoyarsk were not really displaying a poor understanding of customer service (as a general concept this was something still very alien to Russian businesses) so much as a complete lack of business sense. All the restaurants we went to were shut for lunch. I would not describe myself as an entrepreneur, but even I could see their business plans were flawed.

So we parted company with Eugene and Yuri in the street. It was all rather rushed and unsatisfactory. Eugene seemed happy to be going home; I had the feeling that he had joined us because he had been asked to, as part of Centre Pole's arrangement with us, rather than out of any personal desire to explore by bike. Nonetheless, he had entered into the spirit of the trip, and again easier communication between us might have revealed something different. Yuri was in his element, undaunted by the hopeless condition of his bike and generally laughing and interested in everything around him. He said he was thinking of coming out again later in the trip to ride some more, maybe at Blagoveshchensk. Who knows what state we might be in by then, two months further on?

We returned to the flat, and once Sasha had explained to Oksana how busy we were getting organised to leave the next day, we settled into a four-hour session of bike cleaning and replacing worn parts. Over dinner (more spaghetti and puree, but with some dried mince this time – who says expedition food has to be dull?) we cracked open a bottle of cheap fizzy wine to celebrate the half-way stage and Sasha's arrival.

Sasha was only 21 but had already travelled further than the majority of Russians could ever hope to. Earlier in the year he had joined an international group of students in Iceland for the Gore-Tex International Youth Camp, but his most significant overseas trip had been when he was 17, to the United States. It had had a profound effect, from the moment he had stepped into the airport toilets while in transit in New York bound for Seattle and been brought to tears, not, as had almost happened to me on more than one occasion since arriving in Russia, because of the overpowering pong, but for precisely the opposite reason. The toilets were so clean. As an indicator on the scale of potentially attainable lifestyles, airport toilets are probably quite a rarity, but I imagine they are very high on the list of how people get their first impression of a country, especially if they have just stepped off a longhaul flight, so perhaps they should all be spruced up a bit. Flowers, pleasant music, decent hand dryers, that sort of thing. No loitering shoe-shines, though – they can be very off-putting. Whatever the décor was at the facilities where Sasha touched down, it had made a big impression. If a country took this much care of its public loos, what must the rest of it be like? Luckily Sasha thought that it could get better than this, otherwise he might have been in there for an inordinate amount of time. The rest of his trip to the States had only confirmed his first impression of the West, and since returning home he had worked hard at preparing to make a second, more permanent, visit. (He was not the only one to move to the US permanently as several members of his student exchange group also had the same idea.)

His English was excellent and it was easy to see he was an ambitious young man. At the moment he had put his medical studies on hold for a year to work and earn some money, and he would be with us until the end of the expedition. It would be more demanding than the previous two-and-half months, and there was no doubt Sasha was strong enough (he spent a lot of time at his local gym lifting weights, including the traditional Russian kettle bells) but this was a long-distance event – a marathon, not the 100m – and it would be endurance that counted more than pure strength.

When we left the flat the next morning it was much cleaner and tidier than when we had moved in. Despite her apparent unwillingness to leave us alone, Oksana had been a welcome and very unexpected host. Yuri had suggested after his two-and-a-half hour city tour that she had a pathological need to communicate with people, but as she handed us some small souvenirs to take away and we extracted ourselves from her office with a minimum of fuss, it seemed she was not so bad after all.

The Sayan Ring section was complete. During the planning stages I had seen it as an inconvenient excursion, but the range of vegetation, landscapes and people had made it the highlight of the trip so far. Great mountains, huge valleys and grassy plains; extreme storms and hot sun. It was a fascinating and beautiful region, within Russia but not truly Russian, with different faces and languages. But in the town squares there was always a picture of Lenin or some similar Communist imagery, seemingly out of place and giving the impression of an ideology being imposed. It was definitely worth making the detour from our main route, but it felt good now to be back on the easterly track and making for our next target, Irkutsk.

SECTION 5

~~~

BREAKDOWNS, BAIKAL AND BURYATYA

~~~

We were doing a pretty good job of keeping to our timetable, losing a day here, gaining a day there. Ideally we wanted to be ahead of our plan as we headed east out of Irkutsk so that we had time in hand to deal with any problems. That was the intention, at least.

Sasha had ridden his bike around Ryazan a reasonable amount earlier in the summer, so he was used to it. He had never ridden it fully laden, however. Carrying 25kg a bike handles very strangely, closer to grappling a large and lively sturgeon than enjoying a sleek dolphin ride, and it takes a while to adjust your riding style. A quiet day on good roads would have suited Sasha; unfortunately the Krasnoyarsk authorities had chosen this day to do a lot of resurfacing work on their roads. If civilization's progress can be marked by developments in simple technology designed to simplify and at the same time better organise the lives of a country's citizens, then the advance of the humble traffic cone across Great Britain's green and pleasant landscape ought to signify the achievement of a heightened state of development that other countries would do well to imitate. The ranks of cones guide us; we do not have to think about how to avoid obstacles or obstructions. Alternative routes are planned for us. We just need to relax and allow ourselves to be carried along. You might think that our

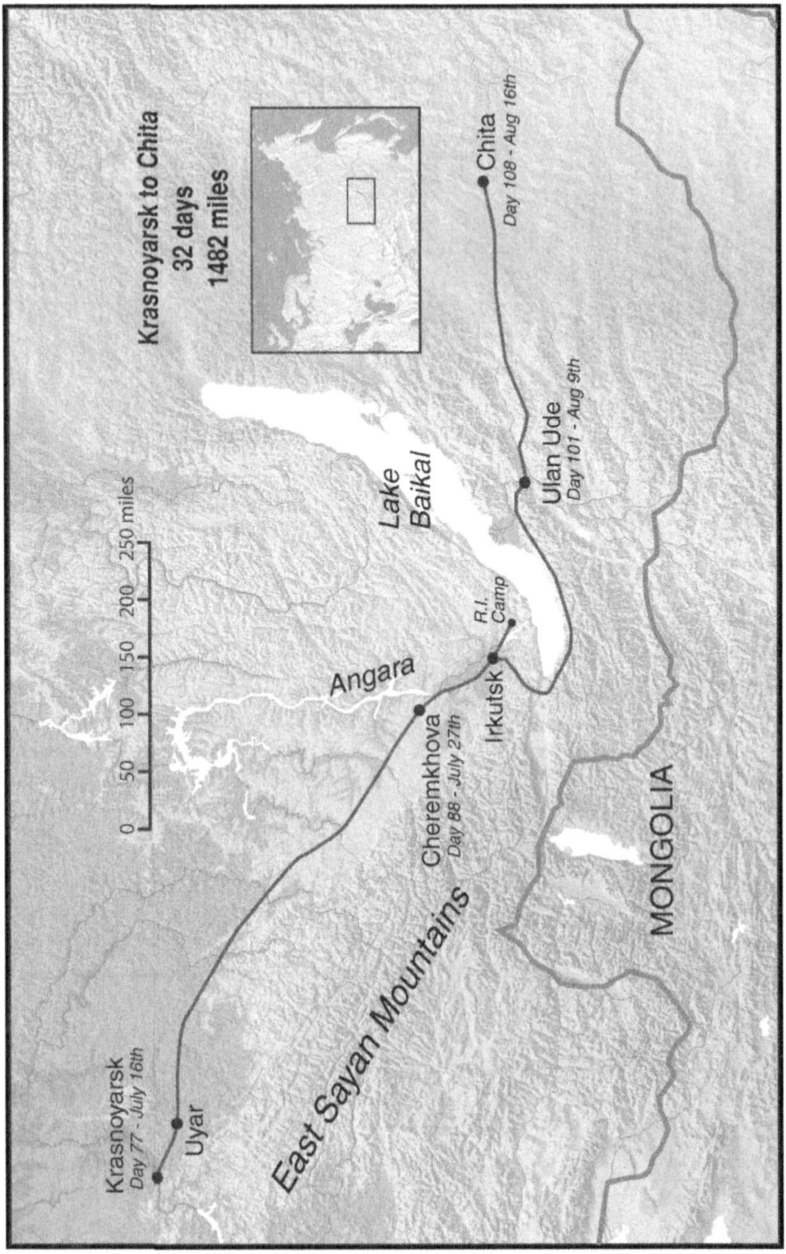

Krasnoyarsk to Chita
32 days
1482 miles
0 50 100 150 200 250 miles
Krasnoyarsk
Day 77 - July 16th
Uyar
East Sayan Mountains
Angara
Cheremkhova
Day 88 - July 27th
Irkutsk
R.I. Camp
Lake Baikal
Ulan Ude
Day 101 - Aug 9th
Chita
Day 108 - Aug 16th
MONGOLIA

cone-culture had been modelled on a similar approach in Russia, top of the pile of countries when it comes to deciding what route is best for its population to take. But no – traffic cones are nowhere to be seen. Using the cone measure, Russia was backward, a civilization that had missed the opportunity to develop highway-based population control measures. Not only that; what did Russian students have to look forward to on a Saturday morning, waking up hungover and not finding two or three pilfered traffic cones sharing their grim bedsit?

The point is, though, that in Russia people are allowed the opportunity to exercise their common sense. To assess a situation and decide for themselves if a risk exists, and, if it does, whether it is worth taking. It is nice to be given the responsibility, and ideally we have the means to act on it. Unfortunately, though, this is not always the case. The risk on this occasion was fairly small: the highway workers had successfully carried out the first stage in their resurfacing work, namely the dribbling of lines of liquid and extremely slippery tar along the road, thus transforming it, in the height of summer, into a skating rink. There was a risk of falling off. Kate and I assessed it, did not like the idea of it, and cycled around the uncordoned-off area, grateful that we did not have to negotiate cones as well as tar. Sasha no doubt arrived at the same decision but his bike handling skills were not yet up to the manoeuvre. He bumbled straight into the danger zone and bang! he was down. It was an ignominious start to his expedition, as he picked himself up and considered the tar adorning himself, his bike and his now-torn panniers.

Overall, the day went well, despite this early hiccup (and spending an hour-and-a-half trying to navigate our way to the edge of Krasnoyarsk). With 75 miles completed Sasha could be happy with his first day, and we pulled quietly into the village of Olgino. We were getting the hang of securing a stay in someone's house. Kate would stand at the front, looking tired and dusty (no need for any acting there), while we knocked on the door. A few stumbled words from Kate or me, just to raise the curiosity of the home-owner, before our local cyclist would step in, asking if there was any milk we could buy or maybe some hot water for a wash. Invariably our soon-to-be-hosts took an interest in us and after a short conversation we would be invited in to enjoy the delights of simple home cooking, a hot sluicing in the *banya* and fantastic Russian hospitality. So it was in Olgina, where Ivan and Valentina welcomed us to their home like old friends. The small house was extremely clean and tidy, with two large rubber plants, a large television set, and a radio tuned to the one station that seemed to be available – 'Lighthouse Radio'. We had got used to it, as every hotel room we stayed in had a radio attached to the wall and the repetitive strains of the channel identifier jingle were becoming etched on our brains. This evening, though, we were being regaled with 'Tristan and Isolde' – a marked improvement, and a welcome cultural interlude in the trip.

We spent a relaxed evening chatting about our trip and what we were trying to achieve. Everyone was in a good mood, despite Ivan's slightly morbid attitude. His wife had died two-and-a-half years ago, and he was prepared to die this year. It was the middle of July, so over half of his final year had already gone. Something might happen at any time, and I did not really want to be around when it did. Luckily, the most obvious manifestation of Ivan's fatalism was only a slight deafness, and I am pleased to say that he was still with us the next morning.

The day dawned clear and bright for everyone. After a warming bowl of delicious porridge and mixed dried fruit, there followed a slightly surreal and extended goodbye. Leaving Ivan's house, we thanked him and Valentina (whom we had worked out was one of his step-daughters) for looking after us so well. As we set off, Valentina followed us down the dry mud road to her friend Tamara's house. We had met Tamara the night before when she called round with some milk fresh from the cow. A second round of profuse thanks and goodbyes followed, and we set off again. We needed to stock up on some provisions so made our way to the local shop, only to find ourselves being followed by Valentina, Tamara and her daughters, who were apparently also all on a shopping excursion. Once everyone had bought their groceries we went through the whole goodbye sequence once again. It was like an intensive language course, repeating the same phrases over and over for about half an hour to drum them into the appropriate part of my brain. I had resisted the temptation to take my leave in ever more complicated ways, developing a straightforward 'goodbye and thank you' into a full-blown 'I bid you ladies farewell and do fully implore that God bestows upon you the full splendour of his blessing and bounty on this most glorious morn,' via a slightly more moderate 'good morrow to you and all your kin.' I hoped Valentina and Tamara had done the same, otherwise my vocabulary development would have become hopelessly confused.

Finally, we set off properly. Then, with only 1.1 miles showing on the clock, we stopped. It was the shortest day of the expedition, and we would not move again for four days. Kate had suffered our most serious equipment failure so far: the rim of her rear wheel had split, along about a third of its circumference. Continuing would risk worse damage to the bike and possibly to Kate, so the only sensible thing we could do was stop. We had made it to the main road, at the turn-off to the town of Uyar. There was a hut at the junction, which turned out to be a local GAI checkpoint. With their machine guns and big boots the traffic police had a slightly paramilitary look, and we were not sure if this was really the best place to stop. So far we had avoided any contact with officialdom and had tried not to draw too much attention to ourselves. We knew our paperwork and visas were all in order, but bored uniforms in out of the way places will find ways to while away the time with unfortunate passers-by if they feel so inclined. Yet here we were, stopping right outside the officers' front door. We could hardly pretend we had not noticed them, and I am sure they had spotted us. Had we walked straight into the lion's den? To make matters worse (for me at least), at this point a bus arrived bound for Uyar; Kate and Sasha jumped on, leaving me to cope by myself with whatever the post-Soviet sticklers had in mind. The door to the hut opened and one of the officers came out to see what I was up to. He had that slightly dishevelled look that manages to make official figures look rather menacing – unshaven, top button undone.

'*Strastvooitye,*' I said in my best Thames Valley Russian ('Hello'). The response was a machine gun delivery, but fortunately of words rather than bullets. I switched to Thames Valley English and pointed helpfully to my bicycle, in case he had somehow failed to notice it and its large bright yellow panniers. A few more broadly unintelligible questions, or possibly comments, followed before the officer realised he was getting nowhere. He turned and pointed, unhelpfully I thought, as I did not really want to go in there, to the door of his hut. I entered, and was met by the gaze of a second officer, who regarded me impassively. Oh, no: good cop, bad cop. Right here in a quiet Siberian hut. The door shut firmly behind me and I was not to emerge for at least an hour.

Motes of dust, thrown up from between the dry wooden floorboards by the first officer's heavy deliberate steps, hung in the sunlight. He made his way over to the small wooden table and picked up the neatly arranged electric flex. I could not say for definite, but I was beginning to form an opinion as to which of the two was Mr Good and which was Mr Bad. Plugging in the wire, the officer paused before turning to me. Maybe it was a trick of the light, but his bristly features contorted into what I could only describe as an evil leer. I had heard stories of exiles suffering punishment by application of electrodes in the gulags and I hoped that Mr Good would step in, but my mind was racing and looking from one officer to the other it now seemed impossible to tell which was which. The flex-wielder took a step towards me; my heart was thumping as he leaned his stubbly face closer and breathed a single, simple word: *'Chai?'*

How could I have fallen for the old stereotype of Cold War policemen? With a large amount of relief I realised that my detention here was not going to be of the 'I'm sure you won't mind submitting to this unnecessarily detailed and intimate examination while we ask plenty of probing questions all in the line of duty you understand, etc etc' style but more along the lines of 'Make yourself comfortable while I put on the *samovar* and we'll have a good old chat about what looks like an amazing adventure you're having. Biscuit?'

Igor and Igor, as they turned out to be, were as charming as one would hope policemen would be the world over. Neither of them spoke English, but without the crutch of Sasha's translation service I found that I had actually picked up more of the local language than I realised, and we managed if not quite to have a conversation then at least to exchange some information. Igor No. 1 was 33 and had been a GAI officer for eight years. Before that he had seen service in Somalia, taking pot shots at planes. Now he worked 12-hour shifts stopping 100 cars a day for 100,000 roubles a month (a new Lada cost 4 million roubles). He was a big fan of Sherlock Holmes but luckily because of the way things had turned out I would not find out if he had picked up any of the pipe-smoking sleuth's investigative methods.

Igor No. 2 was less forthcoming. Instead of chatting he was clearly more of a man of action, and set off on his official motorbike to track down Kate and Sasha. When he roared back into view a while later it was with a grinning Sasha riding pillion, clearly enjoying his brush with the law, and Kate in the sidecar. They had achieved a lot in town, making contact with Centre Pole to explain the situation and also go through the list of other bits and pieces we needed (they had been going to be sent to Irkutsk, but it made sense to get them here). They had also sussed out the hotel and found out how to go about phoning the UK and Australia from the post office – all very efficient. It was still only mid-morning. Although we would probably have been welcome back at Ivan and Valentina's it would be better to be in town where there was easy access to a phone, so we loaded the bikes and ourselves onto Igor's lorry and he drove us to the hotel. After checking in and having a decent lunch in the local *stolovaya* the exertions of the day caught up with us and we all enjoyed extended siestas. In reality it was more likely that Kate and I were still worn out from the mountains and Sasha was feeling the effects of his journey out from Ryazan. Maybe an enforced break of a few days would do us some good.

Day 79: Sunday July 18th – day off, Uyar
Had a great day with Igor no.1 and his security guard friend Vassily. They had arranged last night, when they met Kate and Sasha on their way back from the phone, to take us to the mountains. They picked us up at about 8am, and there followed a very bumpy ride (with Kate on pillion on Igor's motorbike, and Sasha and me in the cart on Vassily's three-wheeler Vespa-type machine) for about an hour back through Olgina and on into the forest. Past family groups lazing by the river, washing carpets and catching fish. (Popped into the large open-air market first; mainly clothes (tee-shirts, tracksuits, shoes, 'western' stuff), some food. Bought a singlet for R2700).

Beautiful pine and birch forest, with very lush and varied herb layer. Agrimony, clover, vetch, umbels, grasses, some strawberries. Vassily said the forest now is mainly secondary, having been cleared previously - there are many big old stumps. It looks unmanaged, but there are foresters who cut the trees and plant new ones (cf Raman in Kubaika).

Amongst the trees there are many large wood ant nests - if you blow on these and hold your hand near the ants, you come away with a very strong smell of formic acid, like vinegar. Sasha put the ants on his body - said it's good for the health. Seems to keep the mosquitoes away - there are loads of them in the forest, and large horse-flies, tiny biting flies, and ticks, one of which I found on me, but it hadn't done anything. Encephalitis is very seasonal, ending mid-July. We followed a rutted track through the forest, opening out into wide grassy clearings a couple of times. At the bottom of one particularly bumpy section there was a puddle and wet mud, and in the mud was the impression of a bear's paw (about size 10!) Very exciting, but we were so noisy on the motorbikes and making such a smell with the fumes that there was no chance of seeing it. Igor said the tracks were of a mother with her cubs.

From here we did some trail-blazing. There was a track somewhere that we were following, but the grasses, meadowseet, raspberries, and hogweed were too high for us to see, really. At least six feet. Sasha and I kept having to leap off, push, and then try to leap back on again. Eventually we stopped in the forest in the middle of nowhere, and followed Igor and Vassily to the top of a rock outcrop (granite covered in rich lichen growth). What a view! Suddenly, from being in dense forest, we could see right to the hazy horizon, across miles and miles of forest-covered hills, with no signs of humans, no car noise, and no aeroplanes. Just the screaming swifts and the noise of the river way down in the valley. Seemed quite Australian to me, that sort of rock outcrop, and made me think of 'Picnic at Hanging Rock'. Interesting shapes in the rocks, made by the water running off.

We decided to go down to the river, which was hard work down the steep and overgrown hillside. The canopy was open, so lots of light results in lots of plants. Lots of dead wood on the ground, too, very rotten, so we had to be careful where we trod. Sasha stripped off and went swimming with Igor and Vassily in the rapids. After a very hot climb back to the top, we prepared tea from freshly gathered bilberries and bilberry leaves, with some blackcurrants, too. Sausage, hard-boiled eggs, bread, chocolate mints (bit unexpected), and delicious home-made rose jam. Perfect. It's great to meet Russians who don't just get pissed on cheap vodka all the time, and who appreciate the value of their surroundings. Igor explained that he comes to the forest all the time on his days off, picking berries etc. The perfect remedy for suffering too much stress is just to be in the forest with the trees and to feel nature (he is working on night shift later, when he will have his machine gun - too stressful!)

Vassily is a member of the environmental council in Uyar, but it doesn't seem that they can really do anything to stop factories etc polluting. The local factory bosses provide dachas etc for important people in the town, so they have them on their side. No possibility of collecting fines.

Set off back along the track, over the bear prints. There was a small stream here with gold in the sediments. Apparently there used to be couple of settlements along the track, but the people were moved during collectivisation. Lenin used to come here to hunt sable.

We stopped to chat to Igor's GAI friend, who was fishing with his family (obviously he was Igor no.3!) and then went to a house on the river and

hired a couple of rowing boats for an hour or so. A bit of upper body exercise to stop our chests and arms withering away completely. Sasha stripped again (Kate doesn't seem to mind) and leapt in, and managed to swim all the way back to the place we got the boats from (about a mile or so.) I did a bit of swimming, but obviously four months out of a pool requires longer than five minutes to overcome! Very refreshing, though.
We stopped briefly at the GAI post (said 'Hello' to Igor no.2 - Sasha got a lift back to the hotel on his official motor bike - no brakes!) and had supper at a different stolo - very good. Fried eggs, mash and rice/meat thing, good soup, and piles of pancakes. At the moment we are waiting for Vassily to come along with some of his slides and some fresh milk.
What a great day! We are all rather pleased that Kate's wheel broke, and are all relaxed about having to spend some extra days here. These unplanned meetings and excursions really make the trip worthwhile. If Kate's bike had been okay we would have zoomed through this area on the way to Irkutsk, maybe thinking 'Hmm, nice scenery.' Now we have a chance to meet some people and find out some more about the country and what they think. Russians are an unreserved lot, quick to start talking to strangers, and happy to accept people quickly as new friends.
We have to ring Eugene at Centre Pole later tonight to check on what arrangements have been made regarding tickets to bring out the wheel. Fingers crossed.

The following day felt like quite a comedown. I had a sense of just hanging around waiting for something to happen and Kate was suffering a bad bout of homesickness. The highlight of the morning was having a shave and going to the shops, where we bought a pack of playing cards to while away the time. It looked like we would be here for at least a couple more days. Whoever was travelling out from Centre Pole with the spare wheel would have to fly to Krasnoyarsk and then catch the train to Uyar – a journey of about 3000 miles – and that was after someone had made the three-hour drive to Moscow to try and buy the tickets at such short notice. We would just have to accept the delay and try to get as much out of this unplanned stop-over as we could.

Between shifts, Igor and Vassily called at the hotel and we sat and chatted or went out to explore the town and its surroundings. As well as being on the environmental council, Vassily had been diligently recording weather information for the past three years. Three times a day he would make a note of the temperature, and also record the air pressure and cloudiness. The day of our mega-ride to Krasnoyarsk his tables showed a high of 34°C – no wonder we had drunk a lot of water. He explained that the weather had been warmer than usual so far that year, which could help us later on. Igor said there was a lot of water in the landscape east of Chita, which is where we knew the road would either be extremely bad or non-existent. If the warm weather helped dry it out a bit I would be happy. Of more immediate concern was the news they had for us about the road between Uyar and Irkutsk. Apparently we had plenty of miles of rough and stony unsurfaced sections to look forward to. It was a good job Kate's wheel had broken here, as it certainly would have failed quite spectacularly after a day or two on stones.

An interview with the local paper went smoothly. Kate and I had got the hang of fielding the awkward questions, so when the inevitable 'Do you believe in God?' was brought up we simply said 'No'. It was by far the most straightforward way to deal with it. We made it on to the front page but remained unaffected by it, as did the local population. Nobody stopped us in the street.

The local church was an excellent example of the plain wooden exterior leaving you completely unprepared for the breathtaking and splendid decoration on the inside. The oversized golden halos of the icons reflected the light so they looked as though they were producing it from within the painted wood itself. In the vestry on its stand was the most beautiful and ancient-looking bible, its pages covered in bold Cyrillic text and complicated illuminations. Again, it was easy to get a sense of the importance of religion especially when you consider that Cyrillic, which Russia guards as a symbol of its difference and independence from the rest of the world, was developed by the church in Constantinople during the 11th Century so that the people of the original Russian lands could have bibles in their own, until then unwritten, language. In the 10th Century Prince Vladimir had specifically adopted Christianity to unite these disparate people, so the church and its icons had given their society cohesion and identity.

At 6.30pm, following an afternoon of playing cards in the hotel room, we were very pleased when Mikhail from Centre Pole turned up. He had the spare wheel, a bag of various other bits of equipment, and also a letter for me from home. It did not take long to switch the wheel over on Kate's bike (the old one was now a useful source of spare spokes), and once the job was completed we all drove off with Vassily in the police jeep to his colleague Katia's *dacha* for a *banya* and a barbecue. Katia and her brother Raman, who tends the *dacha's* vegetables with her, are ethnic Germans. Historically, Germans had either found themselves within Russia's expanding borders by a quirk of geography, or had chosen to start a new life there, such as in the 18th Century when the Russian authorities invited settlers in their keenness to build up the population in newly acquired Ukrainian and Volga lands. Promises made to these adventurous people turned out not to be as reliable as they had hoped, however, and over the following 200 years the treatment of the ethnic Germans and their culture deteriorated. Stalin, unsurprisingly, worked hard at demolishing the German identity in Russia. Katia and Raman's family had originally lived in the Togliati region on the western edges of the Urals, but in 1941 they were moved east to settle here. Many others had since returned to Germany, but Katia and Raman had been happy to remain. They had no memories of Germany and no contacts there.

Our last evening in Uyar was very relaxing, especially for Vassily as he had just started his six-week summer holiday. He faced the prospect of long evenings pottering on his own *dacha* and, understandably, seemed perfectly happy with the idea. Over dinner and a glass or two of vodka we chatted about our plans. Our maps were, apparently, rubbish. We had noticed discrepancies between ours and Vladimir's earlier in the trip, but since ours were US Air Force sheets we had thought they ought to be reliable. It would be reasonable to assume the Western military organisations with plenty of satellites would be able to produce a map whose information reflected the reality on the ground. Vassily remained unimpressed; the road information was very out of date, there were plenty of rivers missing, and some of the rivers went the wrong way. We were not expecting there to be that many roads to choose from later on, so we could not say if it would be a problem or not – something else we would just have to deal with if and when a problem arose. The air might cause problems as well, although we would not be able to blame poor cartography for that. We had noticed a haziness earlier in the day on a trip out to a pine plantation with Vassily, who explained it was due to a large forest fire burning to the east. We had not planned for anything like that.

Day 79: Igor (relaxing) and Vassily (rowing) during our day exploring the forests and rivers around Uyar.

Day 81: Greg, Vassily and Mikhail feeling the effects of *dacha* life.

Day 84: Village children entertaining themselves.

Day 87: Sasha and Greg coping with the heat and dust on the way to Rita's house.

Day 93: Babushkas selling beetroot in Irkutsk market.

Day 93: View along the Lake Baikal shore above our swimming spot.

Day 99: Local boys collecting mushrooms around Lake Baikal.

Our unexpected break was over. Leaving Mikhail to retrace his route to Ryazan, Kate, Sasha and I said goodbye to Igor who was back at his checkpoint on the main road keeping an eye out for suspect cars. Between them, he and Vassily had turned four potentially very tedious days into one of our best encounters. Vassily joined us on his scooter for the first hour or so of the ride out of town – his time was his own now he had hung up his uniform for the summer.

It was a day of strengthening head winds, hot sun and haze, which was noticeably worse than it had been the day before. Riding in sunglasses and helmet, with poor visibility and the wind in my ears, I felt quite claustrophobic. The best way to cope with the wind was to do 10 minutes each at the front while the other two tucked in behind for a bit of shelter. This meant we could keep up a reasonable speed, and we covered over 90 miles to reach Kansk by early evening. Somebody might have noticed our arrival as the town boundary bristled with radars. There were six or seven of them turning lazily, picking up echoes off distant objects. We had not opted for stealth bikes, so I imagine a glowing green screen in a bunker somewhere recorded three blips approaching in formation at a very non-threatening pace. Nothing was scrambled to meet us, unless the city's defence system was extraordinarily low-key – on our arrival we asked two girls about a possible camp site, and the place they showed us was so unsuitable that we carried on for a mile or so beyond Kansk to look for somewhere better, leaving its citizens undisturbed.

The tarmac came to an end at lunch the following day. It really was hard to believe that we were on the main road across Russia as the stony, dusty route stretched ahead of us. No rain had fallen for 10 days and the land was quite dry. The dust just added to the poor air quality and to try and relieve our red eyes Sasha bought some drops in the chemist's. We were cycling through the continuing headwind and haze all day, so it was impossible to avoid the effects. Traffic along the road was intermittent, but large lorries loaded up with hay rumbled past from time to time, kicking up such a dust cloud that it was impossible to see or breathe. We just had to stop and wait for it to blow away.

I was lucky to escape a near disaster in the afternoon. The nuts and bolts securing my front pannier rack needed checking regularly, especially on the bumpy sections. I had not done this since arriving in Krasnoyarsk and now as I headed downhill too quickly and hit a large dip the front rack bounced into the right hand side of the wheel.

Jamming something into your front wheel is never a good idea at the best of times, never mind in the middle of Siberia many miles from the nearest medical facility. Amazingly, and luckily, on this occasion it was the pannier rack which bore the brunt rather than my head – one of the struts was ripped off as it collided with the spokes, ending up badly twisted and bent. It took a bit of brute force to sort it out (along with some of the ever-present roadside wire), but I was just happy I had not gone over the handlebars.

A mile or so later we arrived in Cheryemshanka, a very small village of only about nine houses. A lady called Fienya answered the door we knocked on, and after an unusually long conversation we were invited in to stay. Fienya had been widowed nine years earlier and her four sons had left home. After her initial reluctance to take us in, she seemed to like the idea of having guests, and another female, around the house. 'Stay here forever,' she kept saying as she plaited Kate's hair. If any of us had been budding directors of teen horror films we might perhaps have seen the makings of a B-movie plot. Luckily our imaginations did not work that way and we spent a restful night.

We had crossed another invisible line on the ground and I was now eight hours ahead of London. Kate was back on the same time as her family near Perth, Western Australia. It was immensely satisfying now to unfold the map completely and see how much ground we had covered. There was no doubt things were getting tougher but I was completely into the swing and rhythm of the expedition and felt very comfortable about my abilities to cope with whatever came along. However, we still had a long way to go and could do without equipment breakages like the incident with my rack. We needed to look after ourselves as well, to make sure we were not wearing out. Kate woke with a cold and Sasha was suffering the sore behind of a new-to-expedition-cycling team member, as well as being generally tired. There was always a gap, though, between what we wanted the situation to be and its reality.

Day 84: Friday July 23rd – Cheryemshanka – Oblyepicka
58.6 miles (total 4830.9 miles)
Some parts of the road seem to have been roughly cobbled, with edging stones - terrible to ride on. We passed through some small villages and towns - some of the people seem very bored. What do they do all day, especially the younger ones?

At about 7.30pm we arrived in Obleypicka (on the T-S railway). Tried our opening lines at a house: 'Water to wash, please?' We got that, and interested conversation, but then only suggestions of where to camp. We went through town to a small lake to wash - it was full of kids swimming, so we didn't really want to sleep next to it. Kate found a place nearby, so we went there, smiling and saying 'Hello' to people we passed. At the edge of the houses we stopped, and were just about to knock on another door when a young woman we had greeted came up and invited us to stay before we'd had a chance to say anything. Brill!, especially as we had lots of maintenance to do. Sasha had a puncture (twice) and so we had some tubes to check; the chains needed cleaning and oiling; and, major equipment failure of the day, my front bottle cage completely sheared off - very poor. I managed to refit it, swapping it with the one on the downtube and using two of the plastic jubilee clips (pump fittings). See how long it lasts.

The woman whose house we're in is Tanya. She says the road is unrelentingly crap from here. Marvellous! She is a primary school teacher, and also works in the playschool. She has always lived here. She didn't speak very much in the evening - I thought she would ask us all about our trip, especially after asking us in. She is going to go and live in St. Petersburg after the summer (her brother lives there).

Old episode of 'The Sweeney' on TV.

The following day as Sasha was riding along, both the top fixing points of his rear pannier rack broke, and the whole ensemble of rack, panniers and various other pieces of attached equipment fell backwards. Suddenly he found himself dragging an anchor behind him.

The smoke and haze from the forest fire was getting worse, with visibility down to about 400 yards in places. There was actually some work going on to build a new road; a wide swathe had been cut through the forest, more or less parallel to the old road, and we were able to make fairly good progress along it. There were sandy patches which bogged us down, but it was generally smoother than what we had been riding on before. Stopping for lunch in Kamyshet Sasha found a tap and stuck his head under the stream of cooling water for about five minutes. The days were continuing very hot and although we could always find enough water to drink in the logging camps and villages we had to avoid the effects of overheating. Tarmac reappeared here and lasted until lunch the following day. Everyone we asked had a different idea of what the road ahead would be like, so ultimately it did not seem worth asking about it. There was no alternative route available.

We were aiming for the town of Tulun for our overnight stop. The best strip of unsurfaced road often seemed to be at the very edges of the piste and we would usually be quite spread out and using both sides of the track. Suddenly a van drove between us, which would not normally have been anything noteworthy except this one did not have Russian number plates. We had not seen a foreign vehicle since the very first week, and the driver of this one had obviously not seen a group of cyclists in this area. The red brake lights came on and as we pulled alongside a head popped out of the windows on either side. The number plate had looked French and the van did indeed contain two Frenchmen, Rémi and Patrick, along with their local guide, Aleig. They pulled over for a chat. They had driven from Paris and were *en route* to Ulan Bataar, making a programme for children's television along the way. It turned out they were heading for Tulun as well – there would no doubt only be one hotel in town, and we arranged to meet them there later. This turned out to be another wonderful stroke of luck; not only were Rémi and Patrick professional television producers and cameramen who could sort out our video equipment and provide us with some more tapes, which they happily did, they were also thoroughly pleasant and helped us sort out our stay in Irkutsk.

We stayed up far too late chatting in the hotel room, finally turning the light off at 1.40am, only for it to come on again at 7am. Fortunately we had had separate rooms, as it was Kate's turn to have a dodgy stomach and a disturbed night. After completing our interviews on camera for French television we set off, promptly heading the wrong way. This was all resolved with a minimum of fuss and we were soon out in the countryside again. Patrick filmed us from the van, which did not look like a particularly easy or comfortable thing to do as he had to contend with the doors trying to close on him while he shouted instructions to Rémi to speed up or slow down as necessary. But he got his shots of us bumping over the railway crossings, bumping along the road, filling our water bottles at a well (quite an easy one) and having lunch (easy to film but not easy to eat – tinned caviar and seaweed). The wells in the villages were very deep and tended to have a roof, so the sun never shone down them. Despite the very warm summer the shafts still had a lining of thick ice and drinking too quickly from a freshly filled bottle was guaranteed to produce a painful head-freeze.

During lunch, Patrick and Rémi were quick to display the advantages of a van over a bike for long-distance travel. While we settled down on the grass and passed the tins around, they pulled out collapsible chairs and a table, set up the kettle, and deliberated over exactly what they should choose from their well-stocked box of supplies. They then ate it off plates using proper cutlery. Obviously we were enormously jealous, but their overall experience would be different and was not what we were aiming for on this trip. 'A chair' did make it onto my list of items most missed, though.

We parted company after lunch with a very vague plan to try and rendezvous in Irkutsk. At this stage nobody seemed to know where anyone would be staying, so it would all be rather hit and miss. Plus, they would get there a couple of days ahead of us and might have organised an excursion up the shore of Lake Baikal. So we said our *au revoirs* and watched the Renault zoom off. Frankly I was surprised their van had made it this far in such good condition. Apart from anything it had very low ground clearance and was heavily loaded with everything from groceries and camera equipment to an inflatable boat and outboard motor. Plus the garden furniture set. Having seen the size of the ruts we had encountered so far it was impressive that they had got through. As it turned out, the van made it all the way to Mongolia and safely back to Paris some months later. Even Patrick's creature comforts were well-worn by then.

By the end of the day's ride we were absolutely filthy. I had been wearing the same tee-shirt every day for weeks – not only was it full of sweat and grime but it was now beginning to rot. For some reason I had stuck with the old cyclists' tradition of white socks, guaranteed to betray the fact that I had not washed them since Krasnoyarsk. That was just me. Kate was a mess, too, and Sasha, who had only been riding for six days, already looked like he had been on the road a month. Perhaps that was why he got nowhere despite chatting to all the girls hanging around on the outskirts of Kimyelteu – he was only after somewhere to stay, of course (it was 8.30pm and we had decided to call it a day as we were still about an hour-and-a-half short of our target, Zima) but clearly was not making the right impression. Suddenly a young lady called Rita appeared and we were given no choice in the matter – we were going to her house. She was rather striking with her spiky blonde hair and bright blue Lycra leggings, and despite her diminutive size she seemed to be in charge. Her house was one of a short row of cement pre-fabs, a small neighbourhood on the fringes of the town. Children played in the dust and the many dogs barked behind their fences. In England I would no doubt carry straight on past a place like this, quickly forming my own impression of the residents and probably feeling slightly wary. On this trip, and travelling in the way we were, we and all the people we met could all be taken at face value. A scruffy neighbourhood here did not mean the same as a scruffy neighbourhood at home, and it was very refreshing not to be judging anyone – this was how they lived, this was how they dressed, and this was how incredibly welcoming they were.

We cooked dinner outside on our stove, and then Rita's mother cooked dinner for the large number of people who seemed to be milling around inside, so we had double rations. A couple of teenage boys brought a rabbit in. I could not follow the conversation, but I guessed they were not discussing what a pleasant addition the rabbit made to the family's collection of cuddly pets. The boys wandered off, only to reappear ten minutes later with the same, but now freshly skinned, rabbit. Very comfortably full after our two dinners we retired to the *banya* out in the vegetable plot. The dust and fatigue was washed away and I felt I could just loaf in the warm humid atmosphere for the rest of the night, but our hosts might have got a bit worried. Back in the house we played cards until gone midnight.

Rita had reckoned Irkutsk lay a further 210 miles down the road, which more or less matched our own estimates. If things went well we could do it in two days. Two very late nights in a row certainly did not help, and as usual there was conflicting information about the road. Sasha chose today to feel ill (dodgy milk, apparently) and skipped lunch; he considered hitching a lift, but in the end a dose of antibiotics and painkillers perked him up and he hung on until the end. The good news was that we had had tarmac all morning and at lunch a policeman told us that the new road to Irkutsk now reached the far side of the town we were in. Apparently, although the newest stretch was not yet officially open, plenty of vehicles used it already and we happily added ourselves to their number. After the previous few days of bumping along over the stones and grit, the smooth tarmac felt like cycling heaven. Kate and I had chosen a town a long way ahead as our target for the day when we thought Sasha would be hitching, and we decided it was still achievable especially as the surfaces had been so good all day. The new road bypassed all the towns and Cheremkova, which we were aiming for, was now five miles off the main route. As we had covered just over a hundred miles it seemed sensible just to pull off the road after the junction and put the tents up. A light drizzle – the first rain for three weeks – began to fall as we retired for the night.

The following day we covered the remaining 96 miles into Irkutsk with no problems (other than having to wear two pairs of shorts again) and checked into the Intourist hotel at the extortionate rate of $40 a night for me and Kate. Even Sasha had to pay $12. But we thought we deserved some comfort and hot showers – possibly our last before Vladivostok – and it was only for one night. That was the plan, anyway. We had a contact in town, Igor from the Vityas Club which ran outdoor activities, but so far we had been unable to get in touch. There was also the possibility of staying with the Raleigh International group which was based about 15 miles away nearer Lake Baikal. Since getting their details from Jane Penn in Yekaterinburg I had sent a couple of faxes asking if it would be okay to stay with them but there had been no way of receiving a reply so we had no idea if they knew about us or if we would be welcome. Then there was the possibility of seeing Rémi and Patrick again and joining up with them for a few days. We were planning on having a week off here, and the one thing we did know about our accommodation was that it had to cost a hell of a lot less than $52 a night (and $2 a beer), or the expedition would come to a premature end here due to a sudden financial crisis.

For the time being, we would enjoy our almost salubrious surroundings. Naturally, the service was atrocious. In the restaurant, the long list of items on the menu was quickly whittled down to the few that were actually available. Tomato salad sounded good so I ordered it, foolishly expecting hefty slices of beef tomatoes with torn basil leaves and a dusting of coarsely ground black pepper, the whole arrangement glistening with a coating of smooth extra virgin olive oil and accompanied by thickly crusted bread hand-made only this morning in the flaming ovens of the very windmill which had ground the grain. What I was served bore, as I should have expected, no relation to the above. True, the dish before me did consist of tomatoes. I could not fault the chef on that score. 'Tomatoes' is what the menu had said, and tomatoes is what I got. In fact, the menu had said 'tomato', and I had three, so you could argue that I was better off than

I had a reasonable right to expect to be *vis à vis* the provision of fleshy red South American fruits. The quantity of tomato, by any measure, was not an issue. It was the use of the term 'salad' that gave me pause. Salads can be warm, cold, crunchy, chewy, nutty, fruity, crispy, creamy, green, red or yellow. There is no definitive salad. However, speaking as someone who enjoys a decent side-dish or palette-enlivening entrée, I would suggest that a feature common to salad in all its marvellous varieties, something in fact that could go some way to help pin down the very essence of a salad, is a freshness and lightness of the main ingredients. The main ingredients, indeed the only ingredients, of my salad were the three tomatoes, and they were neither fresh not light. Recently released from the confines of their tin, they may well have been enjoying their time as a salad, but in my book three large whole tinned plum tomatoes, with watery juice, is the starting point of a good Bolognese, not the end point of a lavishly prepared and uplifting vegetable medley. Nonetheless, I was on an expedition and all food was worth eating, so I put aside my first course preconceptions and tucked in.

The hotel was busy with foreign tourists, and it was strange to hear lots of people – mainly Canadians and Americans – speaking English. Most were on some sort of organised group itinerary, the very antithesis of what we were doing. We met two young Americans travelling independently on the Trans-Siberian express from Japan to Europe, stuck in Irkutsk because of mistakes with their tickets, and a pair of Dutch and German students working on ecological projects at the lake.

In all, we spent eight days in Irkutsk, the longest break away from the bikes and enough time to really forget about the cycling for a while. It would have been an expensive week but a couple of lucky events on our first day turned it into a very cheap and relaxing time. The situation evolved quite rapidly. We had managed to get in touch with Igor, our contact at the Vityas Club, and he had arranged accommodation for us at $15 per night. It was the best offer we had so we agreed to take him up on it and to meet him for lunch in town. Leaving the hotel, we were approached by a lean man with a fine head of rather unkempt hair and a well-developed beard. He seemed to know just who we were and what we were up to. Rather than being anything sinister, though, it turned out that he was Bogdan, the solo Polish cyclist who we had first heard of two weeks earlier on the way into Krasnoyarsk. Apparently he had been on our tail ever since Ryazan and had overtaken us when we went south to the Sayans. Somehow we had passed him again without realising it but now our paths finally crossed. He had an awful lot of equipment, at 60kg about twice what we were each carrying, but satisfied himself with a lower daily mileage. As he was travelling alone he had to do everything by himself, so it was sensible to tackle the journey at a more relaxed pace. In Kazakhstan he had resisted a mugging; travelling solo did bring more risks than being in a group, but Bogdan was not about to let getting roughed up a bit get in his way. Mongolia was the next destination for him on his round-the-world journey.

He joined us for lunch with Igor. We had stopped by at the post office on the way but there was no message waiting for us from Rémi and Patrick, so their whereabouts remained a mystery. Settling in at the restaurant, unsure of the value of looking at the menu and chatting aimlessly about how awful the weather had become as the rain beat against the windows, we were pleasantly surprised to see the mystery resolve itself as the two Frenchmen strolled in. They joined our table and we all swapped stories of the last few days. Apparently their contact at the university had fallen through, so they had gone along to the Raleigh International base 15 miles out of town and had found somewhere to stay there. The good news was that our faxes had got through and Chris, the Raleigh expedition leader, was expecting us. We had a hasty team discussion and explained to Igor that we would now not be accepting his kind offer as we had found somewhere cheaper. He recognised that this was not a personal slight and we finished an amiable lunch with the prospect of organising an excursion or two with him later in the week.

Bogdan headed off. Once he had sorted out his visa for Mongolia he would be under way again, another free spirit curious about the world and keen to explore it in his own way as his fancy took him. Meanwhile, we loaded our bikes and equipment into the French wagon and made our way along the very hilly road to Blue Bay and the Raleigh HQ.

Chris was extremely pleasant and accommodating. His base was one of a number of wooden buildings spread throughout the pine trees near the shore of the Angara river about 15 miles downstream of where it flowed out of Lake Baikal. It was a typical Russian holiday camp set-up, with a *stolovaya*, sauna/*banya*, and various accommodation blocks apparently dotted about at random. Most of the Raleigh volunteers were out in the field on their various projects, so there was plenty of space to make ourselves at home. And it certainly was very homely, with plenty of books and magazines, good music and, importantly, comfy chairs. It looked as though we might find it difficult to leave. Add to this a collection of new Brits to talk to and it looked perfect.

During our week here, as well as all the usual organisational things we had to do, we wanted to explore the area around the lake. On the map, Lake Baikal does not look all that big. Its long and gently curving slit-like shape (393 miles long but on average only 30 miles wide) does not compare with the much broader and stockier Caspian Sea or the collected blue of North America's Great Lakes. Below the surface, though, Baikal is the superlative lake. It is the deepest in the world, measuring approximately 5360 feet (1640m) at the deepest point (the Caspian is a mere paddling pool by comparison, with a maximum depth of only 3200 feet, or 980m). It is the oldest lake in the world, formed 25 million years ago when tectonic forces started tearing a hole in the earth's surface that is generally held to be the precursor of a future ocean. The depth of the fissure is far greater than suggested by the water depth – the water sits on top of sediments, accumulated over millennia, that are estimated to have a thickness of 10000 feet (3000m). The region around the lake remains seismically active, and Baikal contains more than thirty hot springs; more surprising than that is the fact that the lake is steadily growing wider at a rate of up to just under one inch (2cm) per year.

If all the streams and rivers that feed the lake were suddenly to dry up it would take 300 years for the water to drain via its sole outlet, the Angara river, which is perhaps not unexpected when you consider that one fifth of the world's melted fresh water is trying to pass down one plughole. As with other aspects of the Russian environment, the lake's immense size might at the same time be a blessing and a curse. It is so big that polluting industries, such as the large pulping mill sitting at its southern end producing dioxins since the 1950s, can argue their impact is negligible given the scale of the resource they are using both as a raw material and as a waste disposal facility. The argument is that a bit of damage in one area will not matter as there is plenty of untouched environment somewhere else. Another view is that the lake is so big it can absorb these impacts and in effect metabolise and dilute them sufficiently for there to be no overall effect. Until the lake's abilities to withstand this pollution are fully understood it makes sense to take care of the lake and the environment that supports it. The drainage basin of the waterways that fill it covers approximately 212000 square miles, which is slightly larger than France. In the lake itself there are 1500 indigenous species – plants, animals and fish found nowhere else. Given the volume of water there are no doubt plenty of other species hiding in the depths waiting to be discovered. Even some that have been known about for a very long time still pose questions to the scientists. Baikal is home to the only known species of freshwater seal, the nerpa. It is a small seal, living mainly in the northern reaches of the lake where the winter ice lingers longest and provides the right environment for giving birth to pups. It is thought that the seals have lived in Baikal for about two million years, but just what they are doing here, and how they arrived thousands of miles from the nearest sea, is a puzzle scientists have yet to solve. The predominant theory is that altered drainage patterns during a previous ice age meant that Baikal waters flowed west to the Mediterranean – there are apparent relationships between the Baikal nerpa and Caspian seals.

The small town of Listvyanka lies at the start of the Angara. Sasha, Kate and I, along with Rémi and Patrick and a couple of Raleigh staff, headed there to visit the small museum dedicated to the lake. Exhibits describing the geology, palaeohistory and fauna in and around the lake were crammed into the small building providing a fascinating and comprehensive source of information. Fortunately we were able to appreciate it – all the notices were in Russian, but Sasha translated for us. This great natural wonder was not yet thought to have any international tourist appeal. Scientists, though, came from around the world to prod it and stare into its depths. An American team had recently sent a bathysphere to a depth of one mile (1637m), and during our stay we tagged along while Rémi and Patrick interviewed a couple of Japanese scientists who were taking core samples of the sediments. They also spoke to Mr Grachov, head of the Limnological Institute, about his work. He was quite proprietorial and seemed keen to keep a close eye on, if not control, all the research projects that were going on. This approach did not go down well with all the scientists – one independent US researcher we met was keen, and determined, that his work investigating land use and conservation plans for the lake and its surroundings should carry on without any official recognition or input from the Institute.

Sasha and Patrick seemed keen to carry out some research of their own, but it was not seals and pollution levels that attracted their interest. Sasha, being a native, was well used to the appeal of the beautiful Russian ladies, and Patrick, being a Parisian, had more than his fair share of charm. Between the two of them they set out to seduce Irkutsk and promote international relations. As with so many similar plans, the idea and intention often prove more complete and satisfying than the execution and conclusion. However, I cannot fault the boys' determination. The first two girls Patrick brought back (at the same time) resisted his advances, but the next day while we were in Irkutsk enjoying that local rarity, a carefully prepared and interesting lunch, a girl called Ira came over and stated chatting to us. This was more encouraging as she had made the first move, and before long Sasha and Patrick had arranged a date with her and her sister. At 10 o'clock that evening the two Romeos returned to town for their rendezvous. The details become rather fuzzy here; somehow Ira and her sister were replaced with a very pleasant hairdresser who came back for the night, only to be swapped back again the following evening. It was all getting rather confusing, and poor old Rémi had to suffer the disturbed nights in silence. For some reason, Ira and her sister brought along a plate of smelly cured fish with them – maybe Patrick and Sasha's approach had been so hasty that the girls had not had time to finish their supper, or perhaps a plate of potent piscatorial pick-and-mix is a traditional gift on a first date. We left them to it to sort out.

We were all keen to see Baikal at close quarters, but our attempts all seemed to fail. One idea was to take a boat to Olxhon island, 150 miles to the north and a place of ancient spirits and shamans, wild shores, sandy bays, wooded valleys and marshes. Planning to stay there overnight and explore the landscape and archaeology, we drove into town early and headed for the quayside. The only boat of the day had left 10 minutes earlier. This was our only opportunity to travel up the lake – the boat trip took six hours, so there would be no point trying to get there and back in a day and we had left it too late in the week for another two-day trip. An alternative was to travel towards the southern tip by train along the western shore. Setting off with Patrick and Rémi at 8.30am we drove to Listvyanka and took a ferry the short distance across the mouth of the Angara. We had at least managed a boat trip this time, but when we reached Port Baikal on the far side it was to find that the day's train had already left at 6.30am. This was all very frustrating, but we were not easily put off. Shouldering our bags we struck out along the railway line and followed the track for half-an-hour or so, confident that we would not meet any trains. At what seemed like an appropriate point we turned off and headed uphill to get a fantastic view across the lake. On the way we had to go past a family cutting hay. It took a while to persuade the lady that we were not going to trample her precious meadow, and her son Oleig showed us the way through the wonderful species-rich and flower-filled grassland and birch trees to reach the vantage point. Under a clear blue sky and hot sun the lake spread out below us. The wind was light and only the smallest ripples lapped at the shingle shore. 25 miles across the water, the mountains of the eastern shore rose swiftly giving us an indication of what lay ahead for us. It was a calm scene, and it was difficult to imagine the extreme localised weather that the lake's environment could generate. We would find out about it soon enough.

Having taken in the view from above the meadow we dropped down to the water's edge. One of my ambitions when I set off from St. Petersburg had been to swim in Lake Baikal, and now I stripped down to my shorts and ran into the cool, clear water. To swim in open water is so much more than just to exercise. Counting out lengths in the diluted bleach of an indoor public pool will get you fit, but immersing yourself in the wild natural water of a lake, river or sea will both relax and invigorate you. It works not just on your muscles but on your mind as well, no doubt helped by the usually refreshingly low temperature. Rémi was a keen swimmer and had obviously been looking forward to this moment as well. As he luxuriated in the feeling of plunging into Siberia's sacred lake he let out a great cry and beamed like a child.

The rest of our time in Irkutsk was spent on the usual admin and repairs, but at least this time it was made more enjoyable by having the Raleigh people to talk to. Two of the groups returned from their field projects while we were there, so the base was a noisy, busy place. Shopping was the typical mix of large outdoor markets selling a wide range of fruit and vegetables, and large airy shops with bored shop assistants and an unpredictable variety of goods to choose from. It took a while to get used to the back to front way in which you have to buy things in Russia. You pay first, get your receipt and then present this to the person behind the appropriate desk to collect your item. It is good for those on a budget as it makes impulse buying very impractical, but other than that it seems completely daft. The town itself had some beautiful buildings. Right in the centre was a collection of old wooden buildings, their gables and windows decorated with intricate carving. They had clearly survived since the last century; how much longer they would last was unclear – some of them seemed to be subsiding quite alarmingly. More recent stone buildings displayed lovely detailing and wrought iron balconies. The suburbs were drab as usual, with the 'half-finished' appearance I had seen elsewhere. On a short slope in the space between some flats, for instance, a flight of steps had been built. But there was no pavement at the top or the bottom, and everyone just walked around them anyway.

Travelling from Krasnoyarsk to Irkutsk, the weather had been hot and dry. Finding enough drinking water had not been a problem for us so we had been able to enjoy the warmth and sunshine without having to worry about the possibility of drying out. The local Buryats, though, were not as keen on it, and the shamans had apparently been performing rituals to encourage rain. My scientific background does not allow me to believe in this sort of mumbo jumbo, but occasionally events make it difficult to say for sure that there was no connection between the rituals and what happened next. The rain on our first day in Irkutsk and a few localised thunderstorms suggested there was a change in the air. Then the heavens opened, with three solid days of torrential downpour. Whether because of the shamans or Baikal's atmospheric patterns, it had been an impressive display of weather. Gratchov drove out to the Raleigh HQ especially to tell Chris and his team about the mud slides along the road on the southern tip of the lake – the groups would be setting off to their new projects the following day and we were due to leave, too, along just that road. After a week off I was keen to get going, but setting off in the pouring rain was not really what I had in mind. We could not stay in Irkutsk any longer, though, as it was now early August. Within a few weeks the temperature would start falling and the days would be getting shorter. We did not want to make the remaining two months any more difficult than they needed to be. In any case, we had only had one decent stretch of riding since Krasnoyarsk over three weeks ago and I wanted to show some more easterly progress on the map.

Our long break had come at a good time, though. Kate and I had now been in each other's pockets getting on for up to 100 days and although we were both fairly easy going characters we appreciated the opportunity to talk to other people. Sasha's arrival into the group had altered the dynamic as well. Until now our Russian companions had been happy as support cyclists, helping out with any local problems and fitting in with the comfortably relaxed style of the trip (with the exception of Eugene's constant demands for *chai* at annoying moments). Sasha was noisier, pushier and, because of his excellent English, more inclined to let us know what he thought of our plans. Kate had the whole trip sorted out in her head and did not want any more contributions on what we could achieve day by day. Sasha was also very fit and strong and often rode at the front of the group, which goaded Kate's competitive nature. She was not given to emotional demonstrations, though. Describing the ride into Irkutsk, I noted in my diary: *Kate's competitive streak showed today on the hills into Irkutsk, when she got left behind and then came steaming past with a deep scowl on her face. She admitted later she was very angry - normally she just goes quiet (not necessarily just when cycling, this is), lowers her head and 'humphs' if someone does something she doesn't like or agree with, rather than challenging them.*

Undertaking physically demanding expeditions in a small team in tough conditions can challenge even a well-established friendship. As a situation under which to develop a relationship in the first place, especially with a new person joining part-way through, it is not the best choice. Kate never seemed completely comfortable with Sasha (which was unfortunate, as he was with us for two-and-a-half-months) and admitted to me later that she felt he bypassed her and spoke to me more, but the three of us now made up the team and we had to make allowances for each other's traits. Leaving Irkutsk we knew we had the expedition's toughest riding ahead of us. However that might affect each of us we had to do our best to put personal differences to one side and concentrate on making the trip a success. The beauty of travelling by bike was that we were each on our own mode of transport. If I did not feel like chatting I could just leave a gap between me and the others and ride along with my own thoughts (or annoying songs).

So the time came for us to pack up and move on. Torrential rain and mudslides did not add up to enough of an excuse to stay put, but they certainly did not help our progress.

***Day 98: Friday August 6th – Irkutsk to Victor's dacha
58.9 miles (total 5307.9 miles)***
We eventually set off at about 11.00am - it was still raining hard. The caving group returned, beaten by the weather - the lake was too wavy for the hydrofoil. The group walking in the Sayans, led by Tony J. and Phil, set off okay. Rémi and Patrick set off to drive to Olkhon - I think they may have a few problems. See them next in Paris.
After getting a few more supplies from RI we set off, with plastic bags on our feet. Kate's computer wasn't working. It took ages to get to and across Irkutsk - we couldn't see going downhill because of the rain. Crossing the dam in Irkutsk, Kate had another attack of her cramps; the wind was whistling in the trolley-bus wires; rain was stinging the side of my face.
Today was a very hard day - loads of steep and long hills. Cold, wet and tired, basically. We still managed to do about 65 miles, which was our target, but 17 miles was before town. We met a French couple - they had been walking in the mountains, but it was too wet. They were off to Novosibirsk by train to walk there.
The night was spent in Victor and Luba's dacha. He built the house in one month with his brother. It is in a dacha 'village' - only one house is occupied all year round. The building was warm and dry, with a good 'white' stove. [A white stove is one that incorporates sleeping ledges above it so that the occupants can stay warm throughout the winter nights.] Victor is still wresting land from the taiga. We slept in the hay loft - very comfortable. Told hopeless jokes.
My left knee has been aching a bit, and my legs are very tired - it was a very hard day. Each time we stopped, my legs would seize up, and then have to cope with a big hill.

***Day 99: Saturday August 7th – Victor's dacha to river Bidrinnaya
87.7 miles (total 5395.7 miles)***
Left Victor's about 10.00am. The road was hilly again into Kultuk at the southern end of the lake. We had lunch in a decent stolo there - fried rice, and very tasty meat, with crusty fresh bread. The weather was better. Very windy (tail), and cloudy, but dry. There is loads of water around - rivers are well up and flowing fast, full of flotsam. We saw some mudslides, but not as serious as we had thought they would be. Great views across the lake to the western shore, with cliffs. Still hilly in the

afternoon, but not too bad. Flat towards the end of the day. Camped next to the river Bidrinnaya by some dachas, 12 miles from Takhoy. Had a good banya. The Bidrinnaya is still flowing very fast and high, but has dropped about 6 or 7 feet since yesterday. The man whose banya we used was in the army cycling team.
I was a bit fed up today - didn't really want to talk much. Tired. I want to get on with the cycling and reach Ulan Ude and Chita on schedule. Sasha's swearing gets on my nerves a bit - sometimes he seems to be trying to impress. Bit too American at times. Maybe he'll calm down a bit now that Patrick has gone.
Loads of people are out gathering berries and mushrooms in the forest. We had mushrooms at Victor's, and picked some wild raspberries today.

After heavy rain that night the morning dawned dry and very windy, but the ground all around was extremely wet. As the rain returned in the afternoon and the nearest town was too far for us to reach by the end of the day, we were beginning to wonder what sort of night we might have camping amid the swampy fields. It was not an appealing prospect, squelching about in the gloom and preparing supper in the drizzle, but there did not seem to be anything marked on the map that looked a likely place for us to aim for. In these circumstances, the best thing to do is resign yourself to the situation and then once you have stopped worrying about it something will often come along. On this occasion it was a collection of buildings in the trees at the bottom of a decent hill. They turned out to be a pioneer camp, a summer camp for 6- to 17-year-olds. These had been popular throughout the Soviet Union (Sasha used to go to one every year) and would give the children a holiday while making sure they got a good grounding in the ways of Communism.

We were taken in and shown a room for the night before being given dinner. Our quiet arrival was very different from the reception we got the next morning. The whole camp (about 150 children and teachers) formed up around the square in their teams for the usual daily prize-giving ceremony. The previous day's achievements such as potato peeling or sweeping the tennis courts were recognised by awarding small gifts to the team which had performed best. There was also a prize for the winner of that most Soviet of past-times, the chess competition. While this was going on, we were standing quietly at the front, and as the children got more excited at the prospect of winning

Day 102: Drying out our US dollars on the floor in Valodya's grandmother's flat, Ulan Ude.

Day 103: Greg and Sasha contemplating the way ahead through the floods.

Day 106: Stage 1 – set up your hay-cutting camp, sharpen your scythe and get cutting.

Stage 2 – Transport your hay home.

Day 107: Ana, our host in Tataoorova, with her three sisters, niece and brother-in-law.

Day 111: Scrubbed and rested after our stay in Chita, with Olga.

the next prize and more curious about who the three strangers were, the atmosphere of anticipation grew. Finally, after all the prizes had been announced and the day's notices read, we were introduced to everyone as the camp's special guests. The camp trumpeter blew an enthusiastic fanfare as traditional Buryat charms were hung around our necks. It was quite a special moment. To the casual passer-by it might have looked as though our visit had been carefully planned, whereas it had in fact been a complete fluke. We were extremely grateful for the hospitality but were pleased when the proceedings were drawn to a close and we had not been invited to address the gathering. Walking back to the room, though, I was surrounded by kids who looked as though they wanted to chat. I could not talk to them, and they could not talk to me, so we just looked at each other. Sasha saved me, but we were mobbed again when we came to leave, and had to sign loads of autographs. It was all rather bizarre – I had never been the focus of a clamouring crowd before and I am not sure whether I enjoyed it. The rock star career would have to be put on hold for a while if this was the sort of reaction I would have to deal with. Mind you, I could build a career based on playing the trumpet like the camp's resident one-man brass band, I suppose, which would allow me to call myself a musician without the inconvenience of having a huge and dedicated fan base. We could have happily stayed at the camp all day and it would have been great talking to everyone, with Sasha's help, once the excitement had died down, but we had to get to Ulan Ude. As the trumpet parped us on our way, I could not help feeling that the camp could perhaps benefit from a visit from some of the residents of Asterix the Gaul's village, who would always silence Cacophonix the Bard's musical accompaniments in a polite but firm way.

The road to Ulan Ude was thankfully flat, following the Selenga river, and with a strong tail-wind we arrived in good time. The weather seemed to be clearing, with patches of blue sky even making an appearance for the first time in a while, but we could see the effects of the rain all around, with extensive flooding along the Selenga valley. As we approached the outskirts of the city the roads were blocked by floodwater and we had to load ourselves onto the back of a truck along with local pedestrians to ride a few hundred yards through to dry ground.

We had arranged to stay with Dennis, Raleigh International's local contact. His flat proved difficult to find, but in a lucky coincidence as we were roaming around searching for it who should walk past but three Raleigh staff we had met the week before. They were on their way to meet Dennis as well, and they seemed to know where they were going so we followed them. It was one of the few occasions during the trip when someone was able to give us completely accurate directions. In the end, as there was quite a number of Raleigh people in town, we ended up staying somewhere completely different, in Valodya's grandmother's flat. Valodya, Dennis and their friend Sergei were in charge of organising all of Raleigh International's transport, accommodation and communications in Ulan Ude – quite a responsibility for these young men.

Having done plenty of organising ourselves in Irkutsk, our day off here was quite relaxed with time to explore the city centre after a decent and well-presented lunch in the Baikal Hotel. Ulan Ude is the capital of Buryatya. A little over three hundred years ago it consisted of a wooden fort strategically placed to collect the valuable tribute of furs from the subjugated local tribes and also to exploit the trade routes from China and Asia. Like most of the larger towns and cities in eastern Siberia, its fortunes really took off with the arrival of the Trans-Siberian Railway. Once the first train pulled in in 1899, the population grew and now the 360,000 or so inhabitants are engaged in a range of industrial and cultural pursuits, including maintaining Ulan Ude's position as the centre for Russian Buddhism. The Buryats are notable for holding on to their Buddhist religion throughout the Soviet period despite the closure of all their temples (along with churches, synagogues and mosques). Many have reopened, and in 1992 the Dalai Lama visited the region to bless Russia's first women's monastery.

The central square was probably the best I had seen in a town so far – the surrounding streets were clean, there were tended flowerbeds and the buildings were attractive. It actually looked like somewhere it would be pleasant to sit and spend some time. The population seemed quite un-inebriated as well, although they had other vices. Relaxing on a bench we were approached by Arjan, a 51-year-old Buryat and former boxer. He was retired now, his career interrupted by heart disease, he explained, as he lit another cigarette. As we were talking we had a strong feeling that we were being watched, although given what stood across the square from us this should not have surprised us. The dominating feature in Ulan Ude is the statue of Lenin. Most towns still had them, usually about life-size and with the man either pointing the way to workers' liberation or holding open his overcoat (whether this was to let the world see the quality of his tailoring or to display a disdain for the local cold weather was never completely clear). The local statue, though, was a one-off. It consisted solely of Lenin's head, and far from being life-sized, which would not have worked very effectively as a piece of dramatic urban art, this piece of monumental bronze and masonry was 25 feet high. Perched on his Adam's apple, the director of the Revolution gazed out of enormous eyes across the city. To help win over the local population and encourage them to feel more at ease with their former absentee landlord, the sculptor had used the fairly basic trick of giving the eyes a definite Oriental slant. It may have fooled some people, but whatever effect it had you could not deny the head's unavoidable overwhelming presence.

Our equipment had got fairly wet over the last few days (and heavier as a result), so we were welcome of the chance to dry it out. Tents and clothes blew gently on the washing lines in the square in front of the flats. We were happy to leave them out in the public space, but we had other important things to dry that we did not want to spread out so obviously. There were no cash machines in Russia at the time of our expedition, so we had to travel with large quantities of US dollars on us in cash and change them into roubles as the need and opportunity arose. The rainwater had worked its way into our carefully wrapped bundles of banknotes and we now had a few hundred soggy dollars in a variety of denominations. We were not about to peg each one to the washing line to create some sort of display of monetary bunting to celebrate our arrival, so the only alternative was just to spread them out on the floor in Valodya's room. His grandmother seemed to be of unimpeachable character and we were confident that not a single note would go missing, although it was only when we came to clear it all up that we realised what seeing the equivalent of so many months' wages must have felt like.

As well as being a pleasant city, Ulan Ude was notable for the absence of *pelmeni*. Since entering Siberia just over two months earlier, *pelmeni*, in all its shades of blandness, had formed a large part of our diet. During our ride over the Urals we had enjoyed some variation as the *pelmeni* morphed into *manti*. Now, in the heart of Buryatia, we made another brief culinary departure. Dinner on our first night with Dennis and friends at the Intourist hotel was an expensive affair (4,800 roubles each, approximately £4), but the food was delicious. Two types of creamy salad and a hearty stew appeared on the table and we tucked in hungrily. Then the waitress brought out a plate of meat dumplings, and I had a quiet thought to myself along the lines of 'Well, I can't say I'm overly surprised to see a collection of sorry-looking over-cooked ravioli-like items since we've had them more-or-less every day since June'. It turned out, though, that not for the first time I was being a bit hasty. Dennis proudly explained that these were a traditional Buryat dish called *pozi*. Clearly cut from the same cloth as *pelmeni*, they did have their own characteristics – they were larger and were a different shape, more like a tri-corn hat – and in the world of pasta that is enough to warrant a separate classification. More impressive, though, was that there was a special way to eat them. Whether this was a result of their design, or an ancient Buryat had had an urge to eat in a particular way and applied himself to developing a dish that satisfied his creative hunger, is unclear. Maybe it betrays a long-forgotten cultural link to the Cornish tin miners of yore, whose pasty lunches had a good thick edge to their crust so the dirty hands of the miners would not make a mess of the bit they ate. Perhaps the Buryats, after a mucky morning's herding and in the absence of cutlery and easily accessible hand sanitation, took a page from the Cornish cookbook and adapted it to the vernacular cuisine. The result is that your *pozi* has crimped corners of pasta that are used to pick it up by in order to bite into it. Not that a single *pozi* is as large as a pasty. It is a little-known fact that pasties are the size they are so that in the gloom of the mineshaft, lit only by the flicker of a tallow flame, it is fairly easy to locate and retrieve a dropped one successfully without too much fuss and fumbling – an important consideration given the calorific demands of an afternoon at the tin-face. By contrast, Buryats worked up on the surface under the bright and wide Siberian sky, so the potential to lose a dropped snack would have been much less. Hence, no need to make them big for easy spotting. Not to mention the potential structural integrity problems of an over-sized pasta envelope struggling to contain a large portion of moist mince.

 Having pinched the *pozi* corners carefully between finger and thumb, much as one would a fine china cup of lapsang sushong, but with two hands, and taken a small bite, you then drink the juices that have collected on the inside. Today with cutlery and plates available to everyone, the next stage is to set the *pozi* down and carry on as normal, but that is probably a relatively recent development. I expect it is only dedicated anthropologists who will be able to prove any of this complicated theory with any certainty; all I can say is that the similarities and apparent coincidences are too uncanny to ignore.

While *pozis* and *mantis* were regional, there was another aspect of Russian cuisine that was countrywide, namely the consumption of fat. Over the bitter winter months a high fat intake is a good idea, providing plenty of calories to burn and generate heat. When the weather warms up the intake can be reduced. It may be this is what happens, but if it is then in winter Russians must consume a hell of a lot because they were still tucking into it enthusiastically during our time there. *Smetana* seemed to be the favourite, a thick sour cream. When we set off from Yuri's place in Krasnoyarsk back in July, with the mercury nudging the low thirties, his mother had presented each of us with a large glass of *smetana* full to the brim. I might put a blob on my baked potato or stir a small spoonful into my soup, but the idea of drinking a tumblerfull of sour cream had never occurred to me before.

I experienced a more solid type of fat during breakfast at Valodya's. His grandmother had laid out plates containing a variety of different things for us to try, and I went for what I thought were the slices of cheese. As soon as I had popped it into my mouth I realised that I had made a mistake and that it was not cheese but a lump of pure bacon fat. As it happens, it was rather tasty, and I helped myself to a couple more. I was happy I would burn them off over the next few days.

We had actually seen a reasonable amount of cheese, but the quantity was not matched by the variety. In fact, across the whole of the country, from Europe to the Pacific, I only spotted two types of cheese. How could this be? People kept dairy cows and we had even stayed on a large dairy farm. Surely among the country's huge population there had been someone over the years who had come up with a third type of cheese. Even by accident. If I left a bowl of milk out for a week I am confident that even I could start production of a cheese of some sort, but this just does not seem to have happened in Russia. Or maybe it had. Perhaps pre-Revolution Russia had been the cheeseboard of the world, and then something sinister had happened. Speaking about France in the 1950s, de Gaulle, the then President, said 'How can you govern a country with 246 varieties of cheese?' Stalin must have caught a whiff of this and, seeing the implications for his own country, immediately instigated the ruthless oppression of the dairy industry. With cheese output reduced to the now-familiar two varieties he was able to control the population absolutely and bend them to his will. It is easy to see why Monty Python's 'Cheese Sketch' became such a rallying cry for the anti-Communists, its improbable list of cheesy comestibles presenting a utopia of choice to a people who had had the joy of cheese kept from them for so long.

The rain had stopped, but news about the river was not good. It was still rising at 2cm per hour, apparently, which, given the fact that many areas were already flooded, seemed quite alarming. Shortly after we left Ulan Ude we climbed a hill and saw the full extent of the floods for the first time. They were the worst for 20 years, affecting a huge number of people. The previous day we had called in at a polyclinic to try and interview some local doctors about healthcare in the area, but all spare personnel were out helping the 15,000 people in its catchment area who needed medication for such things as intestinal diseases. Back at water level some of the roads we wanted were closed to traffic, but bikes are more manoeuvrable than cars and trucks so we ignored the first few signs and made it through. Ultimately, though, we reached a spot where the road curved away around the foot of the hills and we could not see how far the flooded section lasted or how deep the water was. We had no choice but to get off and push our heavily laden bikes up the hills and across country for nearly an hour before we could rejoin the tarmac. When the road finally turned away from the river we stopped for lunch, choosing a dramatic outcrop of rock from which we could look back over the flooded landscape.

That night we stayed in a poorly appointed hotel in Khilok – no showers, and the people in the room next door lent us their hotplate so we could cook dinner; what does it say about the state of hotels in a country when guests pack hotplates in their luggage? – and the following day rode through the wide and flat (and thankfully unflooded) valley of the Arey river. It seemed as though the whole area was devoted to hay production, but there were no large combine harvesters rumbling up and down. The outputs of the record tractor-producing years seemingly beloved of the propaganda era did not appear to have filtered through to this area, and all the people dotted across the landscape toiled away with their scythes. It was a Saturday, and many had clearly come for the weekend, with either a tent pitched or a temporary shelter erected with some fresh hay thatch. As always seems to be the case, a hot sun beat down on the labourers. They seemed fairly unconcerned by it, but it was looking wrong to me. Although there had been no obvious junctions, and we were certain we had taken the only road out of town that supposedly led to where we wanted to go, we were having problems matching the evidence on the ground with what was indicated on the map. The road we wanted was shown passing through a number of villages, but we had seen none of these. I was getting the feeling that we were heading in the wrong direction, and the sun's strange appearance confirmed it for me. The sun itself looked okay (blazing golden disc in the sky with no obvious signs of exploding or running out of puff five billion years ahead of schedule), it was just that it was not in the right place.

After a few months on the road I was getting the hang of using the sun to work out our direction. This is not to say that I would feel confident trying to emulate the extraordinary navigational achievements of, say, Vasco di Gama, but I had got past the basic stages of 'morning, sun in front, good; morning, sun behind, bad'. I could match time of day with the sun's position (making the occasional correction for time zone changes – we had crossed into another one two days earlier) and was able to judge whether we were on track or not. We were following a fairly simple solar rule though, since our route ran more or less due east for now, which meant that the sun should never really have appeared on our left (an unfortunate consequence of this was that our cycling tans, daft enough at the best of times, looked even worse than usual after being lit predominantly from one side while in cycling shorts for five months). On the day in question, in mid-morning the sun should have been on my right shoulder, but it was square on my left side, which meant that we were heading more or less south. This was not supposed to happen for another 700 miles. Roads twist and turn, of course, but we had been heading this way for some time with no sign that it would change any time soon, so we stopped to check what had happened. A quick conversation with a few drivers (always a good idea to get at least a third opinion) confirmed that we were in fact on a new road, and after hearing from more than one person that it would join the road we thought we were on in the not too distant future we relaxed and went back to contemplating the scene and imagining how many people it takes to cut the whole of Siberia for hay by hand.

The new road was fine to ride on but it meant we went a long way before passing through anywhere, so picking up food proved difficult.

It was 60 miles before we reached a village worth stopping at, and what was on offer was not very appetising. After Sasha had negotiated with the lady in the shop to open it for us, all we could buy was some biscuits, horrible fish cakes and awful grape juice. The bread, though, was fresh, having been delivered a short time before. We did better in the evening in the village of Tanga. A small lake behind the wooden houses provided a pleasant camp site, and as we had arrived in good time everyone was feeling relaxed and in good spirits. Suddenly two girls from the village wandered up carrying a large basket. We had not knocked at any doors here, so they must just have been curious to find out more about us. Lena and Oksana were very welcome visitors – their basket was full of goodies including milk and cream (got to keep the fat content up), mushrooms, rhubarb jam, cucumbers and onion tops. These simple gestures were always very generously made and even in the most run-down-looking places we were offered something. The girls sat and chatted for a while; Lena was 19 and had tried unsuccessfully to get into the medical institute in Chita. Now she said she had heard it was a bad place, with female students suffering unwelcome attention from both lecturers and male students, and she did not want to go. Sasha took a bit of a shine to her and we left them to discuss medical matters.

This was the latest negative information we had heard about Chita. It seemed that the farther east we went, the less people thought of the towns that lay even farther east. At this rate, Vladivostok would be a smoking ruin populated by gangs of feral cannibal children. Perhaps people did not move around very much here and preferred to stick with what they knew. Our own experiences did not match this. Sasha, from way back west, felt the people of Siberia were friendlier and more open than those in his region, and judged on the fairly crude scale of number of roots and waves from drivers the Siberians did have the edge. All the bad press had an effect on our expectations, though, and as we approached the centre of Chita everyone looked rather suspicious to me. The city had slowly emerged from a hazy murk, and the grim prefabricated concrete outskirts gave way to a pleasant centre. We would be here for three nights and started looking for a suitable hotel. The first was full, and the second was not open to non-Russians – it was beginning to look as though our evening would be spent roaming the streets for accommodation. Before heading back out the front door, we called in at the hotel bar to wash some of the trail dust away; this turned out to be our best decision for some time. The young lady running the bar was called Olga, and she was very interested to hear about our expedition. Sasha obviously presented our case very well, and soon we found ourselves being offered the use of her flat. Her soldier husband was on holiday with their son in the Crimea and Olga was staying with friends, so we would have the place to ourselves. We did not have to think about this for very long, and happily followed Olga the short distance to her flat, which was conveniently close to the middle of town. Once she had let us in and handed over the key she went back to work. Within about an hour of meeting us she had let us loose – it was incredible, and I was beginning to wonder how long our luck would last. For now though, I was more concerned with putting my feet up. Olga's neighbour popped in to use the phone, and rather than appearing confused or concerned at our presence produced some fish for us, which Kate whipped up into a delicious dinner.

The central post office in Chita was a fine wooden building with a tall tower and, more impressively, working telephone and post restante systems. There was a bundle of letters waiting for us from friends and family; they were six weeks old by the time we received them but it was good to catch up on the news anyway (which was usually that there was no news). I managed to phone home for a more up-to-date exchange of what had been going on, and since Olga had a phone in her flat we could give people a number to ring us on directly rather than going through the moody Russian operator to place an outgoing call. It proved easier, though, to call the UK than Centre Pole (we were expecting the pannier racks from the spare bike to turn up in Chita and needed to check on their progress), and although Kate had managed to speak to her parents they were having problems getting back through to us. When she did finally connect with them it turned out they had written the number down wrongly. The whole incident proved a bit too much for Kate, and although she was trying not to show it I could see that she was a bit tearful. I hoped that after three-and-a-half months of fairly relentless cycling the stresses of the trip were not beginning to take their toll. We had covered 6010 miles so far, but the toughest part still lay ahead of us and we all needed to be comfortable with that idea and confident that we would be able to cope with all the situations we found ourselves in. None of us felt the need to have heart to heart confessional conversations about how we were coping, though; we knew we would all just get on with the job. We were not here to go on an emotional journey of self-discovery but to enjoy the ride, see the country and raise some money. Kate allowed herself a few moments of lachrymose reflection, and who could blame her, and had soon turned her mind back to the matter in hand.

Day 110: Wednesday August 18th – day off, Chita
Last night we heard from Ina at Centre Pole that our stuff has not left Moscow yet! Complete pain. Fortunately we're not waiting for anything which means we cannot carry on, so we will set off on Thursday as planned, and CP will have to get the bits to us in Mogocha. We can't wait for them. Misha is away at the moment, so there's no-one there to kick the collective backsides of the others and get them moving.

Shopping in the morning. Lots of stuff was available in the market, as usual, but no dried fruit or nuts, which are quite an important part of our diet. Not a brilliantly successful shopping trip, and we ended up eating most of what we had bought later in the day. We have been eating quite well in Chita, getting quite imaginative with the stuff we can get. We even had garlic bread this evening, then spaghetti with salami and tomatoes - very tasty. With that and the beer, and 'Neighbours' on Star TV ('Asia's own satellite TV channel') it was almost like being at home!

We managed to find some good maps covering the area from Baikal to Vladivostok and bought a set each, costing the daft price of R10 per sheet! We transferred some of the information onto the US maps we have, then packed the new ones to send to Ryazan, along with my cycling shoes. I finally decided they have done enough, plus I don't have any more glue left to keep repairing them.

Centre Pole rang. Our bits have returned from Moscow. No-one wanted to take them, and it is the end of the holidays so there are no tickets available for anyone to fly out. They will send the stuff by DHL to Mogocha, which will cost either $22 or $220 depending on who out of Kate and Sasha got the message correct. I can't believe it would be $220 - I'd rather they didn't bother, especially as they also have some bits to send to Khabarovsk. We also heard that Eugene who came cycling has been to hospital to have his heart checked. I hope the cycling wasn't too much for him!

In the afternoon we went to Olga's bar in the Ingoda Hotel and ate loads of water melon. She has had it six months and is in the process of refurbishing a second in another hotel in town. She is a very efficient lady, about 30 years old, clearly knows what she wants to do and is prepared to make a go of it despite difficulties with official and unofficial taxes.

Moscow imposes daft things like a tax for being near a bus-stop! Official taxes come to about 20%. I don't know her arrangement with the local mafia. The bar doesn't make any money. Olga's actual job is as a teacher of psychology in the local institute. Her husband is a soldier. She spent a few years in Germany as a kid - her dad was in the army, too - then moved around the USSR a bit. A very generous, sensible, intelligent person, who would clearly be very successful in a country more geared towards private enterprise. She also wants to start a creche for mothers, and wants to see Chita become a major tourist place. It could easily happen - there are wonderful buildings, theatre, good road and rail connections, the central square was actually looked after with planted flowerbeds and trimmed grass.

Met some young people who work in the new casino - it only opened three weeks ago. There was a very relaxing atmosphere in the town square in the afternoon, with people strolling around, and even tourists (mainly Chinese) taking photos.

SECTION 6

~~~

TACKLING THE SWAMP

~~~

From our maps we knew that we were about to enter the worst section of the expedition in terms of roads, or lack of them. We felt we had already coped with some awful stretches – the mud between Omsk and Novosibirsk, the dust, stones and smoke before Irkutsk, and the floods around Ulan Ude. These had each lasted just a few days, though. Coming up, we calculated a section of approximately 1500 miles – one-and-a-half times Land's End to John O'Groats in the UK – with no road marked on the map. There were villages, and the railway, so people lived in the area and moved through it, but just how easy it would be for us and our equipment, we would have to wait and see. We could not tell how connected it all was, and what little information we had found referred to the area as 'swamp', which did little to calm any nerves we might have been feeling about riding into the unknown. From now on our supply lines would be very stretched - each day waiting for replacement equipment to arrive from Centre Pole would be critical in terms of extending our stay in the region. We needed to get through to Blagoveshchensk, where the roads reappeared on paper, with minimal delay to avoid being stuck in the wilds as the snow started coming down.

Leaving Chita seemed to take a very long time, and not just because we had to turn Olga's flat back from the bicycle workshop that it had become into a presentable living space again. By the time we had

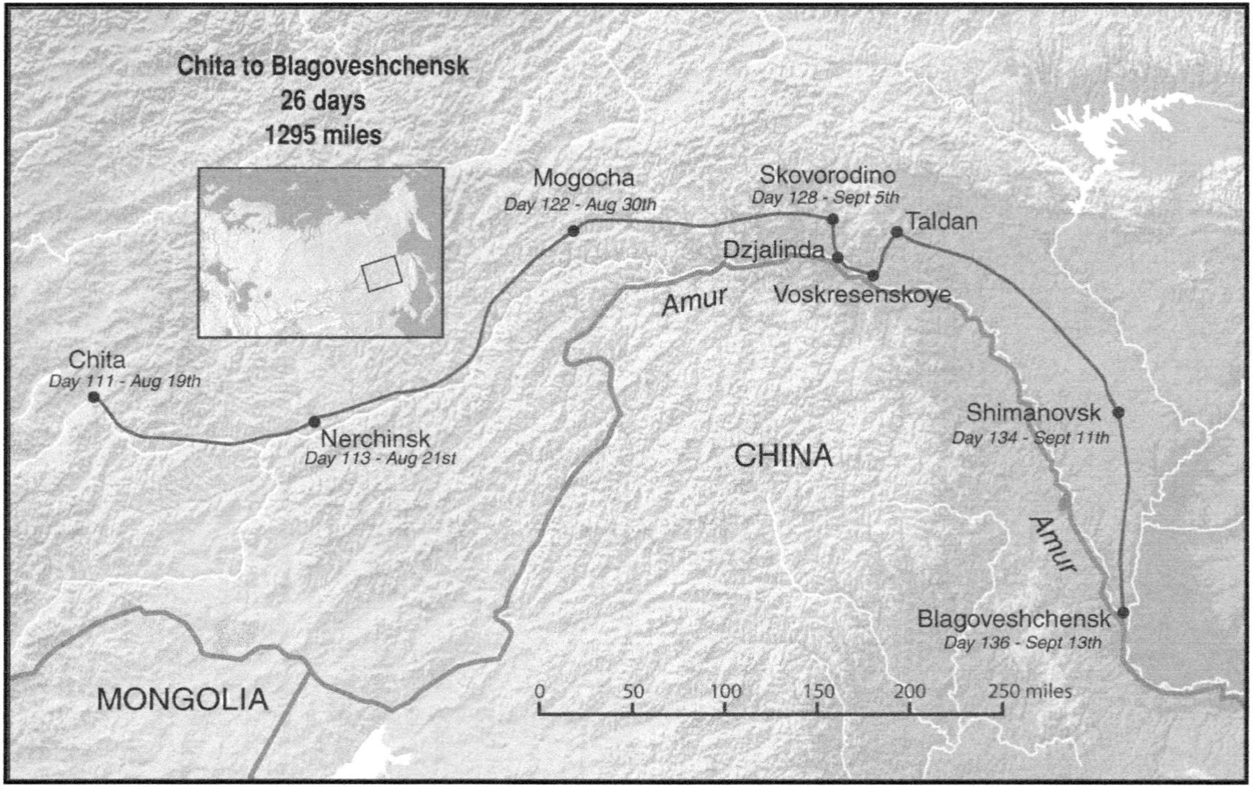
Chita to Blagoveshchensk
26 days
1295 miles
Chita
Day 111 - Aug 19th
Nerchinsk
Day 113 - Aug 21st
Mogocha
Day 122 - Aug 30th
Skovorodino
Day 128 - Sept 5th
Taldan
Dzjalinda
Voskresenskoye
Amur
Shimanovsk
Day 134 - Sept 11th
Blagoveshchensk
Day 136 - Sept 13th
Amur
CHINA
MONGOLIA
0
50
100
150
200
250 miles

done that, and eaten, posted the parcel to Ryazan, met Olga, had lunch at her bar (tomato salad, noodle soup, fried cabbage and meat, and fresh oranges, all carefully prepared and presented as usual) and said goodbye, it was 1.30 in the afternoon. We set off feeling relaxed though, which was important.

Information about the route from here proved difficult to get hold of. We had learned early on that there was little point asking about anything more than a day or two ahead, partly because of our speed of travel and partly because if we asked someone about somewhere outside their local area their answer would be unreliable. It was better to talk to a few different people about what lay just around the corner. Because there was no continuous road between Chita and Blagoveshchensk, though, we would not be able to meet anyone who had travelled all the way along our route. Every few days over the coming weeks a gathering dust cloud would announce the imminent arrival of the latest convoy of up to about eight Japanese cars hammering along from the Vladivostok quayside to their future owners in Moscow. The only parts of these cars that had a 100% chance of surviving the journey intact were the headlights, which were carefully covered in cardboard against the stones and other debris. To complete their journey the convoys would have to load themselves onto the flat railway carriages for certain sections (no doubt to the relief of the future car owners) as it was simply impossible to drive the whole way. This seemed extraordinary to me, that in this country, a world super-power, it was not possible to travel by car from one side to the other. You would think this was a fairly straightforward mark of a country's level of development, alongside things like medical, industrial and social advances (not to mention traffic cones). You cannot have everything, I suppose. Anyway, in this eastern part of Russia it was the railway that was the main highway.

While Yermak and his Cossacks had rapidly brought Siberia under Russian control from the late 16th Century, travelling along the rivers to penetrate the wilderness, it was not until much later that movement around this enormous region became practical and comfortable. The first proposal for a railway across Siberia actually came from an American called Collins in 1857. His idea, and those of many who came after him, was rejected, until eventually the go-ahead for a scheme was given in 1891. Over the next 25 years, gangs of Russians, Asians and Europeans endured awful working conditions as they cut the route of the railway through the taiga and across the steppe. Altogether, tens of thousands dug, chopped, carved, built and toiled to bring the railway into existence. The final section was completed in 1916, and Russia finally had a continuous line of communication from coast to coast.

From now on we would be following the railway closely, a convenient compass in the Siberian landscape. But although the tracks could be relied upon to point us in the right direction their presence did nothing to indicate how flat or hilly the landscape would be. As soon as we left Chita the road rose and fell into the distance, making my knees complain as my eyes enjoyed the extensive views. I remembered Anthony and his company called 'I Will Not Complain International'. Its name was very apt, particularly during the next three weeks. Whatever the terrain was like, however steep or never-ending the hills, however flooded or non-existent the track, we had to remember that from the day we left St. Petersburg, although we could not predict accurately what their nature or extent would be, these were the conditions that we were always going to encounter at this point. We could not fall into the demoralising 'If only...' state of mind, where everything would be okay if only the road were lovely and smooth; if only we did not have to wade through knee-deep puddles; if only the path were not massively eroded; if only the route were free of obstacles. The truth is the obstacles were the route and they were always going to be the route. When Kate and I had planned the trip, we were not putting together a journey across the selected pleasant and easily accessible areas of Russia. We were travelling across the whole country, whatever that involved. That was our aim. We could not pick and choose which sections to cycle and which to cover maybe by train. Today would be beautiful tarmac with a tailwind; tomorrow would be endless hills negotiating a horrible surface of ruts and grit. That was the nature of the journey, and on the worst days we just had to adjust our expectations and not focus quite as much on the mileage but make sure we put in a good day's effort that got us as far as the conditions allowed, dealing with each day as it came. Keep pedalling. Keep pushing, slipping, sliding and wading. I will not complain.

Our resolve was not quite as perfect as all that, of course, and there was a fair amount of swearing along the way, but I was happy with my attitude towards the cycling. I managed not to see things as obstacles or negative aspects along the route, just as sections that needed to be completed.

Three days out of Chita we did actually meet someone who had travelled a decent amount of our next section, and he was moving even more slowly than we were. Cycling along the road from Shilka to Nerchinsk we spotted a figure in the distance. We did occasionally see people walking between villages but something about this one seemed a bit out of the ordinary. As the person came closer we could see that he was dressed in an ankle-length patchwork denim tunic, a broad-brimmed hat and open-toed sandals (displaying his brown socks). In one hand he clutched a dark red leatherette pouch, and in the other a six-foot staff topped with a crucifix. A fine full beard blew in the wind. He was not your typical Russian. In fact, he was not Russian at all. As we drew closer Sasha called out a local 'Hello', which was met by a twangy 'Hiya!' which stopped us in our tracks. The strange-looking person before us turned out to be George Walter, a Catholic pilgrim from the USA. He had walked from Barcelona to Jerusalem in 1970, returning to the States to cover Pennsylvania, Mexico City, California, Anchorage and then over to Russia. When we met him he was between Magadan, on the east coast, and Irkutsk, where he was aiming to spend the winter before continuing down into Afghanistan, India, and back to Jerusalem. His average distance was 20 miles per day, getting 950 miles per pair of tyre shoes. We chatted for about an hour, partly because George was grateful for the opportunity to speak English, and swapped information about the route. Apparently there had been a lot of rain in this region this year, which was bad news for us, and for one section he had to go by train into Mogocha as there was too much standing water. That was the route we wanted to follow, but we reckoned that George was travelling so slowly that by the time we reached the area where he had experienced the worst of it, which still lay 300 miles ahead of us, things would have improved. We filed his information and parted company, wishing each other well with our adventures.

For now, our progress was not too bad. There were many miles each day without any tarmac but the tracks were in a reasonably good condition. To help us along for a few days we even managed to maintain the decent diet we had enjoyed in Chita by doing some foraging. One evening we supplemented our soup with a bunch of wild thyme and some freshly gathered mushrooms. I would not have the confidence to pick wild mushrooms, but Sasha knew which ones to avoid and he happily tucked into the soup. I thought it would appear rude to wait until the morning to see how his health was before having my own supper, so I dished out a bowl for myself as well. Pudding was custard with wild rhubarb, another potentially toxic meal but carefully prepared and delicious. Best of all, in the village shop next to where we camped the first night after Chita there were actually oranges for sale. There was no way we were going to let an opportunity like that pass us by so we bought a bagful. However, we did not eat them. Not immediately, at any rate. They were too valuable for that, and would be tucked away until some future low-point in morale, at which they would be brought out and considered for consumption. They served as some sort of measure of how bad things were. Having seen the orange, I would pause for a moment and reflect on the day. Was I really so cold/tired/fed up/uncomfortable that I needed to eat it? I only had one, after all, so I really had to have a good excuse, and how frustrating would it be to see Kate and Sasha gleefully tucking into their small globes of revitalising citrus after a *really* tough day, realising I had scoffed mine to make up for feeling merely a bit puffed out? Sasha clearly felt that all this agonising over a piece of fruit was more trouble than it was worth, and gave his orange away to George the pilgrim. At least *he* could abdicate his decision to a higher power.

The Russian for pilgrim is *strannik*, and George had sensibly learned this very early in his journey so he could explain his appearance and purpose to inquisitive people he met. Since Sasha had joined us it had become easier for me to pick up Russian words and phrases, and I was determined to make the most of the opportunity. There was an important phrase that I wanted to master which made reference to another religious figure. Sasha took a while to pin down the Russian equivalent, and then it took some time for the unfamiliar vowel combinations to set in my mind, but after many attempts I got the hang of it and was eventually able, after expressions of satisfaction following a hearty meal (or being caught unawares by a rising bubble), to ask confidently, *"Yesho chai, svyashennik?"* – More tea, vicar?

In Nerchinsk we spent the night in the hotel. We booked in easily enough, but the straightforward paperwork was cancelled out by the lack of facilities. There was no running water, hot or cold, and the restaurant was closed. We could not do anything about the water, hence our trip down to the river for an alternative city centre washing experience, but since the note on the restaurant door said it was open until 10pm and it was currently only 9pm we felt that that situation could be changed. Once we had complained, the owner appeared and invited us in. The restaurant was lively, and it turned out to be a private birthday party that we were now crashing, with plenty of good food and drink available and a crowd of well-oiled guests. Katia, the birthday girl, had clearly enjoyed a lot of toasts. I fell into conversation with Igor. His family was originally from Germany and lived farther west near the Volga; forty years ago they moved (or were moved, I was not sure) east and settled here. We were chatting comfortably and the fact that we had joined their party did not seem to present any problems for much of the group. One of the guests, who was very drunk, seemed unsure if he was happy for us to be there or not, though. When he started thumping Igor I decided it was time to leave. Sasha was nowhere to be seen at first but we tracked him down in the kitchens, where he was in negotiation over some food. We made our excuses and were happy to leave unbruised and in possession of a large dried sausage.

Our experience the following day was much more relaxing. The scenery had been superb all day, with great views stretching far to the horizon over treeless rolling hills and agricultural land under a clear blue sky. Mid-morning we cycled off the end of the last decent bit of tarmac we expected to see between here and Blagoveshchensk. In the afternoon, one of the standard-issue Lada saloons came bowling along the track kicking up a plume of dust. It stopped alongside us and Slava and Anatoly stuck their heads out of the window to say hello. They were a friendly pair, giving us a loaf of bread from their back seat and arranging to meet us in town later. Chernishevsk was 15 miles farther on. The whole hotel looked closed this time, not just the restaurant, but again first impressions were deceptive. There really did seem to be a whole different cultural approach to doing business in this country. Inside this particular hotel it was hard to say if the work going on was restoration or demolition. We hoped for the former and checked in. Once installed we did the sensible thing and cleared out for the evening. We drove with Slava and Anatoly to Slava's parents' house and spent a very pleasant few hours having a *banya*, a welcome shave, and dinner. We were getting used to eating plenty of cucumbers and tomatoes at people's houses, and tonight these were accompanied by good bread, garlic, very salty pickled mushrooms and pancakes with jam so loaded with sugar we could hardly get it out of the pot. The house and garden were well looked after, with abundant flowers, a healthy-looking vegetable plot (we were given some of the garlic crop to take with us) and a lively collection of pigs, hens and the cow.

Compared with what we have in the UK, life in the villages seemed basic, although it might be better just to think of it as simple. Travelling through Siberia we always had sufficient food and what people put on their tables for us was always a source of amazement and sometimes embarrassment. Maybe the way to look at it is that what we have in the UK and the West in general is a vulgar and bloated lifestyle in which we are bombarded by choice and over-availability. After spending time living a more stripped down life, Kate and I both came away reassessing the need and perceived importance of much of what we had at home. One consequence I had not reckoned on was the confusion I would feel when back at home trying to do some shopping. Standing in front of the shelves in the supermarket trying to buy some milk I found myself incapable of making a decision. All I wanted was a pint of milk, and I suddenly had to choose not just between whole, semi-skimmed and skimmed, but there was also vitamin-enriched, homogenised, sleep-enhancing (extra melatonin), and flavoured. I did not even have to settle for humble cow's milk, as a carton of the goat variety jostled for visibility on the shelf. There was milk for now, milk for later in the year (UHT) and milk for some time next year (powdered). It was overwhelming. I just wanted 'milk'. I know I thought the lack of cheese varieties in Russia was odd and I do think the good citizens would have enjoyed the pungent experience of tucking into a truckle of Stinking Patriarch, but whereas all cheese is definitely not just cheese, milk is, from pretty much any angle, just milk, and to be confused and almost defeated by such a bewildering selection as I had been presented with in the supermarket seemed absurd.

It would be easy to romanticise the way of life in Siberia, though, and I did see plenty of villages and hamlets where honest, hard-working people led straightforward lives in beautiful rustic surroundings. The reality was that life was tough, conditions often were basic and in the winter the temperature dropped to around -20°C. It was interesting to see it and experience it for a while, but I would not want to live here, and I imagine that there were quite a few people who did live in the villages who wondered how they might manage to move somewhere more comfortable.

On Day 115 the dirt track disappeared. We had reached the town of Zjerekan after a bumpy morning on a gritty track during which Sasha's rear pannier rack had broken again. These latest repairs meant it was now attached to his bike only by wire. Three of the four attachments on my rack had been replaced by wire as well. As it turned out, these fixings proved far more resilient than the original versions and we had no further problems. As we carried on east my actual rack itself started to break; old spokes came in useful for repairs here and again the repaired rack was good until Vladivostok (and in fact beyond, as I used the same bike on a couple of later trips as well).

Lunch in the *stolovaya* in Zjerekan was perhaps the worst of the whole expedition. The beginning and end were acceptable (soup and strawberry ice cream), but the middle part was so revolting it more than cancelled out the other two. The meat cutlets smelled quite offensive and tasted foul, as did the *pelmeni*. In a strange reversal of the usual situation, the hotel next door had one of the cleanest toilets I had seen so far.

Knowing that the condition of the track would deteriorate from here we went to the railway station, not to buy tickets but to study the timetable, note down information about the villages that lay ahead and work out the distances. Within four miles of leaving town, the road, which had been a muddy and rutted grit track bulldozed across the wet landscape, ran out and became no more than a muddy set of tyre tracks. It was still a route though, and was clearly regularly used. The most difficult part came when our way was blocked by a river and we had to make our first foray onto the ballast of the Trans-Siberian Railway, pushing our bikes up the embankment and across the bridge. Standing above the damp landscape and surveying the indistinct track, I did experience a moment of anxiety, thinking to myself that if this was as good as it would get then the next three weeks would be very interesting.

A few muddy miles later the village of Kavyetka came into view, a jumbled collection of wooden houses and buildings close to the railway and home to about 90 people. Knocking on a door, we bought some milk and ended up staying there for the night. The owners (Vladimir and his wife) were joined by their grandsons Igor and Yuri over the summer, so the house was rather busy and we cooked outside to avoid getting in our hosts' way. It was a simple operation but the situation nearly boiled over. Over the last few days Sasha had been irritating me; at the end of a tiring day's ride, his cockiness and pushy attitude frayed my nerves and I could feel my fuse getting shorter. We had had an argument about the relative weights of our panniers and whether all the stuff I was carrying was important (such as my short-wave radio; I had told him it was as I was away for over five months). This latest difference of opinion was about what foods can and cannot go together to make a meal. If you are at home enjoying the benefit of full kitchen cupboards then food combining might be a reasonable approach to adopt, but when operating under the constraints of Russian expedition catering there would not seem to be any point in bringing it up as a subject for discussion. These trivial things took on greater significance than they deserved and threatened the cohesion of our team just as we were approaching the section which would need us to work best together. I would have been surprised to reach Vladivostok without the occasional ruction, but shouting at each other would solve nothing; I would just have to bite my tongue, and hope Sasha would do the same (with his).

Day 116: Tuesday August 24th – Kavyetka to Zilova
17.2 miles (total 6326.6 miles)

Today was our first proper day without any real roads. We followed a rough track varying from a decently visible track to just a set of tyre tracks. Very wet in places - we had to wade across a couple of not very warm rivers, thigh deep. I took my boots off for this, but promptly stood in some deep water after the second crossing, so didn't achieve anything. It was very hard work, riding a bit, pushing and lifting the bikes, and we were all very tired in the afternoon.

Lunch was had in the small and isolated village of Archiskoyi. An old lady gave us milk, bread, jam and cucumbers, and then took an axe to a chicken which the dog had caught. Sat around airing our feet and watching three local girls (about 10-12 years old) playing around and showing off. The mother of one of them was obviously unimpressed, and kept chasing her to tell her off - the girl hid in the woodpile.

After lunch, we had five miles into Zilova along a new unsurfaced road - bliss! Earlier in the trip we would have cursed it, but it seemed like the best tarmac today. Zilova is the last decent town before Sbega, where the road starts, about 60-75 miles from here.

We checked into the railway station bedroom (R1650) - no water. Washed the bikes in the river, and ourselves, though inadequately - it was very cold and running very fast. We cooked in the ticket office, secretly filming the 20-year-old girl working there. She is doing three months' work experience before completing her studies at the 'railway institute' in a town somewhere east of here (24 hours by train).

The countryside today was very pleasant, despite being so wet. Beautiful plants and flowers - loads of dark blue gentian-type things and general swampy vegetation. Yuri would enjoy this bit! After lunch, we rode through a very wide valley full of haystacks. Even when apparently miles from anywhere we would see one or two people cutting hay. At one point there was a hut with a group of blokes sitting eating, and a few horses - it was only four miles along the track, but it seemed a long way. It had taken us a couple of hours to get there.

Everyone was in a good mood this evening. We had stopped very early in the afternoon, so had a chance to relax properly. Apparently (!) there is some sort of new track more-or-less all the way to Shega - we shall see in the morning. If true, though, it will save us some time and effort.

Day 117: Wednesday August 25th – Zilova to Uryum
67.0 miles (total 6393.7 miles)

What a day! Quite extraordinary. Once we had picked our way through the railway sheds, bounced over the rails a few times and dodged the oily puddles, we did actually find ourselves on a decent road, apparently only a couple of years old. Basically it was a hoggin track bulldozed out across the countryside. We could make a good speed on it. Out of Zilova we followed the same valley as yesterday afternoon - really beautiful, with open birch woodland on the slopes of the quite substantial hills, and very rich hay meadows on the lower areas. Lots of gangs working on the railway - we always got a wave from them, and from the train drivers. After about 12 miles the new track turned to a muddy trail, so after a short distance we went down onto the railway and bounced along that. One train went past the other way - they are very big when you are right next to them! The freight trains move relatively slowly, but you get enough warning even of the approach of the faster passenger trains, and there is plenty of room to let them pass. Walking all the way along the railway would be a very interesting way to see the country, and there are plenty of villages to stop at. Crossing the bridges is probably the only problem (they are guarded by the army) - we will no doubt have to deal with that one later on.

At the village of Ulyakan we stopped for a small lunch - the good road had been going again for a while. After this we had to cross a large river. It was possible to wade through, as Sasha found out for us - he seemed happy to plunge in and check. It was deeper than those we had crossed previously, and running a bit faster, plus it was a bit too far to carry the bikes. So we followed the path which went over the railway bridge - I wish we had spotted it earlier! This was our second river today - the first had been much smaller. It is very distressing when you are riding along and suddenly the road just disappears into a river! In a drier summer this part of the trip, though awkward, would be so much easier and more comfortable. There is nothing worse than wet, and therefore heavy, socks and boots.

We arrived in the village of Uryum. Sbega, apparently, was still anything from 25-38 miles away, but we had plenty of time assuming the track was still okay, so we set off, threading our way through the building site on the edge of town (new flats, all in pre-cast concrete sections; building from a kit), and, with some railway workers confirming that we were on the Sbega road, happily carried on.

After ploughing through a stream we came to a junction. Obviously there were no signposts, and no-one to ask. Sasha forged ahead along the right-hand track, which both Kate and I wouldn't have chosen because it went away from the railway. However, it was in better condition than the one on the left. Following this it seemed we were heading farther and farther in the wrong direction, but we couldn't see where we were going because of the forest and mountains. We eventually persuaded Sasha to turn around and we went back to the junction and down the other, very wet, track on the left. It went downhill and came to the railway, and joined with a rough track running parallel to it. We decided to follow this one since we knew it would go the right way. However, it really was in a very poor condition, with loads of large stones, ruts and puddles. After half an hour we decided to return and follow the original road again, believing it to be the continuation of the new road to Sbega. Alas! it was not. After seven miles of the steepest, most difficult and most eroded sandy and gritty track imaginable, the track dumped us somewhere in Siberia. The view from the top was beautiful, and we saw a chipmunk, but we didn't really know where we were. Also Kate had a huge bonk on the way up (a very serious one - it ended in tears; fortunately we had bread, meat, cucumbers and halva. I think we all needed it; for water, though, we had to resort to

scooping some from a rivulet beside the track), and I had a bonk on the way back to the top.
It was getting late and we decided to head back to the village. There were only 1½ hours of daylight left, and we used all of it. We arrived at 9.30pm, not knowing where to stay, and too tired to want to camp. A stocky bloke with a moustache and a bucket of mushrooms suggested we try the workers' camp up the road. It turned out to be the best thing we'd done for days! Banya, hot and very tasty food, clean linen - superb! Great people.
It was actually the HQ of the local gold mining group, nearly 500-strong. There are many mines spread across this area, and this group has been going 20-25 years. The main chap is Valodya - we had some vodka with him at supper - I didn't mind as he wasn't pissed and was obviously a sensible, intelligent bloke. Most people just want a hand finishing their bottle. We decided to have a day off tomorrow. Beautiful weather - sunny, clear. Very warm. Cloudless evening.

Although there were about 500 people in the group as a whole, there were only 11 at the base. The others were out at the various active mining sites in the area. Given its distance from anywhere of any significance, the HQ grew all of its own food in well-stocked greenhouses with crops of tomatoes, cucumbers, cabbages, beetroot, dill and garlic, among others, all coming along well. Strung up like paper chains in the kitchen, recently harvested mushrooms were slowly drying, and Maria the cook was even curing her own meat. The gang did not stay here over the winter but it looked as though they would manage without too many problems if they suddenly found themselves stuck by an early snowfall.

In the past there were thousands of Chinese here working the ground for gold. China only lies about 150 miles to the south across the Amur river, and over the end of the 19th Century a large amount of gold was smuggled across the border. Today, the group we stayed with came mostly from the far west of the former USSR, from Moldova and Ukraine. For eight months of the year they move thousands of miles from home lured by the prospect of high earnings. Each month they can make $1000, ten times what Igor the policeman in Uyar was earning.

We decided to take a day off and spent the time relaxing and trying unsuccessfully to play a competent game of table tennis and snooker.

Day 113: When we asked about the bathroom facilities, our hotel in Nerchinsk directed us to the river.

Day 114: Leaving the tarmac behind, on the way to Chernishevsk.

Day 115: Sasha brewing up dinner in Kavyetka on the edge of the swamp.

Day 118: Early stages of a boozy dinner with Svetlana, Misha and Nikolai at the goldminers' camp, Uryum.

Day 116 (shortest day, 17 miles):
River crossing 1 – wading across.

Day 120: River crossing 2 –
wobbling across to Nanagriy.

Day 120: This is the main road across Russia at this point.

Day 120: Waiting for a boat to take us across the river at Sbega.

Once again we unpacked everything and spread it out to dry, discovering some items I thought I had lost but which had worked their way into the dark recesses of my panniers. Valodya was extremely helpful; in the morning he asked if we had anything that needed fixing, and I gave him my front pannier rack and a handful of well-worn brake blocks. Later in the afternoon he reappeared – the rack was as good as new and the brake blocks had been re-shaped so they were usable again. He waved away the profuse thanks with a typical 'It was nothing' remark before zooming off to Chita for a month. We were lucky to have caught him at the base, but we were left in the capable hands of Nikolai (Valodya's brother), Svetlana (his daughter) and Misha (his son-in-law), who treated us to a slap-up dinner complete with plenty of singing and booze. The performances were very uneven; Nikolai was in fine voice, performing traditional Ukrainian songs with enthusiasm, but between us Kate and I could not come up with anything more stirring than 'Bounce your Boobies', a traditional Aussie hockey tour favourite. It did feel a bit hopeless that I could not manage a single homegrown song. People ask what being British or English means, and the answer is usually along the lines of 'having a sense of fair play' or something similar and not exactly unique to one particular country. 'Being in touch with the country's cultural roots' might be a better answer. It would be no more unique to Brits than the other answer, but it would remove the need to try to define a national character because people would just feel a subconscious connection with the country through cultural continuity. Kate was doing well to maintain any sort of continuity; the vodka (both officially produced and 'own brand') and sparkling red wine were taking their toll, and the room was spinning for her before the meal was over. I was barely any better, but I had managed to reduce my alcohol intake marginally by the simple but effective approach of sticking my finger in the glass as it was being topped up. This would not have had much effect if we had been drinking pints of beer, obviously, but in a shot glass a finger represents an opportunity for significant volume reduction. Mealtime drinks are not sipped in Russia. Each one is knocked back as a toast, even the sparkling wine, and this goes on throughout the meal. By the time the first three have begun to dull the edges, there are another three queuing up to knock holes in your grasp of a clear reality. It is an approach to drinking that requires dedication and practice, not one that can be embarked upon from a standing start, which was unfortunately the position we were in.

Kate and I, and even Sasha, paid the price for our eager overindulgence and the next morning we decided to take another unscheduled day off. We all felt terrible all day, with delicate heads and rough stomachs. Rather than lounge about feeling sorry for ourselves we rashly decided that the best thing to do would be to join a bright-eyed Misha on a 75-mile drive in his lorry along bumpy tracks to visit one of the active gold mines. Most of the tracks in the region are built and maintained by the miners; they are in a reasonable condition but the maps do not show them and there are no road signs. If you do not know where you are going it would be very easy to end up a long way from anywhere. Misha's navigation was fine, and despite my fragile physical state I enjoyed the trip. The landscape was mountainous and remote, with the track we were following the only permanent sign of human activity. From time to time the mountains would recede to leave a wide, high valley of hay meadows with a river winding across the scene. It was like a lost world, hidden among the Siberian peaks. This is perhaps what appealed to the ruling powers when they chose it as one of the places to send the exiled Decembrists in 1826; among the trees at one point we saw the ruins of a prison that had housed the plotters, broken down and being reclaimed by the landscape.

The Decembrists were a group of intellectuals (the so-called *intelligentsia*) and liberal-minded army officers who staged a poorly planned coup against the newly installed Tsar, Nicholas I, in December 1825. The Tsar was determined not to allow the reformist ideas developing in Europe at the time to take hold in his own country, and when the plotters led a large demonstration of some 3000 people in St. Petersburg's Senate Square the palace's loyal soldiers were ordered to open fire. It brought the movement to an abrupt end, and over one hundred of the agitators were exiled. Ironically, because of their education and position in society the exiles did a huge amount to improve the cultural standing of the developing cities that they were sent to. Irkutsk, Krasnoyarsk and Ulan Ude all benefited from the concerts, schools, debates and private tutorials that the Decembrists established and ran. One of the key factors in this process was the fact that, very unusually, the wives of a number of the exiles chose to follow their husbands eastward, renouncing any claims to titles and riches in the process. It all helped develop the Decembrists' cultural status, and in 1925 Senate Square was renamed Decembrists' Square.

The land here contains large quantities of gold. We were told that the mine we visited produced 2kg a day, which sounded like a lot to me. Unfortunately none of the profits from this lucrative industry seemed to be used to restore the land after the destructive extraction process, even though this was a requirement for renewal of the mining licence. Backhanders were a common part of the process, as I was told 'off the record' by the young man in charge. He had only left college four years earlier, but his father was the big boss in Chita.

It was beginning to feel like a very long day, and I was definitely flagging. Misha stopped on the way back to collect some lumber, and we also picked up a couple of elderly local hitchhikers, who endured the rest of the journey standing up behind the cab. Where they had come from was a complete mystery to me; if we had not stopped they would have had a very long walk back to Uryum. Perhaps they could have called in at the camp we had spotted earlier where a group of archaeological students from Chita were busy stewing up a cauldron of berries. It would not be easy, but if you knew what to look for the countryside would provide plenty of food – something that had sustained the Decembrists and enabled them to turn this huge area from a natural prison into a viable home.

We could not afford any more time in Uryum, but it was hard to leave. Svetlana kept appearing with more food for us to take (tins of milk, tomatoes, cucumbers, smoked meat, tinned meat). It was a struggle, but we eventually managed to persuade her that it was just too heavy for us to take all of it, at which point she suggested sending a food parcel ahead to Mogocha. This unconditional hospitality and generosity seemed to be getting more marked the farther east we went. But with our hangovers gone and our bikes loaded we had to face the latest obstacle – walking along the railway. The news from the goldminers was that there was no road reaching Sbega from Uryum and we would have to push our bikes along the ballast of the Trans-Siberian railway. Our experience of this five days earlier had only lasted a few yards but this time we would need to cover about 15 miles. I had no idea what to expect; I did not imagine it would be particularly enjoyable, and I was not disappointed. There were some positive aspects, though, which are worth pointing out first as I do not want to give the impression that it was all hardship and no benefit. When following the railway we knew we were definitely travelling in the right direction; having picked up the information in the station in Zjerekan we knew how many villages there were along the tracks; we could keep up a steady 3½ miles an hour, so we had a good idea of where we would end up after a given time; and from the convenient practical side of things, railways mean bridges, meaning we could keep our feet dry when dealing with rivers. Even better, the trains scared the bears away. I had been disappointed by the lack of wildlife so far; there had been plenty of birds but all we had seen of large mammals (except for the fawn that suddenly appeared by the roadside on the way out of the Sayans) was a set of bear footprints. The forests were alive with bears, deer, martens and even elk, but they were staying well hidden among the trees. People we met often mentioned that they had seen a bear or two recently and I was keen to spot one, but at the same time I was happy for the trains to deter them so we were not faced with the problem of actually having to deal with an encounter.

So much for the good points. There were plenty of downsides to walking along the railway. Pushing a fully loaded bike is awkward at the best of times, but bumping along the ballast and sleepers made the process especially exasperating. The sleepers were not the right distance apart to match my stride, and because of the front panniers I had to hold the bike out to the side, meaning I was pushing unevenly with my shoulders and back. From time to time the sharp teeth of the pedal would bite into my calf as I lost my coordination. This all made the process uncomfortable and at times painful, but the worst negative aspect, which we always had to have at the front of our minds during the total distance of about 100 miles that we covered like this, was that we were on a railway – not somewhere I would normally choose to be, even without a cumbersome bicycle, and an environment that by definition included its own potentially very serious hazard. We were not walking on the outside of the rails either, since the ends of the sleepers and the sloping ballast made it impossible. There were two sets of tracks running parallel; the best place to be (from the point of view of the easiest walking) was in the middle of one set or the other, or failing that between the two sets, although this strip tended to collect the rusting empty tins and broken bottles that passengers threw from the trains once they had finished their on-board picnics – a perfect recipe for multiple punctures, as I found out. By choice, then, we would put ourselves directly in the path of the trains, while pushing a heavy and unwieldy bike. On the face of it this was not a sensible thing to do, but there was no other choice – for certain stretches there simply was no road.

Anyone who has seen one of the Trans-Siberian trains will know that they are both very long and very tall. They make a big enough impression when you are standing next to one in a station; being down at ballast level when one of these monsters comes rumbling past, the feeling experienced is one of frailty and insignificance. When two go past in opposite directions at the same time and you are standing between the two sets of tracks, the sensation is more than doubled. The main thought going through my mind on these occasions, though, was the hope that none of the passengers flushed the toilet.

The drivers never seemed particularly surprised to see us, and always tooted and waved cheerfully. As there were no fences along the line and the railway made a good dry route I imagine it was not that unusual for people to use it as a footpath. We wanted to use it as little as possible, so getting information from people we met was more important than ever. Sometimes what they pointed us towards seemed no less risky than the railway – approaching Nanagri a man cutting hay indicated the track we wanted, which was safe enough, but within a short distance we had to cross a wide river using a bridge that looked like something out of an Indiana Jones film, a plank and wire construction with 'home-made' written all over it. It swayed gently as we crossed it one at a time, negotiating the missing planks as the river flowed swift and dark below. Generally though, anything was better than the ballast; some days later two boys shouted across to us that we should be following the path on their side of the tracks. It turned out to be a footpath about a foot wide through the grass, perfect for us to ride along but bizarre to think of it as effectively the main road across Russia at that point.

At Sbega we encountered another problem. Earlier in the day we had picked up the dirt road at Djalonda and followed it during the afternoon through extremely hilly but beautiful countryside, enjoying the peacefulness of it when we stopped for a tea-break. We were moving along comfortably, but at Sbega our progress was interrupted when the road disappeared quietly into the river. It did at least pop out again on the other side, which was encouraging, but the river was too wide for us to cross and we could not see how deep it was. It highlighted a dilemma: stick with the railway and get the bridges, or use the road when it appeared and risk wet feet. It was clearly always better to use the road, since we could make faster progress; we just had to make sure we were not heading off along some goldminers' track into the interior. Luckily at Sbega the village of that name was immediately over the other side of the river, so we just propped our bikes up and sat quietly until somebody spotted us. We did not have to wait long, and after Sasha had explained our predicament a man rowed across in his metal dinghy with his two sons to give us a lift. One of the boys moved up to the bows as the craft came towards the shore on our side, ready to jump out, rope in hand. Unfortunately the boat bumped into the bank and with a splash he was pitched overboard. He came up laughing (his brother found it amusing as well), and I was happy to see the locals having problems of their own as they negotiated their own surroundings. We appreciated the impromptu ferry but it was not provided out of the usual spirit of generosity – we had to pay 2000 roubles for the privilege.

It had been a hard day, but we were all in a good mood as we set up camp in what looked like an area that had been dug out to provide some of the material for the road. It was stony, but flat and dry and high up a hill, which turned out to be a good spot the following morning as we woke in warm sunshine and looked down into the valley full of heavy mist. Sasha blew the embers of the campfire to life, and as the morning cup of tea was brewing I contemplated the vast landscape spread out below. From here directly northwards, in the 1400 miles to the Arctic Ocean there were only 10 or so towns. To the south, it was 80 miles to the Chinese border, with no settlements of any note. Turning 360°, all I saw was hills and taiga forest. It was wilderness on a huge scale, a glorious counterpoint to the crowded urban landscape I was used to. Equipped with food, water and puncture repair kit I was happy to set out and explore it, as we were travelling west to east we did come across more towns, so we were not exactly trail-blazing, but it was still remote, and there was definitely a feeling that we were on the boundary of a large zone of emptiness.

A seemingly insignificant incident showed how delicately balanced our situation was, though. In an area like this, when things are going well it is easy to take your equipment for granted. But if any of it fails or is lost, a comfortable situation can quickly become more serious either because of a direct effect on your ability to keep moving safely and easily, for example, or because of an effect on morale that can magnify any team relationship issues or damage your motivation and ability to deal with the conditions you find yourself in. Cycling along the track on the way to Kisly-Kluch, Kate noticed that her waterproof jacket had fallen off her bike. As Sasha and I waited by the roadside, she rode back to look for it. We waited for about an hour altogether, chatting and dozing. A jacket might not seem that important; not having it would not stop Kate cycling, and between us we did have enough kit to share around. But it was the act of losing it, an annoying lapse of concentration, that was important. We all had to be reliable and able to look after our own stuff. If one member of the team demands an unequal amount of support from the others, in a way that is different from when the expedition's goals and methods were set, the outcome of the venture can be seriously put in doubt. It is a long way from losing a jacket to failing to make it to Vladivostok, but when Kate returned empty handed after an hour of searching she was clearly very upset. I wanted to capture the moment on film but Kate could not speak without her voice catching, and she turned away from the camera. Maybe she was just angry with herself for losing the jacket, or because it revealed a fallibility both to herself and to me and Sasha. She did not talk about it then or afterwards, so I did not hear her side. It did not change my view of how capable she was, but it did show that the effort of this trip was having an effect beneath her usually phlegmatic surface.

There was not much to see at Kisly-Kluch beyond the usual ramshackle collection of wooden houses. The shops were all shut and we needed to buy some food, a simple thing that looked like becoming more and more difficult until decent roads returned, which was not for another 300 miles by our reckoning. An old lady appeared and we asked if she had any tomatoes that we could buy, to which she replied that she never saw any there. Tomatoes were one of the few vegetables we had seen pretty much everywhere, fresh and pickled, so her answer was rather surprising. However, she was obviously not feeling ungenerous as she invited us in to her house for bread, jam and tea, and also produced a pot of potatoes. We left these, as Sasha pointed out that they were probably what she was having for supper and it was plain from her house that she really did not have much to share, despite her willingness to do so. As we ate some bread and jam, the lady chatted about what she saw around her. All the men drink a lot, she said, especially the younger ones. It had not been like this when she was growing up. In these small villages, far from each other, a world away from the big cities and wrapped in the long cold nights of winter for half the year, what is there to do? Her husband's hands displayed a possible symptom of the men's relationship with vodka. Two of his fingers were missing from each hand. It was not that uncommon – even Yeltsin, the President, had lost a few digits – and although I was not 100% sure it was directly related to alcohol it seemed reasonable to suggest a link. Maybe it was from operating machinery after a liquid lunch, or frostbite after a drinking session in winter and thinking that some vodka made them immune to the cold. Every year, when the snow melts, the bodies of wandering drunks are revealed, frozen where they stumbled and fell asleep in the drifts; they are known as *podsnyejzniki* – snowdrops. In Russia, the number of deaths connected to alcohol is a staggering 50% among 15- to 54-year-olds, which has prompted drastic action by the government. In 1985, Soviet leader Gorbachev tried to introduce strict controls on production and consumption. It was a complete failure, with people resorting to extreme measures to secure a hit. Drinking perfume became widespread and resulted in restrictions on the amount it was possible to buy. More worryingly, we heard how desperate people would spread boot polish on a slice of bread and leave it for a few hours so the solvents would migrate into the bread; they would then scrape off the polish and eat the bread. Vodka was clearly such an integral part of the Russian character that to try to remove it would produce a worse situation than the one that existed before. Populist politicians tried to capitalise on it – the right wing presidential hopeful Zjirinovsky seemed to be promising an easy supply of cheap vodka for everyone as a way of attracting voters. Mixed with his stirring rhetoric and a determination to regain Russia's glorious empire and push on to the shores of the Indian Ocean it produced a heady cocktail that might easily appeal to the disaffected Afghanistan veterans and fans of unsophisticated broad-brush politics.

The problem was that vodka (literally 'little water') had been around for too long. Vodka produced from grain first appeared in the 15th Century (before then, Russians had been satisfied with beer and mead), and it was not long before the distillation of this fiery drink came under the control of the tsar. The state monopoly on production remained in various forms for four hundred years, oscillating between rigidly enforced total control and more relaxed periods when the aristocracy were allowed distilleries as well. The quality of the product was generally high, but there was no standard until late in the 19th Century, when the ideal alcohol content was described and applied nationwide. It took a year and a half of research to arrive at the optimum balance of water and alcohol – the details of the experimental approach used to determine just what the optimum would be are not clearly described!

Vodka brought in great amounts of revenue to the government, but occasionally a feeling of generosity took over. In 1830 Tsar Nicolas I rewarded a humble carpenter, who had single-handedly repaired the angel 400 feet above the ground on the top of the Petropavloski Cathedral in Saint Petersburg, by tattooing his neck with the imperial eagle. Nothing immediately appealing about that, you might think, but what it meant was that from then on all the carpenter had to do when he went into any tavern was tap the tattoo to claim his free drink. Across Russia today flicking your neck is an invitation to your colleague to join you for a drink – or, more probably, some drinks. While a session will more than likely leave you feeling rather fuzzy-headed, just be thankful at least that since 1885 it has been possible to buy vodka in something smaller than a two and a half gallon bucket.

Day 121: Sunday August 29th – 12 miles after Shega to Penykovaya
58.6 miles (total 6491.7 miles)

At the end of the day we reached a small group of houses - more semis and even a terrace, clustered on the railway - Penjkovaya. We were just about to put up the tents when a bloke (with only one hand!) showed us to an empty home in the terrace. The bloke who used to live there had gone away somewhere - people didn't seem to know where. Anyway, it was perfect for us. There were a few things lying around - hardhat, slippers, picture of Sophia Loren, one bed, one chair. We fired up the stove and got the food going. Soup with spaghetti for a change, then rice pudding with raisins, custard, fresh milk - delicious.

Sasha and I washed in a very cold stream. The lady next door invited Kate to the banya, but not Sasha and me - don't know why. Then, just as I was finishing in the stream, her husband walked past and said 'Banya?' Bit late now, I thought. The lady then walked past and said 'Cold, isn't it?' Apart from that they were a friendly couple.

Another beautiful sunset - firey clouds above the wooded hills, with trains labouring up the hill opposite. The moon was very bright, and there were millions of stars. It's a real shame that it is so difficult to appreciate the night sky at home.

The next morning we had the first frost of the trip. The puddles had a glaze of ice and the grass was crisped with a jagged white fringe. It was a gentle reminder that even though it was still August, summer was rapidly coming to an end. If autumn was concentrated into a few short weeks in the same way that spring had been we really did not want to spend any longer in this area than necessary. We had to reach Khabarovsk as quickly as possible and then our route would turn sharply south, with the weather becoming more influenced by our proximity to the coast. We needed to replace some worn out pieces of equipment and had arranged a rendezvous with Centre Pole in Mogocha, a reasonably-sized town about half-way from Chita to Blagoveshchensk. It was a short day's ride of 25 miles to reach the town, where we checked into the hotel and were pleased to find a note from the Centre Pole contact. Reading his message, though, it looked like we had missed him and we zoomed off to the railway station to catch him before he set off back west, but there was no sign of him there. Sasha suggested pinning a note to the station door; it seemed a slightly desperate thing to do but it was our only option, so Sasha quickly scribbled something and we returned to the hotel to consider when another drop might be arranged and contemplate which bits of our bikes were most likely to fall apart next. We were disturbed by a knock at the door. News of our note had reached the courier and to our relief here he now was, clutching a bag of goodies. Kate got a new speedo and Sasha fixed on a new rear pannier rack. I decided my front rack was now okay, thanks to Valodya's repairs at Uiyum, so chose not to replace it. We were also able to unload some video tapes and camera film and send them back to Ryazan.

To make our expedition as official as possible (and thereby give us as much paperwork as we could gather to wave under the noses of any awkward uniforms along the way) we had not only been in touch with the Russian ambassador's office in London (and been invited in to discuss our plans and be given official recognition), we had also contacted the mayors of St. Petersburg and Vladivostok. At the start of our journey Kate and I had been received at the town hall in St.

Petersburg where we had handed over a letter from the mayor of Manchester, its twin town in England. We hoped to do something similar at the end, and I had persuaded the mayor of Milton Keynes, where I was living at the time, to write to his counterpart in Vladivostok. This letter was in the bag that came out to us in Mogocha. I was not fooling myself that I might initiate the formal opening of diplomatic relations between the two cities, but it added another sense of purpose to the trip and would help round off our arrival in Vladivostok with some sort of ceremony. Our final destination was still a month away – almost on the horizon but far off enough for us not to start thinking about it just yet, so I filed the letter away carefully, hoping it would not look like some obscure piece of origami when I retrieved it from deep within my pannier nearly one thousand miles later.

Day 123: Tuesday August 31st – Mogocha to forest camp 60.4 miles (total 6576 miles)

A good start, but then downhill. The morning was very cold and foggy. We went to Mogocha market to buy Sasha some gloves. The first section of road along the railway was good, until our first tea-break at Toptogari, and for a short while after. Then we turned off down the road to Amazar, and it was very bumpy. My pannier bounced off, breaking a clip and landing on the video camera, which now doesn't seem to focus. Disaster. We'll just carry on filming and see what comes out, but this could be the end of our media star dreams! Kate's pannier came off and broke her new computer. At lunch I noticed that the primus was leaking petrol in my bag. In the afternoon I got a puncture. But, apparently there is a gold miners' road to Yerefy Pavlovich, which would save us lots of time, but we need to check with some other drivers in the morning to make sure we don't get lost. The alternative is to go into Amazar and follow the railway. The road we've been on today left the railway at Semizyornaya - it used to be only a winter road, but a few years ago was improved. Most good roads here are built by the goldminers.

I had an attack of liver pains after lunch, too serious to cycle - the same as at the end of the Sayans. Sasha tapped and prodded and said my liver was enlarged. I don't think the meal in Uryum helped (a real liver-killer - alcohol, fatty meat and potatoes, and chocolate). It lasted about half an hour, and then was as if I hadn't had anything. Don't know what causes it, but it is extremely unpleasant.

Nobody we asked could agree on a distance to Amazar, and we ended up camping somewhere in the forest - there are lots of bears here, apparently. A bloke talking to us about the road said he had seen six yesterday! Another perfect evening. Not a single cloud; completely quiet except for the stream; beautiful sunset; brilliant full moon almost too bright to look at; delicious chocolate rice pudding. Tomorrow morning will be very cold, I think.

I was very annoyed today about all the equipment cock-ups, especially the video. Who wants a programme showing a trip two-thirds of the way across Russia? And we didn't really get as far as we had wanted to go today. But we have managed okay up until now, so I'm sure none of this will prove to be a set-back. Tomorrow we must decide whether to follow the railway or whether to go along the old road - the quality of the road and the frequency of places where we can get food will be the deciding factors.
A curate's egg of a day.

September arrived, and immediately autumn was upon us. The fragile leaves of the dense birch forest were yellowing and beginning to fall; berry bushes carried their red crops prominently, attractive to people, bears and other animals who would soon start stocking up for winter. All around, the taiga was beginning to take on beautiful tints of golden, red and orange – a wonderful muted palette into which the local population, in their grey, khaki and generally faded clothes and weathered wooden houses, fitted perfectly. The last of the swallows were still flying, their tumbling liquid calls the final connection with the summer warmth that was now passing. Very soon they would turn south, as we would too at Khabarovsk.

September 1st is the day all Russian children return to school after their long summer holidays. It is a day of celebration, and in the town of Amazar we saw the young pupils in their spotless uniforms, all scrubbed faces and neatly combed and pony-tailed hair, heading off with beautiful bunches of flowers to present to their teachers. We had stopped in town for lunch having decided to follow the road beside the railway after speaking to some local motorcyclists at the junction. They had told us the alternative route passed through a sensitive area near the Chinese border, with big rivers and no bridges. Apparently there were also mines, so after about two seconds' thought we had made our choice. Thanking them for their information we set off, leaving them to carry on repairing their punctured tyre. It looked like it would take them a while as they had obviously left their puncture repair kit at home and were busy stuffing the motorbike tyre with reeds and grass cut from the verge. No doubt this was a tried and tested method (and one we would do well to note, just in case) but rammed vegetation does lack the natural resilience of a nicely inflated pneumatic tube so I was sure the men were anticipating an uncomfortably bumpy ride home.

Lunch in Amazar was fresh bread with tinned fish and juice – decent enough but not very exciting. We were loafing about, watching the world go by when a Ural motorcycle suddenly pulled up amidst the usual attendant haze of blue exhaust. Its rider stepped off and walked over to us purposefully, clutching a crumpled bundle of newspaper. We had no idea of his intentions, but as he started talking to Sasha both of them were smiling broadly so I knew the conversation was going well. The man held out the newspaper and Sasha opened it to reveal some fresh cucumbers and carrots. It was an unexpected, very welcome and completely unsolicited gift. We had not eaten a fresh carrot for four months and the prospect of crunching into one was incredibly appealing. I have no idea what prompted this person, who immediately became known as 'Carrot Man', to come over and chat. He had had to go home first and pick up the vegetables, so although it was a spur of the moment act it had involved some thought – he had not just wandered over because we were standing nearby. His gift was so simple yet completely appropriate, and the way it was offered was so unprompted and unconditional, that for me Carrot Man came to symbolise everything that was so wonderful about the Russians.

Having handed over his present, he then went on to give us information about a new road that had recently been built from Amazar to a new bridge. Unfortunately we still had to deal with a 12-mile stretch of railway walking, but our new friend had a contact, Viktor, along the tracks in a settlement called Kolokoljnogi, and he rang ahead to let Viktor know we were coming. We stashed the carrots and cucumbers safely and set off clutching our other gifts, a couple of bunches of flowers – very pretty but under the circumstances not as useful as a good bunch of fresh root vegetables. The afternoon was very warm and we were wilting as we made our way along the ballast. Sasha kept nipping off, seduced by the glimpse of a possible track, but always reappeared shortly afterwards as it turned out to be another false hope. Kolokoljnogi appeared at about 7.30pm. Despite the recent good weather the village was very wet, with a small stream running through the middle of it and planks laid out to walk on. Viktor returned with his cow and directed us to what seemed to be an old office, which we soon turned into our home for the night. While Sasha sorted out the stove and got the place warm, I followed the path a shot way into the birch forest to fill some pans with water from the stream. Everything felt good – I always enjoyed autumn, with its mix of warm days and crisp nights, the turning leaves and ripe fruits, and walking into the forest I had a sense of relaxation and contentment. Back at our digs we were enjoying more friendly neighbourliness, with pots and pans lent to us and milk donated so we could prepare a sustaining rice pudding. At 10.30pm the bread train pulled in, a mobile shop that kept the few residents of this small collection of houses resupplied and connected to the wider world.

The following day, any feeling of relaxation soon passed. The rain was pouring down as we ate breakfast, topping up the sogginess of the village and resulting in the huge puddles we would experience later in the day. The deluge did finally stop before we set off but the prospect of a 15-mile walk on the railway did not fill me with joy, and after only the first five miles I was already feeling very fed up and rather tired. These sections along the railway did not put any of us in a good mood, and it would not take much for one of us to snap. At Potaika halt Sasha wound me up just a bit too much and we had an argument about asking people for directions – hardly the world's most significant subject. His tendency to suggest an alternative idea that he thought was obviously more correct than mine was getting to me; maybe it was a cultural difference that was coming across badly in translation, maybe it was just Sasha, or maybe I was letting our situation make me short-tempered. Whatever the reason, the result was an animated exchange of views that did not resolve anything except to vent a little frustration.

Cucumber and garlic sandwiches constituted possibly our worst picnic lunch during the expedition, and we tucked in at Chichatka having covered 12½ miles. With only a few houses and the station there was not much to see and not many people about. The sandwiches did not really satisfy us physically or emotionally, but a quick conversation with the station-master sorted that out as he lent us his hotplate and we rustled up some soup. Yerefy Pavlovich was the next proper town, lying about 45 miles away. On tarmac that would be an afternoon's ride but here in the swamp and forest we would not get there until at least the end of the next day and maybe later – it all depended on whether there was anything resembling a decent track. While we were having lunch we chatted to three men who were also heading there, but not by train. We had not seen any other decent transport outside the main villages for a while, so were curious about how they were getting about, and when we saw what they were using it did not fill us with confidence about the state of the route we were all about to follow. Parked next to the station was their transport of choice – not a standard four-wheel-drive, and not even a souped up one with extra ground clearance and over-sized tyres. For these chaps, nothing less than a tank would do. It was a civilian version, admittedly, with no gun turret, but basically it was a tank. The frustrating thing was that after a few passes up and down by one of these even a decent track would soon be reduced to a churned and rutted mess, so it is a closed feedback loop. From what they said, though, it seemed that the 'decent' stage had been passed long ago, but at least there was a track and it meant we did not have to spend the rest of the day on the railway. Apparently it would be in very poor condition for about 10 miles, but at this point anything seemed better than struggling along the ballast – had we been shown just how bad the track was we might not have been so hasty in our choice.

It varied from rubbish to appalling. The rain had caused huge washouts in places, with eroded areas three or four feet deep. Elsewhere the water just filled the ruts resulting a sort of water-based Russian roulette as we gambled on a route through the watery minefield. If I got it right, the puddle would be just a few inches deep and I would make it out the other side having suffered nothing more than a few splashes. If I got it wrong, the puddle would turn out to be a small pond and my front wheel would sink deeper and deeper until the panniers were completely submerged. All this happened too quickly to really do anything about, so it was just a case of trying to keep upright and either power through hoping that my wheels had reached the bottom, or step off into the water, haul the bike to relatively dry land and set off again following a different line. Not only was this a disaster for the bikes, with the chains and gears rapidly being stripped of lubricant and water finding its way into the wheel and pedal bearings, but it was not doing my feet any good either. The constant dunking and wet socks and boots meant that we were in danger of succumbing to 'non-freezing cold injury', otherwise known as trenchfoot. Having properly fitting boots would have helped. My old cycle touring shoes which I had been gluing back together over the last couple of months had finally given up in Chita, and I had switched over to a pair of fabric walking boots (which apart from anything meant that I had a large amount of new space in my panniers – quite why I had carried the bulky things all the way from the start rather than send them out later I do not know; I am sure there had been some logic involved in the decision at the time, but it had long since disappeared). In the relaxed surroundings of the shop they had seemed fine, but in the intervening months either the boots had shrunk slightly or my feet had grown, and now my toes were pushed up against the ends just enough for them to feel tight. This did not help my circulation and when I took the boots off after a wet day's ride my toes looked like wrinkled white walnuts.

The road (although it did not really deserve the title) ran beside the railway for a short distance before turning away into the forest, a wild beautiful scene of dense pine trees and thick low berry bushes, where it became more or less a stream with water running along it off the hills. If you are trying to reach a particular place and are not quite sure if you are on the right route it is easy to become anxious; if you are just heading out and are happy to see where you end up you cannot get lost and it is easier to feel happy in your surroundings. We were somewhere between the two. Making our way through the forest it seemed like we were heading deeper into the unknown. There were no other routes to follow, though, so we must have been heading in the right direction. This was confirmed shortly after when the ambient sound of the trickling water running over the gravel was pushed aside by the growing growl of the tank's engines as our lunchtime companions chewed up the miles and caught us up. A brief chat and they were gone, assuring us that the 'proper' road would appear shortly. It was all relative. When we did reach the end of the forest track it was at the point where work on a new road pushing in from the east had temporarily finished, but the only thing that really distinguished the two was the width of the path through the trees. The new road took up much more space and looked like it would be a main route one day. But for now, these were just the preliminary works and the ground was still seriously eroded. We carried on for another couple of miles and came to the village of Mala Kavaly. Ira, the head of the local railway station, found us an empty house and we went through the routine of getting the stove going and spreading out our soggy kit in the hope of having something dry and comfortable to start the morning in. With the tank long gone and the sun going down behind the trees there was a great sense of tranquillity in the hamlet. Smoke curled from chimneys, suggesting warming stoves, and wood piles stood stacked and ready for winter.

Day 126: Friday September 3rd – Mala-Kavaly to Yerefy Pavlovich
29.2 miles (total 6670.5 miles)

Terrible sleep - barking dog, Sasha tripping over Kate's bed, Kate's bed making lots of noise whenever she moved. Warm morning. We didn't leave until about midday, after cleaning the bikes, fixing punctures etc. There have been lots of equipment casualties over the last few days - my pannier clips, the video, a puncture, Kate's computer, pannier and shoes, my front rack again (a different bit), Sasha's pannier clip, Kate's pedal is a bit wonky, Sasha's and my headsets are wearing out. It's all happening! Will the bikes last!?

The ride into Yerefy Pavlovich was easy, through lovely scenery - it made a change to be able to look at it rather than at the road. Flat valley, swampy with an occasional haystack and birch trees. The leaves are now falling. It put me in a good mood - I love autumn.

Once in town we went to the mayor's office. We thought she had arranged dinner for us, but no, so we had a crap meal in the stolo – a pathetic amount of meat (100g) for R227. Out of 39 light fittings none worked, then three bulbs blew up anyway. Cockroaches and lots of flies. We had actually had lunch there, too, and that hadn't been too bad. Crap shops here as well - we can't find any food to take with us for lunch or snacks.

Day 127: Saturday September 4th – Yerefy Pavlovich to Urusha
56.4 miles (total 6727.2 miles)

Another couple of bloody disasters - I dropped my camera this morning just outside Sjegachama causing it to spring open, exposing the film and wrecking the mechanism. Luckily I had changed the film yesterday and had only taken a few photos. Still, I will have to rely on Kate now for photos - she doesn't always see the same photo opportunities as I do, so we'll see what we get.

This afternoon my front pannier rack broke yet again. I had a bit of a crash, losing my balance on the central part of the track, and the front pannier knocked against the ruts and ripped the attachment for the rubber clips on the back. I presume the rack broke at the same time. I survived with a bungey for a while, but the rack eventually hit my wheel and broke. It was the same side as had broken before. I had to finish the day with one bag on my back, resulting in a sore back, and one strapped onto the rear rack. I'll have to sort out something better for tomorrow and try to get it fixed in Skovorodino.

Apart from that it wasn't a bad day. Beautiful weather and scenery (except for one heavy shower in the afternoon). The road was better than I thought it would be - mostly gritty dirt track, with some muddy bits, but generally pretty good. We followed close to the railway all day - get waves and toots from the engine drivers.

Kate was very slow today. She doesn't seem to have much confidence in mud. She fell in once, and invariably has to put her foot down when she comes to any tricky part, which slows her down and is a pain if you are behind her. Usually it just means that Sasha and I have to wait a while until we can see her coming, then we set off again. I was enjoying dodging around the puddles in the afternoon, except for the bag bouncing on my back. The roads remind me of leafy autumn lanes in England. Except for breakages I was in a good mood all today.

We had lunch in a small station hamlet. A freight train had stopped, with a wagon of cars and lorries going to Vladivostok. One had a washing line attached. The people just sit in their cars for the train journey. We had some tomatoes bought in the morning from Yerefy Pavlovich, and some cutlets bought from the stolo there (actually not too bad), and some not very tasty dry biscuits (R50/kg) from Sjegachama, where we stopped at about 10.45 and waited for the shop to open.

We reached Urusha in good time — our first view of it was from across the valley, with a rainbow over the town. We found the workers' apartments and moved in (R1100 each). Cleaned the bikes in a stream, had a hot shower (two nights running), then some good spaghetti Bolognese and strange Russian mousse (vanilla semolina with lemon). Coconut chocolates as an expensive treat - R900/300g

Skovorodino is only 60 miles away according to one bloke we asked (seemed a reasonable bloke; he showed us the way to the appartments), so we may get there tomorrow if the road and the equipment are okay. Bad stomach again today - sort of diarrhoea.

The following morning saw no change in the road, with the usual mixture of stretches of grit alternating with mud and puddles. We were hoping to reach Skovorodino, which looked a decent-sized town on the map. The plan was to have a day off, our first after nine days of very tough riding, and give the bikes some much needed care and attention. Sasha's rear rack, newly installed in Mogocha, broke. He ought to have left the old one in place; using wire to mend the broken attachment points clearly worked better than the original bolts as it meant the rack could move slightly and absorb the bumps better. My rack had no bolts attaching it to my bike at all by now, and was giving no problems. Strangely enough, Kate was the only one of us who had no problems like this and she was using an alloy rack, which everyone had advised us against because if it did break we would not have been able to get it welded. The rest of us all used steel ones, and they all broke; Kate's survived intact.

Another reason to get to Skovorodino was to do some shopping. Our stocks were getting low, and although I knew there was not much on offer I needed a bit more variety. Lunch consisted of bread, one egg, mayonnaise and stale bread sticks – calories but no comfort. We had stopped to eat on the far side of the railway bridge over a wide river. Again the road had taken the direct route through the river and we had to scramble up the embankment. It was hard work hefting the bikes up, and Kate scouted around for an easier route while Sasha and I made it across. Eventually she reappeared, a bit tearful, saying she had not known where we were. I think we all needed a day off to relax and have an opportunity to look at what we had achieved over the two-and-a-half weeks since Chita, and appreciate the effort involved. Fortunately not long after lunch the road improved; it was still rammed grit, but it was now two lanes wide – a veritable highway which we could zoom along at 15-18mph, enjoying the autumn warmth in our shorts and tee-shirts.

As we rode into the outskirts of Skovorodino we were pleased with our progress and made for the hotel. Despite staying in empty houses recently we had somehow been spending quite a lot of money. Hotels were becoming more expensive, and we had finite funds. The idea of not being able to afford our journey home from Vladivostok was not one I wanted to dwell on. Our costs on this evening were kept down as a result of meeting Alexei. He chatted to us while we were checking in and seemed very impressed with our journey. When we learned that he

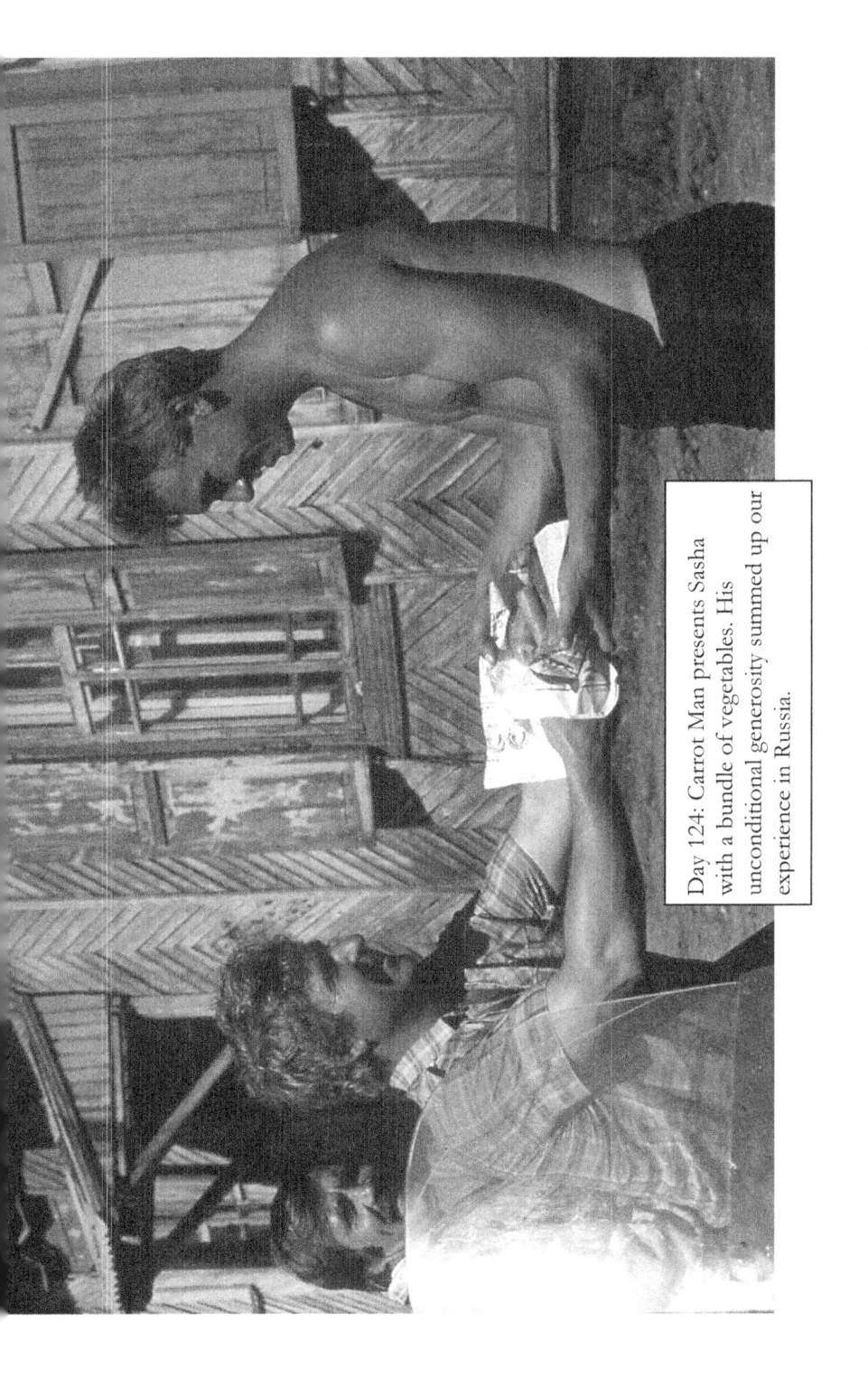

Day 124: Carrot Man presents Sasha with a bundle of vegetables. His unconditional generosity summed up our experience in Russia.

Day 124: Walking along the railway after Amazar. Sasha is holding the flowers we were given in the town.

Day 124: Trans-Siberian Express meets Trans-Siberian Cycle Expedition.

Day 125: Serious erosion on the main route to Mala-Kavaly.

was an army engineer with a road-building detail we thought that at last we had found someone who could provide us with some reliable information not just on the existence but maybe even on the quality of the roads, since he may have built some of them himself. Imagine our surprise, then, when he confidently explained that the decent road we had enjoyed that very afternoon was, in fact, rubbish. (He had clearly set his road quality bar unattainably high (based on some benchmark known only to himself, given the average quality of what we had experienced), and unless he moved to Tarmac World I felt he would never be satisfied from a transport corridor point of view.) Not only that, but the road from here to the major city of Blagoveshchensk did not exist. This really was confusing. We had just made our way from hamlet to hamlet through an area that on our maps had no roads marked. From Skovorodino there was most definitely a line tracing its way east. We chose to ignore everything Alexei had to say about the roads – it seemed the best thing to do. On the financial front, though, he did prove more reliable, helping us avoid spending money by sorting out our evening meal.

The first thing to do before eating was get cleaned up. While we had been getting acquainted in the hotel lobby, a jeep-load of his fellow road-builders rolled up (fresh from constructing more fantasy routes, no doubt) and we all piled in to head for the *banya* and a good scrub down. Unfortunately when we got there it was shut, but it did look as though our negotiations with the man on the door were going to be successful. Suddenly, an awesome and most definitely not-to-be-negotiated-with woman appeared from the shadows, screamed something that I had no hope of understanding (although the enthusiasm of her delivery did everything necessary to get her message across), pushed the man aside and slammed the door in our faces. For a second we all looked at each other in stunned silence before bursting out laughing – proof that great comedy transcends cultural boundaries. With the public *banya* option firmly and irreversibly closed to us, we all got back in the jeep and headed over to the local railway workers' buildings. Here the showers were hot and we had no problems getting in, and nor did what seemed to be the majority of the townsfolk. Sunday evening family wash-time was obviously a popular event. If I were the *banya* owner, I would sack the guard-woman on the door and get the place open for business.

Suitably clean we drove to the house of Viktor, one of the soldiers. He and his family had only been here three weeks, and he was no doubt looking forward to a less risky assignment than his tour of duty in Afghanistan had turned out to be. While there he had been injured in the chest and leg, requiring a four-month stay in hospital. Dinner of soup, tomatoes and meat was prepared, followed by mugs of hot chocolate. No vodka in sight, which made a pleasant change.

The following day was fairly inactive, with bouts of dozing punctuating the few things we did rouse ourselves to do. Spotting the machine yard next to the hotel I took my front rack in to see if it could be mended again. The person I spoke to, Eugene, seemed confident that he could fix it, and sure enough later that afternoon he appeared at the hotel with his handiwork. The result of the day spent wielding his welder was an astonishing piece of ironmongery, or, more accurately, ironmongrelry, since in its new incarnation one side of the original had been replaced and my formerly sleek and lightweight rack had become a clunking hybrid of aluminium and iron. Isambard Kingdom Brunel's formidable *Great Eastern* contained only marginally more iron in its sea-going hull than I now seemed to be carrying, but I was now the proud owner of an original piece of Soviet-inspired over-engineered kit that looked as though it could withstand anything that NATO might have wanted to throw at the Warsaw Pact. My rack could trace its lineage back proudly to the extraordinary Caspian Sea ekranoplans, the gargantuan and gravity-defying military Tupulovs, oversized and triumphant civic statuary, and, I dare say, to the heavy-hanging drapery of the Iron Curtain itself. And who knew? – maybe all the weight that was concentrated in its struts would result in such a significant lowering of my centre of gravity that my bike would enjoy greatly enhanced stability – not, I expect, to the extent that I could perform Blondin-like feats of high-wire daring, but enough to keep me upright over the bumps. I loved it, and happily paid Eugene the four dollars we had agreed. I then retired to the hotel room and spent the next hour patiently filing away at the rack's superstructure until I could actually manage to fit my pannier onto it.

The road we wanted to follow from Skovorodino to Blagoveshchensk ran parallel to the Amur river, which formed the border with China. It had not been on our original plan – the road on the maps we had used to put the trip together was farther to the north, but this newer one would save us a few days. The only problem was that it ran through a sensitive area and we were unsure whether we would actually be allowed to use it. If we had been feeling reckless we might have taken the risk and just headed off, hoping that any soldiers and officials we would surely meet along the way would be suitably impressed by our story and overlook the usually important issues of national security, happily waving us on our way. Even if we could not talk our way through, we might have reasoned that a period of arrest and incarceration in a remote Siberian cell would certainly raise the profile of the expedition. But there was also the strong possibility that following our release we would be put on a plane out of the country. With only three weeks to go to our planned arrival in Vladivostok this was a risk we were definitely not prepared to take, and we dutifully made our way to the border guards' base to see what permissions we needed and how to go about getting them.

Our question to the head officer was very straightforward ('Can we ride along the road next to the river?') and he was considerate enough to provide us with an equally straightforward response ('No!'). It was not what we had wanted to hear but there was no discussion invited. We were, however, allowed to go as far as the enigmatic sounding Post No.8, just beyond the small town of Dzjalinda; from here we would have to turn north to join the other road at Taldan. It was the best, and only, offer we had. We felt the officer had been very helpful, and he said he would phone the Dzjalinda office to let them know we were on our way (not so they could keep an eye out to make sure we arrived safely, but so we could not try to slip past unnoticed).

Apart from a brief section of appalling mud and puddles for a couple of miles because of roadworks, the route was reasonable quality dirt and took us through a landscape with plenty of steep hills. Skovorodino did seem to mark the end of the truly awful stretch with no road at all for many miles, but we clearly had some way to go before we could expect tarmac to last all day. Arriving in Dzjalinda for lunch we called in at the police station to have our passports checked. The policemen were very serious to begin with, but they relaxed and we chatted about the road. It was an easy conversation to have and enabled us to get over official introductions, but as for being any use… After the police, we went to the border guards' post and were met by Sergei, the second in command. Sitting in his office, I wondered what strategically important secrets were hidden from the prying eyes of passing spies behind the unassuming piece of curtain hanging on the wall behind his desk. No high-tech sliding James Bond panels here; and, I hoped, no ejector seats or shoes with concealed toxic daggers. My best guess was a map covered in wiggly Dad's Army arrows detailing proposed forays along the border, but there was no likelihood of Sergei suddenly seeing our presence as an opportunity to seize the diplomatic initiative and swish the curtain aside dramatically in an act of international *glasnost* to reveal everything that the Western powers had been straining to get their hands on for years. With its material apparently more weighed down than a House of Windsor hemline, nothing short of a hurricane would have deflected the curtain from its duty, and so the plans of manoeuvres and troop deployments remained a secret. Or maybe it was just the HQ's shopping list for the week. We shall never know.

While all these thoughts of international intrigue swirled in my head I did my best to keep a poker face. I could not contain my excitement at what happened next, though. A pot of herb tea and a plate of biscuits had appeared. Sergei poured and handed out the cups, and invited us to help ourselves to biscuits. Based on our experiences so far, this would have been a moment of disappointment, my expectations of a taste and texture sensation squashed as surely as the aged biscuit between my teeth. Sergei's biscuits, though, were a revelation. Although they were plain, I could tell as soon as I picked my first one off the plate that it was in a different class from the others of the previous four months. I raised it to my mouth and bit, and was amazed as my teeth were met not by the spongy half-hearted resistance of a stale biscuit but by the determined solidity of a fresh one. A harder bite, and crack! I was through. On the left and right I heard crunching coming from Kate and Sasha. The conversation had paused while we each enjoyed a private moment before turning to each other to share this absurdly simple pleasure. Fresh biscuits! The plate was cleared in what we hoped was a politely short time, and Sergei got on with telling us where we could go.

Post No.8 (*Voskresenskoye*) was 22 miles farther along the road and would make a sensible target for the end of the day. We thought we had been given some sort of special permission to ride along this section, but it turned out that anyone could use this road – it was the part east of Post No.8 that was out of bounds. The only restriction on us and other civilians was that we must not cross to the southern side of the barbed wire that ran parallel with the road and which marked the limit of 'The System', a strip of land 300m-800m wide which ran down to the banks of the Amur river. It was an easy rule to stick to, and as it turned out any curiosity we might have felt about the area's strategic role was satisfied a couple of weeks later when we had our opportunity to get up very close to Russia's military apparatus.

A strong tailwind helped us cover the miles through the beautiful open scenery without too much trouble, and the heavy rain showers we were keeping an eye on passed to the north of us, so we arrived at our destination dry and in good time. The base consisted of the military buildings and parade square and some civilian quarters. We were put up by Alexander and Tanya, potato farmers who had recently moved here from farther north. He had constructed a workshop out of two old railway carriages with a roof joining them, and these were our quarters for the night. With some senior officers from Khabarovsk on site the commanding officer was apparently rather nervous about our presence, so we had to keep a low profile. We were allowed into the barracks to have a quick shower and then had to retreat to the workshop. The garrison was busy with some square-bashing; if this was the fighting force that would be unleashed from behind Sergei's curtain it looked like he would do better keeping it under wraps. Unless of course syncopated marching was the new surprise tactic designed to bamboozle an enemy more used to facing a well-drilled military machine.

We were now heading for Blagoveshchensk, our first proper city since Chita, 850 miles earlier. It was still six days away, and any thoughts we might have had that conditions under tyre would improve after Skovorodino were soon confirmed as being wildly optimistic. At least we had plenty of fuel on board. Tanya had appeared weighed down with some delicious apple jam, home-made flatbread and a bag of cooked potatoes, all of which went on top of the semolina we had just cooked for breakfast. Leaving the Amur river and heading north to Taldan, the road rose and fell over the thickly wooded hills. As I approached each crest I was hoping for an extensive view, but each time the road levelled out briefly the trees would remain densely packed and all there was to see was the track running on into the distance to the next hill. I felt hemmed in and tried not to think further than just one hill at a time. Each one done was one less to do. After lunch in Taldan we turned east again onto a worse road – more extensive mud and unexpectedly deep puddles. The hills stayed with us to the end of the day and I was grateful for the huge quantity of carbohydrate that I had eaten over the previous twelve hours.

The skies had been clear all day, and as we rode into Goudachi at about 7.30 in the evening the temperature was dropping quickly. We did not like the idea of camping but the town seemed very quiet, with no-one around for us to encourage to let us stay in their house. I went for a wander to see what was what and bumped into Ludmilla, an attractive mother of five. By now, I was able to explain a bit more about what we were doing in Russia on our bikes, and once Ludmilla had unravelled my description of our journey she kindly offered us some water for a wash before taking us around to the mayor's house to see if he could arrange somewhere for us to stay. While Kate, Sasha and I got colder and colder as the sun dipped to the horizon, the mayor, clearly a man not to be rushed, strolled back through town to find someone to open up the disused workers' apartments. They were fine for us, dry and with plenty of space, but the electricity was out so dinner was cooked by candlelight. It did make for a relaxed evening, though, and I actually managed to have a decent conversation with Kate about the trip. Whereas I was feeling very relaxed about the whole thing and was particularly enjoying this stretch through the wilder parts of Siberia, she explained that she was keen to finish and had had enough of the mud. I knew that this did not mean that she would be looking for a way to cut the expedition short – she was not a quitter and something drastic would have to happen before she would consider throwing in the towel. In fact, it probably meant she was more determined to push on and get through to Blagoveshchensk and back (we hoped) onto proper roads for the final burst to Vladivostok. I had still not started to think about arriving at our final destination, and did not want to rush the last part just to get there as quickly as possible. I wanted to make the most of each day and make sure I reached Vladivostok in the right frame of mind having had time to think back over the trip before jumping on the plane to get home. And there was still a great deal that would happen over the next three weeks that would make them as memorable as the previous seventeen.

One thing that took up an increasing amount of our time between here and the end was bike maintenance. The next morning in Goudachi began with me and Sasha attaching more wire to our racks to try to stave off their complete disintegration, and very shortly after setting off our machines were filthy again, with the chains making an awful grating noise as the coarse grit made a very effective abrasive paste with the oil. Not long into the day, disaster. Descending to Gonja I hit a bump and my rear pannier flew off breaking both hooks and a spoke in the process. Fortunately Sasha had been out in front, and while he was waiting for me to catch back up he had fallen into conversation with Anatoly, a repair-man at the local hospital where his wife worked as a nurse. A quick rummage through his jumbled storeroom at home produced some stiff electrical wire, which turned out to be just the thing for attaching the panniers. We took a long length of it, planning for future breakages, but instead of setting off again we ended up having an extended lunch break for a couple of hours at Anatoly's house. It seemed to be getting harder to get going each time we were invited in anywhere, and on this occasion who could blame us, with hot tea, fresh bread and homemade bilberry jam on offer? It did mean that we still had about 60 miles to cover between 2pm and 8pm to reach Tigda; a strong tail-wind whipped up the dust but blew us along and we made it as the temperature and the sun were dropping.

Lunch the following day was provided by Nikolai and Gala on their *dacha* near the town of Ushumum. The morning had been spent dodging the numerous potholes on the thankfully dry track. It was impossible to cycle in a straight line and there was always the danger of being caught out uncomfortably by an unanticipated sudden dip if my concentration lapsed. The small wooden house with its carved window frames was spotlessly clean and decorated in what the home improvement supplements back home would describe as an 'uncluttered style'. Here, it was just the way their few possessions were neatly arranged rather than being a conscious decision to create a particular lifestyle choice. The hospitality was faultless and Gala's fresh *chi* (cabbage soup) was the best of the trip so far. After lunch the road disappeared and we were faced with following the railway for 15 miles. When we asked people about the condition of the route ahead they would tend to describe it in the context of travelling along it by car, so the information they gave was not always that relevant. On a bike, even a fully loaded tourer, a foot-wide path is all that is needed to be able to cross the landscape, so when people said it was impossible to get through a particular section because of a lack of suitable tracks they generally meant it was impossible to drive through. For us, though, a footpath worked fine, and for the first five miles or so following our lunch we had no problems as just such a path led us through the grass.

After a while it took us into the trees, where the path faded and disappeared, and we had no option but to lift our bikes onto the ballast and start walking. Everyone was in a good mood; as the afternoon wore on the temperature held up and the hay meadows and birch woods glowed in the early autumn light. At about 6.30pm we still had seven miles to go to reach Tu, a halt on the railway line, and although the light was beginning to fade we decided to push on rather than try to find somewhere to camp. The tracks ran straight ahead and after a while the green signal lights at the station appeared in the distance; we pulled in in the dark at about 8.30pm. It seemed quite a busy station, but there were only four or five houses so it was not very obvious why there should be a collection of sidings here. The signalman did not seem very enthusiastic when he saw us arrive, but once Sasha had chatted to him he became more accommodating and eventually allowed us to sleep on the floor of his office. It seemed like a good place to spend the night, but as the hours ticked by and we became better and better acquainted with the local method of communication between signal box and train driver we realised we would have been better off in our tents somewhere far removed from Tu. At regular intervals along the incandescently floodlit stretch of track that ran for half a mile or so from the signaller's office the large cones of old fashioned public address systems sprouted from the tops of the telegraph poles. There was no public to address here, certainly not at three in the morning, but from the warm and cosy confines of the control room the controller could maintain a lively conversation with the train drivers thanks to these loud-halers, broadcasting instructions and information into the night in a scatter-gun approach. The intended recipient was out there in his locomotive somewhere, as was everyone else within a generous radius for whom this must all have been nothing less than an annoying aural intrusion. No wonder there were only a handful of houses here, and no doubt these were all occupied by railway workers.

After an interrupted night's sleep we managed to set off early to resume our railway walk. My mood the previous day had been good, but the overnight announcements of the signal controller and an early puncture did not set me up well, and after only a few miles I was swearing at the railway track. At least my annoyance was directed there rather than at Kate and Sasha, but there were still occasions when passions ran a bit too high. The day before, Sasha and I had had another run-in when a discussion about the location of the path got overheated. As before, we had to agree to disagree and re-establish the cooperative team spirit; fortunately we always seemed to manage this without too much difficulty. Kate would always work to avoid a confrontation and her overall mood was stable, but I am not sure if it is a good idea to keep resentments inside. Better to let off some steam and release the tensions. Kate confided in me on this day that she was feeling slightly left out of things because of Sasha's approach; she explained that he always asked me the questions rather than her, and she felt he was bossy and patronising. She was also unhappy that he would not let her ride at the front of the group. I agreed with her descriptions and said she ought to point these things out to him. If it meant having an argument at least it would show how strongly she felt about it, but that was not her approach and she never had the conversation.

Another puncture, more pannier rack repairs and an unexciting lunch of bread, tasteless biscuits (definitely not crunchy) and halva later, we arrived at Shimanovsk. I was happy enough to be here but it was September 11th and I really should have been at home. My good friend Mike was getting married and I was supposed to be his Best Man. I had happily accepted the responsibility the previous autumn and he had no doubt been relieved to tick 'secure the services of a reliable and dedicated friend' off his long to-do list. Unfortunately I failed the 'reliable' test a few short months later once Kate had told me about her plans, and I had to ring Mike to let him know that far from getting him to the church on time I would in fact be somewhere in the depths of Siberia. Luckily for me he is an adventurously minded chap, and rather than give me an ear-full for failing in my responsibilities his first reaction was to ask if there was space on the expedition for one more. He was only being half-serious, but if I did nothing else during my brief tenure I do like to think that I successfully tested Mike's commitment to his forthcoming marriage by placing temptation firmly in his way and making him choose between an adventurous journey of self-discovery and teamwork, and an arduous cycling expedition. Needless to say, he stayed at home and, newly-appointed Best Man safely seeing him off, he and Liz exchanged their vows. It was very fitting that the restaurant we eventually tracked down that evening in Shimanovsk was hosting a wedding reception. It was in full swing, and once the very drunk manageress had let us in I could at least join Mike and Liz in spirit. It was a lively evening, luckily without the potential punch-up of Nerchinsk, and we did manage to have a promising conversation with Nikolai, an unexpectedly sober guest, about the apparently good road from here to Blagoveshchensk. We left everyone to it as they headed off through the chilly night to continue their partying at the local disco, wondering whether to risk believing Nikolai or not.

Day 135: Sunday September 12th – Shimanovsk to Sverbodny
84.3 miles (total 7204.5 miles)
Tarmac all day!! We stopped off at the excellent market in town - corn on the cob, peanut biscuits. We even found fresh chocolate muffins - incredible. I broke a spoke in town and we eventually got going properly at about 11.00am.
Windy, hilly, overcast. There was a headwind so we did 10-minute bits each stopping about every 20 miles. There is a different type of forest here - more pine and oak. Going south, things are looking green again. We are making good progress. Kate is having trouble with her gears - the chain keeps jumping around. For lunch we had a picnic by the roadside - bread with sausage bought in the restaurant last night.
It got gloomier and started to rain a couple of miles outside Sverbodny. The hotel was expensive - about R3000 each for me and Kate, and no hot water. It does annoy me - you pay more, and you get nothing more than in the crap hotels. The restaurant next door was very good, but also pricey. It was the first time I've seen a really busy restaurant - Russians out enjoying themselves, and apparently not very drunk. The food was very good, and well-presented - pelmeni appeared in individual mini-casseroles, with a pizza-base lid and tasty soup rather than the usual starchy water. We also had some stew with fried rice. I got back to the room at about 9.00pm and fell asleep, but had to get up to do some bike repairs. I helped Kate - she had a broken link in her chain, so we replaced that, breaking the Cool Tool in the process, and also put two new jockey wheels on from one of the spare derailleurs. I tried to adjust the front cones, but that didn't work. Eventually I got to bed at 12.15am. The mossies kept us all awake. It was pouring with rain all evening - not a good prospect.

A big effort the following day saw us cover 100 miles into a strong headwind to reach Blagoveshchensk. We had noticed quite a few military bases along the route, and as we came into the town we realised that a car was following us. Had we been under surveillance since staying at Post No.8? We were sure we had not strayed into any of the restricted areas. In the end it turned out to be something much less sinister, and rather less exciting. The driver was a man called Gernady, a former racing cyclist and now a coach. He had spotted us by chance as we were cycling in and had been curious to find out more about us. We ended up following him to his offices, where Kate and I relaxed while he took Sasha to the hotel to sort out accommodation. Gernady was the most reserved Russian we had met – when he called in to see us the next morning he did not shake hands, which was unusual, and there was never any hint that we might be invited to his flat for a meal or to stay. He was very helpful, though, taking the time to make sure we were sorted out and giving us fresh tomatoes, potatoes, peppers, pears and pear juice, all of which was extremely welcome. As always, we were grateful for whatever help people were prepared to give us.

Blagoveshchensk sat on the banks of the Amur River. Cossacks had passed through the area in the mid-17th Century but the town had not been established until 1856 in a deliberate act of expansionism. The land north of the Amur at that time was part of China, but Peking's resources were spread too thinly to be able to defend this remote area and the Russians forced an agreement with their southern neighbour to re-establish the border along the river. The town's population promptly developed strong trading links with China and half the population were in fact Chinese at the turn of the 20th Century. The Boxer Rebellion of the early 1900s resulted in the expulsion at gunpoint of the Chinese from the town, and for the next 90 years the two countries watched each other warily across the wide, dark river.

Krasnoflotskaya Street ran beside the river and was a pleasant place to stretch our legs with a relaxing stroll. The 'Fantasy Party Zone' outdoor disco looked to us to be one activity too many, so we continued past and made our way to the local museum. The displays inside covered a fascinating mix of local wildlife and culture, and the building itself was unusually fine. A German company called Kunst and Albers had established a very successful chain of shops throughout the Russian far-east at the turn of the 20th Century, and the museum was in one of their former shops. Overall, Blagoveshchensk was a very appealing place.

Sasha had some personal connections with it: his great-uncle had been mayor in the 1950s as well as head of the local Party, and his brother and sister had both been born here. These facts generated no more than a passing interest, though; Sasha's attention had been grabbed by the cheap prices for jeans and denim jackets.

During our two-day break in the city we were hoping to hear from Yuri. He was planning to join us again, but we had not spoken to him directly since Krasnoyarsk and did not know exactly what he had in mind. There were no messages from him at the central post office, and all we could do was leave one there for him saying when we were leaving, and hope he would pick it up. It did not seem necessary to specify which road we would be following – there was only one going in our direction. We were looking forward to seeing him again.

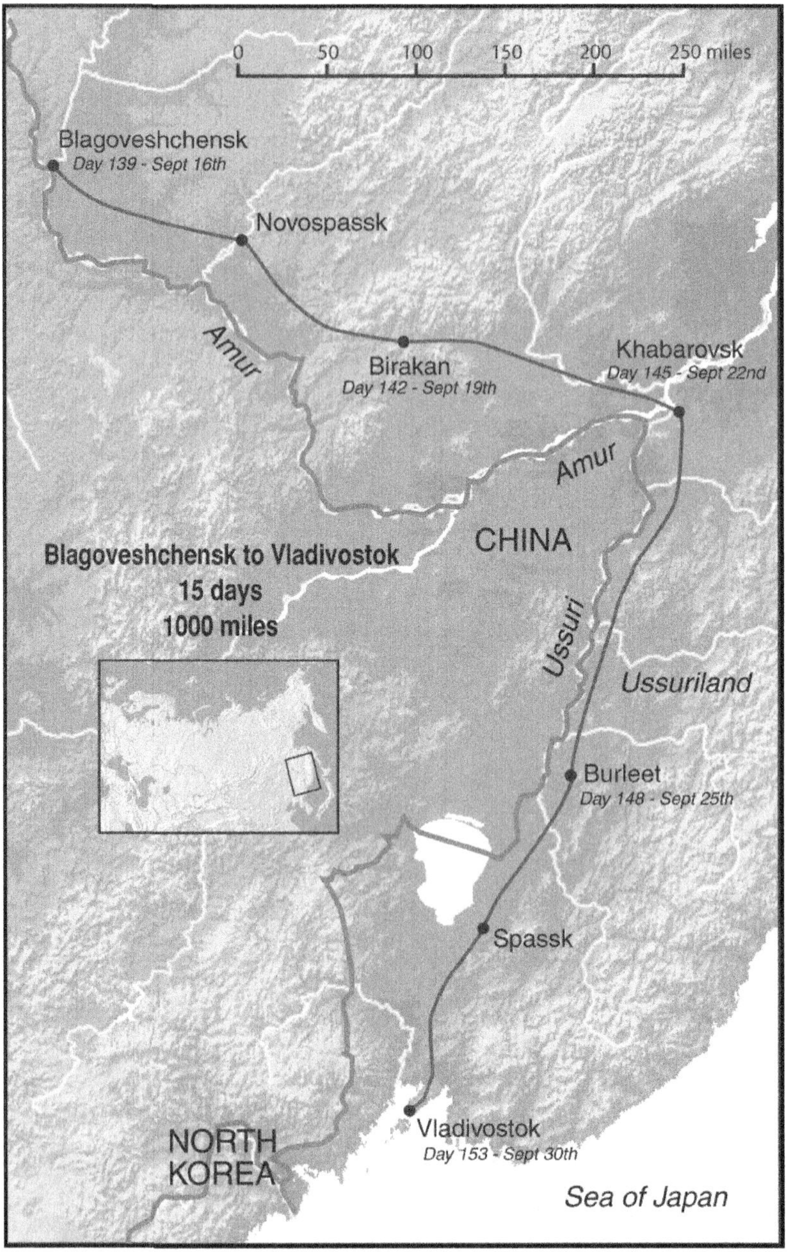
0 50 100 150 200 250 miles
Blagoveshchensk
Day 139 - Sept 16th
Novospassk
Amur
Birakan
Day 142 - Sept 19th
Khabarovsk
Day 145 - Sept 22nd
Amur
CHINA
Blagoveshchensk to Vladivostok
15 days
1000 miles
Ussuri
Ussuriland
Burleet
Day 148 - Sept 25th
Spassk
Vladivostok
Day 153 - Sept 30th
NORTH
KOREA
Sea of Japan

SECTION 7

~~~

LAND OF THE TIGER

~~~

On the morning of our departure Sasha got in touch with the local television company through a contact we had made at the hotel, and a film crew turned up to interview us. After a series of thankfully unprobing questions we pushed off, once again escorted by Gernady who saw us safely to the edge of the city. After a relaxing couple of days, the miles rolled by comfortably with good tarmac under our wheels and a warm sun above us. Everyone felt relaxed and we passed the time singing. By the time it got dark at about 8pm we had pitched the tents, got the fire going and were chatting and watching the countless stars. There was no sign of Yuri, and we had no way of knowing whether he was back at home or on his way to meet us. We would just have to keep going and leave it up to him to work out where we were.

The following day was neatly book-ended by a beautiful sunrise and a stunning, Turneresque sunset. Between these displays of atmospheric splendour we were treated to strong wind, pouring rain and thunderstorms. About forty minutes after leaving the campsite we were overtaken by a local bus wheezing its way to Khabarovsk. A hundred yards up the road it pulled over and a lean figure hauled two large bags and a familiar-looking bike out of the luggage compartment. As we caught up with the parked bus a typically cheerful looking Yuri called out 'Hey, hello friends!' He had managed to convince his boss back at the laboratory that a journey to the far-east would provide an excellent opportunity to collect samples from the local plants, and although his boss had probably not expected anything on the scale of the extraordinary catalogue Joseph Banks had brought back from his voyages with Captain Cook he was almost certainly hoping for more than just the pocketful of seeds that Yuri's rummaging in the undergrowth would ultimately produce.

Yuri had arrived in Blagoveshchensk by train on our last evening there and had picked up our note in the post office. Realising we would not get too far ahead in one day he had calmly checked out the buses and come trundling after us. It was good to see him again; I had enjoyed his company during the Sayan mountains and although I was not exactly sure how he and Sasha would get on given their different characters I was happy that having an extra person in the team, especially one whom Sasha could talk to in Russian after his two months with just Kate and me, would help in terms of the group dynamics. His bike was the same as ever – a broken spoke later this day came as no surprise – but his panniers had been beefed up with additional ironwork. He seemed uncertain after just one day with us about his ability to carry on, saying he felt very tired. I put this down to a mixture of the long journey he had made to reach us and too much drinking during his recent university trip to the Altai. I was sure he was not about to jump on a train back home, and did not worry about his fitness. I knew he would feel fine in a day or two once he had got back into the swing of things.

That evening as the skies cleared we crossed the Bureya river on the ferry and headed into the village of Novospassk, where we were treated to an excellent meal and a bizarre event. We had by now perfected our technique of announcing ourselves as an important international cycling expedition when we arrived in a village and wanted to find somewhere to stay. We would then just ask to be shown to the mayor's house, and they would always be able to sort something out for us with the minimum of fuss. In Novospassk this process resulted in our spending the night in the house of the head of the local collective farm. Dinner, cooked by Tanya the lady of the house, included our first taste of some local delicacies – fish from the Amur river, red caviar and honey. The caviar was delicious – large red spheres that popped in your mouth to release their richly flavoured liquid, and the honey was exquisite – the warmth and taste of summer in the taiga concentrated into liquid gold. Later in the evening I went to the bathroom to get cleaned up and ready for bed. There had been plenty of occasions earlier in the trip when I would dearly have loved to have the use of a well kitted out bathroom, and now in Tanya's house I found myself standing in front of a fine full-sized bath that I would usually have been able to visualise myself slipping into beneath the fragrant bubbles of an exclusive foaming total body cleansing system without any trouble at all. On this occasion, however, I could see I had arrived too late and definitely felt no urge to jump in. Partly this was because there was no space for me, but mainly it was because of what it was that had already taken up residence in the tub. The bath was full to the brim with fish, and we are not talking about a collection of colourful and pretty tropical mini-fish frolicking among the fresh green fronds of pond weed or playfully chasing each other in and out of the plastic faux ruins of a castle or a submerged water mill, scales glinting all iridescent in the refracted light, either. These were large, grey and dead, stacked one on top of the other like, well... sardines, really, except each one of these equalled about 50 sardines. They fixed me with a cold, fish-eye stare. I imagined we had eaten one of their number for dinner, and very tasty it had been, too, and would not have thought a whole lot more about it (other than that there really were rather a lot of them, more than you might reasonably expect someone to catch in a morning's excursion along the river) if it had not been for the fact that when I went back to the bathroom early the next morning the bath was completely empty and there was not a hint of fish anywhere. A large collection of such big fish (which turned out to be Siberian salmon) would be very valuable, and catching them in the rivers was carefully controlled, supposedly, by licences and quotas. Late night fish movements certainly hinted at clandestine activities, a serious thing for someone such as the head of the collective farm to be involved in. I had no evidence to back up any of this, of course, except for a bathfull of fish in the evening and an empty bath in the morning. Maybe the operation had been rumbled and someone had pulled the plug. Whatever the explanation, the whole thing smelled a bit ... peculiar.

Over the next couple of days we encountered more and more roadworks, and became more or less resigned to the idea that we would not reach the point where the tarmac had returned for good. Occasionally, though, the presence of the road crews did bring advantages, such as being able to stay dry during our tea break as the rain beat down hard by sheltering inside the large concrete pipes stacked up ready for installation as culverts. Hills covered in birch, pine and oak proved challenging at times, and the bikes continued to deteriorate, with punctures and gear cables demanding our attention. I told Sasha that he needed to be more careful with his bike and not just try to get to the bottom of each hill ahead of everyone else. We did not have any major spare parts with us and to get someone from Centre Pole to travel all the way out to us here would have been expensive and time consuming.

We were shadowing the railway closely and stayed in rooms at stations and railway workers' rest areas. At Birakan we got rooms and a *banya* – our first decent wash for four days – and the next morning I watched the sun come up over the mountains and climb into a clear, crisp sky. The town spread up the sides of the valley, with older wooden houses higher up and the newer buildings at the bottom near the railway. We cycled back up to rejoin the main road and resumed our easterly heading, frequently teased by the appearance of a comfortable stretch of tarmac. Along the sections where it looked as though roadworks were under way we had usually seen nobody, but this afternoon in the distance through the trees we spotted some large animated machines. After a few minutes we arrived at the active roadworks, with a full range of earth movers, diggers and graders busy preparing the ground for the new highway. Sasha spoke to some of the workmen and was assured that this was indeed the end of the roadworks and we should have tarmac from here on. It was such a significant moment that we filmed it. The tarmac had all but disappeared in Nerchinsk 30 days earlier and except for the odd bit here and there we had had 1500 miles of anything from decent dirt tracks to grass paths, and waterlogged mud to railway ballast. It was a relief for us and our bikes to be back on smooth good road, and we could enjoy cruising along while taking in the view and chatting rather than having to concentrate on dodging potholes.

We had more good luck when trying to check in to the hotel at Birabidjan for the night. The first one was too expensive and the second one was shut, so we carried on exploring the town on the lookout for somewhere else. In the process, we bumped into three young Germans driving a Lada between the twin cities of Munich and Sapporo. Their journey was being sponsored by a German sports television channel, and their camera equipment was compatible with ours which meant we could check the tapes we had shot recently. Since the video camera had taken a serious knock twenty days earlier we had not known if it was recording in focus or not as the viewfinder was showing a blurred image. Slotting a tape into their camera and pushing 'play' we all breathed a sigh of relief when the picture came up crisp and focussed and we knew we would have a proper record of the complete expedition.

The following day we made the most of the road and covered over a hundred miles despite a late start and mechanical set-backs.

Day 144: Tuesday September 21st – Birabidjzan to Nicholaiovka
102.4 miles (total 7768.6 miles)

It was dark this morning when the alarm went off at 6.50. We had to do some work on the bikes - Kate needed a new back tyre (our last nearly-new tyre, only used by Kate between Omsk and Novo), a wheel straightened, and brakes reset. I put a bit more wire on my rear pannier and straightened the rear wheel. I noticed my tyre was worn as well, so had to put one of the originals back on. Yuri was off buying wildlife books. We set off at about 10.00am. The ground was very flat all day and more wooded than I would have expected - the map just shows a swampy area

The first two hours or so were very boring, and I had backache. Yuri and Sasha shot off - I was at the back. This is the worst place, as you have to keep going until the others decide to stop. After the first break, we cycled in a group, which was much better. The pace was very fast - about 50 miles had been done by lunch, in Smitovich. Cheese, tomato and onion sandwiches.

There was a potentially huge disaster just before lunch – one of the rails underneath my seat broke. Luckily I could fix it by moving the saddle forward slightly. We were cycling fast after lunch as well. We stopped for a snack in Partisanskoye and wanted to do about another hour (until about 6.30). We could easily have made it to the Amur today if we'd wanted and if my liver hadn't been hurting again. It always happens just after I've eaten something, and doesn't hurt if I get off my bike and stand up. On the bike it's bloody painful.

We stopped in a grotty small town to sleep - luckily the hotel was closed, so we filled our water bags and carried on looking for somewhere to camp. Nowhere really suitable presented itself, so we kept going a bit more and a bit more. The weather was getting quite cold. We reached Nicholaiovka and went to the railway station. The rooms we'd been told about didn't exist, but the bloke there showed us to the railway workers' rest room - billiard table (no baize, all cut away), chairs, tables, lots of space, basin. Pretty good.

We cooked soup and noodles, rice pudding and chocolate powder for supper. Yuri found some churns in the room, one with curds and one with cream, and helped himself. There were photos on the wall of how to walk along the railway and avoid the trains. Lockers. Diagrams of things that can go wrong with the rails. We managed to get the key stuck in the door, so we may be here for a while.

Fortunately someone turned up with a key at about 7.30 the next morning and managed to unlock the door, thus releasing us from the possibility of having to use the bucket in the corner of the room as a toilet. The fog quickly blew away to reveal a cold clear morning as we cycled to the banks of the Amur river and caught the ferry across to Khabarovsk, our last major stop before Vladivostok. The city sat comfortably on the hills beside the river, with wide tree-lined streets and smartly dressed inhabitants. At the central post office a parcel was waiting for us containing new films and video tapes, a small plaque from Milton Keynes to add to the letter for the mayor of Vladivostok, and more importantly some letters from home for Kate and me.

We found rooms at a student apartment block and ran into two American Russian language students on their placement year, and from them we got our first sketchy information about the developing situation in Mosow. Yeltsin's position as president was apparently being challenged by Rutskoy, the vice-president. A poll on the television news asking 'Who do you consider to be president?' produced 64% for Yeltsin, 14% for Rutskoy and 22% don't know, so Yeltsin seemed secure but there was never any knowing which way things would go in this country. The local old Communists in Khabarovsk held a very small rally by Lenin's statue, but this was the only obvious activity we saw. Moscow felt, and was, a very long way away and the feeling here in the far east of Siberia was that with good links to China and Japan, and excellent natural resources, the region could look after itself. Khabarovsk appeared a confident city – it had previously been the capital of the quasi-independent Far Eastern Republic in the early 1920s, and it looked as though it would be able to cope as part of a breakaway region again. We also satisfied ourselves that if the situation deteriorated we could catch a boat to Japan if we needed to. Although we could not see much enthusiasm for unrest just now the onset of the cold winter with the prospect of associated food shortages might spur those people disenchanted with the current political set-up into action. We hoped to be long-gone by then and back through Moscow on our way home. Apparently it was already only 4°C in the capital – another reason to avoid going there.

Svetlana Shevchencko, Deputy Head of Administration on Social Affairs, greeted us in her office at the town hall. We were not after any help in particular, but it was always a good idea to spend some time chatting to people in official positions so that our arrival was properly noted and potentially useful contacts made. We talked about the trip and the ideas behind it, and hoped we managed to leave a good impression as British and Australian visitors keen to experience Russia. We also got in touch with our contact at the Australian Consulate in Vladivostok. We would be arriving there in about a week if everything went according to plan, and we needed to start getting prepared.

There were only about 600 miles to go, and the ultimate goal of the expedition was now the next city we were aiming for. It was tempting to speed up to try and get there as quickly as possible – Kate certainly felt like that. She said she had had enough – not of the cycling itself, but she felt she had experienced everything the country had to offer and that there was nothing really left to achieve on the trip. Except reach the end, I reminded her, which had been the whole point of starting, after all. This week was perhaps the most important of the whole trip. To rush this last section would have been reckless. We were all tired, and the bikes were worn out. This was just the time to stick to our plan, avoid any unnecessary risks and keep focused on the overall aim of the expedition. In his regular communications with us from Ryazan, Misha Malakhov stressed this approach as well, and if it had helped him become the person who had been to the North Pole more than any other then I was sure it would work for us. Personally, I was feeling very relaxed and if anything would have been happy to prolong the cycling. If we had been offered the means to carry on from Vladivostok and ride into China or across to Japan I am sure I would have accepted it.

The whole of this far-eastern region of Russia had been closed to foreigners up until just 18 months before our visit, and the movements of Russians within it had been carefully controlled, too. It was strategically important and contained a number of military bases; Vladivostok itself was the home of the Russian Pacific fleet. The last thing the local military wanted was young foreigners nosing around their installations, to which my reply would be, 'Well, they should take more care over their security arrangements, then.' Riding out of Khabarovsk we had picked up the main road without any difficulties, avoiding the problems experienced in St. Petersburg by cleverly following the large signpost pointing the way we wanted to go – it was the first one we had seen for Vladivostok and was a cause for some excitement. After a more or less flat and easy morning in the warm sunshine we stopped for lunch near the village of Verino, next to one of these military bases. Through the chain-link fence we could see four air force jets out of their hangars. It was reasonably interesting in an 'Oh look, there's the Red Army' sort of way and we were not feeling especially inquisitive. But then we spotted the large hole in the fence and suddenly we all became much more curious about the place.

There was a motorbike parked next to one of the hangars but neither its rider nor anyone else seemed to be about, and the hole in the fence was just too inviting, so we filed in. I felt like a naughty schoolboy rather than a spy, sneaking about somewhere that was clearly out of bounds, but we were risking more than a sharp whack with a cane if we were caught. I was videoing it all, and was not quite sure how I would explain that to the base's commanding officer should the need arise. The place seemed deserted, though, and we ambled about unmolested. The planes were real enough, as Yuri and Sasha demonstrated by clambering up onto the wings of one of them and posing next to the large red star painted on the tail fin. It was all rather odd and I could not match the familiar images of the Red Square May Day parades, with their ranks of neatly pressed soldiers and gleaming missile launchers, with the run-down and apparently deserted base here. Despite our curiosity and Sasha and Yuri's apparently calm approach to the whole event I did not want to test our luck by staying on the base any longer than it took to have a reasonably quick look around, so once we had satisfied our interest we wandered back through the hole in the fence, returning to the civilian world and relaxing again with our picnic.

Despite our late start and an extended mid-afternoon break while Sasha dismantled, re-greased and reassembled his grumbling front axle, we managed 85 miles and reached Vyazemskiiy for the night, where I greased my rear bearings, Kate replaced her gear cable and Sasha turned his middle chain-ring around in a bid to regain the use of it. The originally triangular teeth had been worn into shark fins, and would not grip the chain under load.

Day 148: Saturday September 25th – Vyakenskii to Burleet 88.4 miles (total 7963.9 miles)

Managed to get up early and leave the hotel before about 8.00, despite the primus spewing petrol and catching fire again. Sasha broke a spoke after about 20 minutes. Foggy morning, slightly hilly. Beautiful trees again, especially a line of rich scarlet Acers with golden poplars behind them near the village of Avan. The fog cleared, giving clear blue sky and hot sun, warm enough for tee-shirts and shorts after lunch at the village of Lermontooka. Did some videoing from the bike and rode into Bikin in the afternoon. A couple from Khabarovsk stopped and chatted. They take groups of Americans fishing in the north, to catch something or other. The man set a world record in July for catching a 50lb fish on a 17lb test line. They suggested somewhere we might be able to camp just over 20 miles out of town. Went to the shop near the railway station and got some bread and chicken stock cubes (to make soup). I was surprised how hot it was in the afternoon, considering it's gone the middle of September.

I set off from Bikin feeling quite tired - my legs take a while to get going after a stop. It was hilly on the map, but actually wasn't as bad as expected - gentler climbs and descents. We watched a dark rain cloud getting closer, but it was only very light rain, and short-lived. We stopped and considered camping near the suggested place, but there were loads of mossies, and a bloke said there was a village in about four miles, so we went there.

We arrived in Burleet and went to the mayor's house. Another Vladimir; very friendly. He invited us in for tea and freshly made cabbage doughnuts and jam doughnuts, with delicious honey. Two types - a clear and light-tasting honey from lime trees (8 species available), and a very richly flavoured, heavier honey from a mixed flower meadow. The latter tasted the same as the scent of flowers. Sasha ate loads and was getting quite carried away. This year, from 20 hives, Vladimir has produced 2 tonnes of honey, which he sells for R1000/kg. Kate is seriously thinking of importing to Australia.

Vladimir arranged for us to stay in a nearby bloke's (Victor) outhouse. There were loads of mossies in it, so we smoked them out with a bee smoker. Chicken noodle soup for supper, with Knorr cube - very tasty. Sasha discovered a 10-litre can of honey in the room. He and Yuri played a guitar and sang songs - it was lovely to listen to them around the fire outside. Then they went off to pull some local totty.
Apparently a tiger has been living in this area for the last five years. It has killed a dog. People have seen its footprints. There is no chance of spotting one as we go along - it would be extremely well-camouflaged now, and there's too much traffic on the road. We have to get used to that again. Apparently Russian summertime ends tomorrow across the whole country. Sasha and Yuri have just come back from the local disco - obviously unsuccessful.
Kate's new gear cable seems to work. Sasha's gears were okay in the morning, but screwed up again in the afternoon - he can't use the middle chain ring again. His rear tyre is splitting slightly - he had to adjust the brakes a bit. My bearings are better, but there are still some nasty noises coming from the gear area!
Bikin - are the residents Bikinis? Bikini region - worth spending some time there. Don't want to wax on about it.
Milk now costs about R300 per litre from the street sellers. Women and girls often have pictures from magazines (models etc) stuck on the outside of their purses.

The news about the tiger was exciting. Ussuriland, in the far-eastern regions of Russia, is one of the last remaining refuges of *Panthera tigris altaica*, the Siberian tiger, largest of all the big cats. In former centuries the various races of tiger ranged from the marshy shores of the Caspian Sea across the full width of Asia to the islands of Japan, south through the Indian subcontinent and down the Malaysian peninsula and Indonesian archipelago as far as Bali. This extensive range was initially fragmented on it western reaches as Central Asia's landscapes dried out and forests and marshlands were replaced by steppe and desert. Once humans appeared, hunting and land clearance also had an effect, but it was not until the turn of the 20th Century that tiger numbers plummeted dramatically. This majestic and magnificent animal, seen variously as 'Godfather' and the spirit of the taiga forest by Ussuriland's indigenous Tungus people or as an 'enemy of man' as China declared it in 1959, teeters on the edge of extinction. Habitat loss, logging, poaching, the trade in skins and body parts (tiger penises, noses and ground bone are still highly sought after in Eastern medicine), hunting and trapping of prey species, and genetic problems suffered by small and isolated populations have combined to bring numbers crashing down. From the 1930s, many reserves were established from India across to the Siberian far east, but resources have generally been too few, bureaucracy too complicated, issues involving local people too involved, and the price on a tiger's head too high (around $25,000 in the mid-1990s). The situation in Russia was not helped by the collapse of the Soviet system in 1991 which led to an unregulated international scramble for the valuable natural resources – animal, vegetable and mineral. In 1993 the Siberian tiger population was estimated at about 420 individuals. The chances of my spotting one of these few remaining wild tigers were non-existent, and I would have to be satisfied with the impressive specimen I had watched in its pathetically inadequate cage in the zoo in Novosibirsk.

Ussuriland is the claw of Siberia that points down towards Korea. On the west, the Ussuri River forms the Russian/Chinese border; on the east are the rugged shores of the Sea of Japan. Since we had started heading south from Blagoveshchensk I had noticed a change in the woodlands as the predominantly coniferous taiga began giving way to mixed broadleaf, with oak, lime, Acers and birch, and honeysuckle scrambling among the grasses. This whole region is a transition zone resulting from a lucky combination of latitude, geography and climate; it is one of the most biodiverse areas of the country, a fascinating area where temperate and sub-tropical species live side by side. Apart from bears and tigers, this region is also where the Amur leopard is found, another critically endangered feline which should have secured its place at the top of the food chain but which had the natural bad luck to be born with a beautiful and highly prized pelt.

After showing us around his beehives, Vladimir presented us with two litres of his superb honey and a jar of curds to see us on our way. We rode on through Luchegorsk (a large town that did not feature on our map at all) and stopped for lunch next to a large cornfield. Our picnic consisted largely of our newly acquired honey and curds, partly because it was so delicious and partly because we wanted to reduce the weight (although all we were doing was shifting it from the jar to our stomachs). Suddenly, from nowhere, three Chinese men appeared and started what they clearly hoped would be a conversation. We did our best, and it was all very good-natured, but it was going nowhere. A fourth appeared; he was older and seemed to be in charge, and after a quick word with the others he sent them back where they had come from. This turned out to be up a tree on the other side of the road. The whole situation seemed very irregular. Had they sneaked over the border (it was only 15 miles away) and entered Russia illegally in search of a better life? The tree may have been more spacious than their cramped flat back in China, but I could not imagine that it satisfied whatever yearnings they had had to improve their lot. Perhaps they were hiding during the day and only emerging at night, to avoid being caught by whomever it was who might be taking too close an interest in them. Our arrival on the scene had pricked their curiosity and tempted them to reveal themselves. On second thoughts, we thought they might perhaps be guarding the corn; it was the most plausible explanation we could come up with, but we did not manage to convince ourselves that it was the right one. It just seemed odd to find four Chinese men secreted in a tree.

That evening we arrived in the village of Tamga. There were still plenty of mosquitoes about, but in Zjana's house where we spent the night the ladybirds threatened to outnumber them. The porch and kitchen were full of the shiny red insects, clustered in clumps and roaming the walls. Zjana took us along to her friend Tonya's place for a *banya*. Tonya was a straight-talking down-to-earth woman, and seemed to be the first person we had met who said she was perfectly happy with what she had. Over the obligatory post-*banya* tea as I sweated gently in the hot atmosphere she told rude stories and kept Zjana's young children in check with the occasional light whack. She seemed quite a matriarch; her husband had died some years ago so she must have got used to being in charge while bringing up her own two daughters. Sasha and Yuri stayed up late chatting to Zjana and were very reluctant to get up the next morning. That was not really anything new; I seemed to be the one who minded hearing the alarm go off horribly early the least and usually got up first to sort out breakfast. An occasional lie-in would have been appreciated, though, and it was frustrating that the others did not share the early morning chores willingly. I was still enjoying the cycling but was tired after four-and-a-half months on the road following a timetable that allowed little time for rest. At lunch the next day in Kirovskiy we discussed the remaining few days of the expedition. With only about 220 miles left including this afternoon's ride we could either cover it in two or three days. Kate favoured two, but the rest of us said three. We did not feel like rushing, and from a practical point of view if we took three days we would arrive in the early afternoon rather than in the evening, which would be better for finding accommodation and getting in touch with the Australian Consulate. Sasha and Yuri's reason for slower progress was more straightforward: they were tired. Luckily Kate did not dig her heels in on this and agreed to the three-day plan, at which point, to back up their argument, Sasha and Yuri dozed off.

I knew Kate was not completely happy with our decision, but she was not one to kick up a fuss about it. In the evening at our camp 20 miles short of Spassk she filed a video report and contented herself with expressing her feelings to the camera. It was not the most well-appointed campsite, next to a section of roadworks and perched on top of a freshly made cutting through the trees. Earlier in the day we had crossed the Ussuri river; would one of the region's elusive tigers come padding around our tent in the night? Hikers and cyclists exploring the wilds of the USA are always very careful to avoid attracting bears to their campsites. They haul their food high into the trees, cook away from their tents, and also change out of the clothes they have cooked in. Siberia is full of bears, and although we had only seen footprints we knew they were around, but we had not taken any American-style precautions. Quite the opposite. We could be accused of recklessness, as each evening we mixed the porridge and dried fruit in a saucepan ready for the next day's breakfast and left it to soak overnight, carefully tucked under the tent's flysheet. It had always been there the next morning, with no signs of ursine snuffling.

I did not know if tigers were partial to porridge or not, but we made no efforts to change our breakfast preparation routine to ward off potentially curious felines. After rounding off dinner with some fresh toast from the campfire spread with the last of Vladimir's honey, we retired to the tents. I scanned the airwaves with my radio, eventually settling on an interesting programme discussing water conservation measures around the world, and concentrated on that so I would not hear any twigs snapping under the footfall of a striped prowler.

Morning dawned with everything and everyone intact, but a bit later than before. It was still dark when I poked my head out of the tent at 7am, so I retreated and relaxed for a while. Last night's radio programme had been interesting but turned out to be completely irrelevant as we proceeded to get absolutely soaked by persistent heavy showers throughout the day. It was water removal schemes that were needed here rather than conservation measures. In fact, this seemed to apply to the whole country. None of the towns we had been through appeared to have decent drainage and water would collect in huge puddles after a downpour, with streams running beside and across the roads. Our afternoon session was not that long, but by the time we arrived in Kremova we were sodden and the bikes were filthy, courtesy of a few miles of roadworks. The hotel was full, so we approached our traditional second choice and once we had given our story to the lady on duty, the railway station was put at our disposal. It was actually the old station; a new one was being built next door, so we found ourselves in makeshift accommodation that was really falling apart around us, not helped by the fact that it was effectively an island after the day's wet weather. We settled into *Krasnoy Oogluk* – red corner. All official buildings had one, an area dedicated to the directors of the Revolution and architects of Communism. Marx and Lenin had been all but swept away by the recent political changes, and they were barely clinging on here as the crumbling plasterwork fell off the wall where their pictures hung, threatening to bring them down with a crash. To add to the humid atmosphere we draped our damp clothes around the room in an optimistic and, as it turned out, futile attempt to get them dry.

With only one-and-a-half days to go, I was still not getting excited about the idea of reaching Vladivostok. Cycling had become my way of life – get up, ride, find somewhere to stay. Life had been stripped of all the unnecessary frills and intrusions that usually distract us and clamour for our attention. The simplicity of how I was living appealed to me – slightly more frequent hot baths would have been appreciated, but I had adjusted happily to two-wheeled exploration. Lunchtime on our way to Burleet summed up for me the pleasures of this way of travelling. As we arrived in the village there was a small crowd of people gathered around a lorry. On the back of it a man stood next to a large wooden barrel, from which he was lifting impressive-looking salmon, gutted and decapitated, their bright orange flesh exposed to the autumn sun. The lorry was his shop, and the fish, each weighing on average five or six kilos, was selling for 1,000 roubles a kilo. Our appearance in the village did nothing to disturb this scene of rural, and possibly illegal, trade. We were able to cycle in, settle down and watch

Day 148: Village life - stocking up on bread, and selling salmon off the back of a lorry.

Day 153: Yuri holds the Russian flag aloft proudly – and upside down – as we cross the line.

Day 153: Riding over, time to relax.

Day 153: 8,304 miles after leaving St Petersburg Yuri, Kate, Greg and Sasha celebrate crossing the Vladivostok city boundary.

without becoming the centre of attention. Being unobtrusive meant we could arrive in a village without descending on it, and that meant we could get a better look at life going on there. That was why I enjoyed cycle touring and was prepared to put up with the discomfort and lack of washing facilities. The salmon man sliced some fish for us to add to our lunch, and as we ate it I thought that suddenly not having to get on my bike every morning in another hundred miles' time would seem very odd, and possibly even something of a let-down.

Progress away from the station at Kremova was slow. The sun was out first thing, but that soon changed as the wind picked up and the rain came down. By lunch we were completely soaked. After buying and eating our picnic we were invited in for tea by a lady called Galina, who perhaps had taken pitty on us in our bedraggled state. No-one was in any particular rush, and by the time we got back on our bikes it was half-past three and we had only completed two hours' cycling. Conditions improved in the afternoon and the sun made a welcome reappearance. Sasha and I had swapped chain-rings earlier in the day as his chain was still slipping, and Kate only had a handful of usable gears. We were faced with the unexpected situation that Yuri's bike was possibly the best of the bunch.

We were not quite sure what road we were on. It seemed to be a new one that did not appear on the map. There seemed to be a few more options available here, with Vladivostok's suburbs and satellites dotted about. We did not want to get lost at this late stage! After another maintenance stop, to repair the sidewall of my rear tyre with dental floss and some fine needlework, we spotted a sign pointing to Kiparisova-1 just off the main road, and headed there. As we cycled into the village a lady emerged from the *dom kultura*, the local cultural centre. After an extended conversation with her, Sasha and Yuri managed to get her original offer of sleeping in the *dom* upgraded to sole occupation of the new house that her husband Ivan was building. It was nearly finished and was perfect for us on our last night before Vladivostok. The only thing we would have changed were the security arrangements, which came in the shape of a large and enthusiastic Alsatian – and I am not talking about a chubby and ruddy-cheeked resident of France's historically disputed eastern border regions. This was the shaggy four-legged variety, all playful licks and whimpers when Ivan was around and leaping snarling fury when anyone else came near the house. Its collar was attached by a short runner to a long wire stretched out straight on the ground so that it could charge madly up and down for about twenty feet, thus extending the area within snapping distance of its impressive-looking teeth. We were not really planning on going anywhere once we were safely ensconced so we hoped that once the dog could no longer see us it would calm down and not leap into action every time it heard footsteps from within.

Ivan had been working on the house for three years and was happy to turn it over to us for the evening. Once he and his wife heard about the expedition, and especially that we were due to finish the next day, they had been very keen to help us out. Later in the evening they called round with a large bag of vegetables, some jam and *smetana* – even with only half a day left it seemed sensible to keep piling in the calories, just in case. More significant than the food, though, was the other gift they had for us. Ivan had been round to the mayor's house and persuaded him to donate his flag to us. It was a fitting gesture at the end of our journey and we tried, with a mixture of success the following day, to do it justice.

In a quiet corner of Ivan's house we set up the video camera and each of us in turn went and committed our thoughts to the tape. Looking at the results later, we all seemed rather subdued and nobody said anything controversial so we may as well all have done it in the room together. We were all undeniably happy that everything had gone as well as it had, but it looked as though fatigue was definitely setting in. In any case, we had not quite reached the end, and there was still the possibility that events on the last day could confound our efforts to reach Russia's eastern port.

The first thing we had to contend with in the morning was a combination of the guard dog and the urge to go to the toilet. Traditionally, the idea of a guard dog is something to keep people out of somewhere, but since we were already in, that need was irrelevant. The dog no doubt felt duty-bound to do something, so it switched its approach to one of keeping people in. Cleverly, this required no extra effort on its part – it barked and gnashed its teeth in the usual way. We were not entirely sure if its chain would allow it to make its way up the front steps to the door, but none of us was keen to put it to the test. The toilet, however, was down the garden path, and one way or another we needed to get to it. Yuri managed to break out via the window, thus avoiding a canine encounter. Sasha was bolder and headed out the front door, prepared to tackle Fido head on. He did have a large spade in his hand, which tipped the odds in his favour, but luckily he did not have to use it as he made himself as small as possible and stuck close to the wall. I bottled out and used a handy bucket in the porch. It struck me that all guard dogs really do is guard themselves.

I switched on the short-wave radio. The news from Moscow was not good. There were large demonstrations, with thousands of people on the streets and barricades around the White House (the parliament building). Tensions were running very high, and the stand-off between President Yeltsin and parliament was about to reach its dramatic conclusion. So far we had seen nothing in the towns and villages here to suggest there was anything going on in the country at all. Maybe in Vladivostok things would be different, with its large military presence. We would find out in a few hours.

Before leaving Kiparisova-1 we called in at School No.9 (the local Municipal Urban Facilities Naming Committee had obviously been having a bad day). The English teacher came out with her class and we did our best to get them to practise with some real native speakers, but the pupils were shy and we did not get anything out of them beyond a few rushed and self-conscious 'hellos'. Even the teacher seemed rather reluctant to strike up a conversation. More children appeared until there were about 40 of them gathered around us, but this time it felt like less of a mob than the group in the pioneer camp near Lake Baikal. Again Sasha had to do all the explaining to them about what we were up to. The pupils' cheerful waves sent us on our way in a happy mood, and we turned for the last time towards Vladivostok. It was a brisk, chilly morning but clear and bright, and we rode along sometimes chatting, sometimes lost in our own thoughts, remembering all the events of the last five months. I did not want to arrive in Vladivostok feeling as though it was just our next destination along the way rather than the end of this whole extended journey. Over the last few days I had been re-running the expedition in my head; so much had happened and we had met so many people since setting off from St. Petersburg 153 days before.

About 25 miles short of Vladivostok we stopped to buy a snack in a rather unassuming looking shop. Lined up on the shelves among the jars of pickled vegetables were a collection of bottles of *champanskoye*, and with a view to marking our arrival in style we bought one. A couple of hours of being shaken in a warm pannier ought to guarantee an explosive celebration. Judging by the state of the ceilings in the many restaurants we had seen these bottles operated on something of a hair trigger. Maybe that was also why invariably only a handful of the light-fittings ever seemed to work, their bulbs shot out by ballistic corks.

As well as marking the moment of arrival we would also want to record it. Since we had no support vehicle and attendant camera crew, getting any spontaneous footage of the whole group doing anything had proved impossible. We had staged some shots during our continental crossing, but they never worked very well, with people disappearing out of the frame, or having to shoot from odd angles. It was looking as though we would be faced with a rather unsatisfactory record of our crossing of the Vladivostok city boundary, when all of a sudden a jeep overtook us, pulled in sharply and a man jumped out. It turned out he was from the local television network. This was just the latest in a long list of lucky encounters that we had enjoyed throughout the trip. The man told us that the city boundary was not far up the road and that he and his colleagues would wait for us there to film us as we rode in. This resulted in a flurry of excited activity; Kate pulled on her pristine expedition tee-shirt and Sasha donned a day-glo cycling jersey from one of our sponsors. He even managed to find a pair of clean white socks. At this rate people would think we had only ridden a few miles around the corner rather than across a continent, so I stayed in what I had been wearing for the last couple of weeks, although even that seemed disappointingly clean. The most important thing to sort out was the flag that Ivan had given us the night before. Yuri leaped off into the undergrowth (as he often had done, when a particular plant had caught his eye) and returned with a sapling to which the flag was duly attached, the intention being to fly it proudly for the last few miles. There was a small technical hitch to overcome first, though, and that was that between the four of us we could not agree which way up the flag should fly. It seemed extraordinary that neither Sasha nor Yuri could say with any confidence how their national flag should look, but it was in fact still not the official flag; although people had been using it since late 1991 it would not be officially adopted until December 1993, a date some three months ahead of where we were now. The old flag had been simple: hammer and sickle go at the top. The new one had nothing in its design to betray its intended orientation, just three horizontal strips of white, blue and red, which was no help to anyone.

Some of us thought white went at the top, others red. In the end we went for red, and Yuri held the flag out as proudly as if he were the athlete leading his national team at the opening ceremony of the Olympic Games. It was a large flag and, as we made our way to the city boundary and the camera crew patiently waiting to capture our arrival, it fluttered beautifully.

Three typical examples of Soviet urban design marked the Vladivostok city limit. The first and most delicate was the tall lamp-post. It was a simple thing, but it had the unmistakable 'Russian-ness' that I had noticed as soon as I had arrived in St. Petersburg. Radiating from the top of the post was a circular splay of arms of varying lengths, each ending in a light, and just below these were two loud-halers, almost certainly not intended for broadcasting useful traffic news to the drivers as they passed by, but no doubt very helpful for announcing record shoe production figures or bumper harvests. The second was the massive town name-sign, a monolith measuring 15 feet high and 24 feet long (making maximum advantage of a name containing eleven, mostly full-width, characters). Each decent sized town had had a similar sign, expressing confidence, permanence, and, at a simple level, an indisputable presence. The farther east we had come, the more significant the signs seemed to be, highlighting the transition from wild and untamed Siberia on one side of the invisible municipal boundary to the controlled and orderly urban landscape on the other. The third object was a triumphant monument of a sailor holding his arm aloft in front of a column.

This was Vladivostok's rostral column, raised in 1960 to commemorate the city's 100th anniversary, which made it a very young Siberian city. Given its situation at the country's farthest south-east corner its youth should not be a surprise. In common with other settlements this side of the Urals its first incarnation was as a fortress, established during the years following the Crimean War to repel any over-curious Western ships. Strategically placed close to China and Japan the fortified town quickly grew into a major trading hub and later the centre for the Pacific Fleet. The rostral column celebrates the seafaring history. Punctuating the 60-feet high monument are the prows of four galleys, protruding bizarrely as if caught up in a severe storm at sea and flung into the trunk of a mighty tree, their battering rams used to full effect. Perched majestically on the top is the *Manchur*, the first Russian ship to sail into the bay around which Vladivostok now sits, its sails set and ready to catch every breeze. Bringing the ensemble up to date at the base of the column stands the Pacific Fleet sailor.

As we cycled the last few miles under a perfect clear blue sky towards these three objects that were so readily identifiable as Russian, no drivers hooted their horns and nobody called out to us. We therefore had no reason to believe that Yuri was doing anything other than engaging in a happy moment of patriotism with anther emblem of Russia. Unfortunately he was not. We had had a 50/50 chance of getting it right and we had blown it, so we got a beautiful shot of the four of us crossing the line side by side with an upside down flag. Since nobody pointed this fact out to us it did not interfere with our mood of celebration and our bottle of local bubbly performed spectacularly well. The TV crew got us all artfully in shot, and we then spent half an hour taking our own photos as we posed next to and on top of the various signs and statues. It was a symbolic finish line since Vladivostok itself still lay 12 miles farther on. Kate only had three useable gears by this stage, so we made our way at a relaxed pace through the hills of the last hour or so of our five-month expedition. We were taking the Australian Consulate as our official end, and at 3pm we arrived outside its front door.

We had defied our friends by not starving, not falling prey to anarchic hoodlums and local gangsters, and not perishing through over-indulgence in home-distilled fire-water. The heat, floods, mosquitoes, mud and absent roads had not got the better of us, and our bodies had come out the far side remarkably unscathed. What is more, we had arrived more or less bang on time. Planning the trip in the warmth of her London flat with only a vague idea of what the conditions would be like, Kate had calculated it would take 152 days: May 1st to September 29th. As I eased myself off my saddle for the last time, having covered 8304 miles, crossed nine time zones and consumed countless plates of *pelmeni*, it was mid-afternoon on Day 153 – September 30th.

EPILOGUE

~~~

We had five days in Vladivostok, and our time was divided between enjoying the city and wondering whether we would be able to leave. On the day of our arrival we called in at the town hall and set up a meeting with the deputy mayor, Vladimir Dubinkin, for a few days' time, before leaving our bikes there and jumping on the trolley bus to get to our accommodation. Opting for public transport on this leg proved one of the expedition's easiest decisions to make.

The meeting with Mr Dubinkin was rather one-sided, being more of a talk from him rather than a chat with us. Nevertheless, he seemed happy to meet us and we completed our official business, handing over the letter and plaque from the mayor of Milton Keynes, before posing for photographs. His office was very helpful, writing a letter for us to take to the Aeroflot office telling them to get us flight tickets for October 5th, even though there were apparently none available until the 15th. Perhaps that was why actually buying the things proved so difficult. The lady rejecting all my cash dollars no doubt resented being bossed about by the town hall and wanted to show that the bucks still stopped with her. Dubinkin also arranged a driver (actually the Chairman of the Municipal Sports Committee) to take us on a tour of the city.

I was very impressed by Vladivostok. Smartly dressed people went about their business and buskers provided a varied soundtrack ranging from traditional Russian music to jazz. There was no sign at all of any political unrest. The city itself spread across a number of hills and was divided by many inlets, and as with more well-known harbour cities such as Sydney and Stockholm this gave the place an airiness and spaciousness that was very appealing. It also provided lots of excellent vantage points from which to admire the view out across Golden Horn Bay, the deep water harbour that probed far into the city and made Vladivostok such a busy and successful port. Container ships lined up patiently for many miles out at sea, waiting their turn to nestle alongside the docks. As Anatoly our driver showed us around, afternoon wore into a beautiful and cloudless evening. Lights came on across the city and the sun set in a perfect display of orange and red. I was feeling very relaxed and was enjoying spending a few days here. The news from farther west, however, did not look good.

We were keeping a close eye on developments in Moscow on Russian television and also the BBC via my radio. The violent demonstrations in the capital had escalated into full-scale fighting between opposing forces loyal to Yeltsin and the parliament. 62 people had been killed in gun battles as the two sides fought for control of the television tower at Ostankino in the north of the city, and the attention had now shifted to the White House. Inside, the People's Deputies were holding their ground, their numbers bolstered by sympathetic militia. But in an extraordinary display of bravura Yeltsin ordered in the tanks to fire on his own parliament. Shells thudded into the upper floors of the White House and black smoke billowed out as fire took hold. As civil wars go it was a brief one, and the People's Deputies surrendered on October 4th. Unofficially the clashes claimed over 2000 lives.

We had heard that Moscow airport was shut and the apparent resolution of the political situation brought no further news on this, so on the morning of October 5th we set off to catch our flight not sure what would happen. As it turned out, planes were leaving on schedule, but our problems were not over.

Tuesday October 5th – leaving Vladivostok

Another Russian system: checking in at airports is different from elsewhere. Rather than checking your bags in when you arrive at the airport and then being free to roam around with just your hand baggage, you have to sit around with all your bags (having had them wrapped up by the brown paper man downstairs - a handy service they could introduce elsewhere) until the flight is called. Everyone then queues through a small doorway, everything is weighed (including hand baggage), then you go and put your luggage onto the cart yourself. It's like going aviating forty years ago.

Having spent ages trying to work out how much excess baggage we would have, after loading Sasha and Valera up to their maximum allowance (since their excess would only be R1000/kg, rather than $3/kg for me *and Kate) we were told that the bikes couldn't go on the plane unless we dismantled them. Aaaarrrggggghhh!! Just when you think everything is organised, some other bloody problem rears up! Fortunately we were able to sort it out fairly easily - we took the bikes round to the freight terminal nearby and booked them on a flight some time in the near-future for R36,000 - not too bad. The only thing is we don't know exactly when they are going, or when they will get there. The easiest thing is to pick them up in Moscow when we go up there to fly home, rather than make extra trips to bring them to Ryazan. So. Stress factor fairly high before getting on the plane, made worse again by English/Russian problems - hard work for Sasha to keep translating everything as well as trying to sort things out, and when everyone has their own idea on how to solve a problem it can be a nightmare.*

Ahead lay nine hours spent at Aeroflot's pleasure. Once Sasha had stuffed his large souvenir salmon, wrapped only in newspaper, into the overhead locker he settled into the seat next to mine. As I clipped my seat belt into place across my lap he laughed, pointing out the lack of help I could expect from it should we find ourselves in the unfortunate position of plunging into the earth from 35000 feet. I consoled myself that between now and that dramatic event I would at least be able to enjoy the best legroom I had experienced on a plane.

The airline and crew seemed to take the view that a nod towards safety was probably a good thing and would help calm those of a nervous disposition, but that there was no point getting carried away. Thus, a seat belt for the few passengers who took some comfort from it, but no sign of any handy card in the seat pocket in front of me depicting escape routes and detachable rafts, and no safety demonstration from the crew inviting me to familiarise myself with the nearest emergency exit or showing how to blow up a lifejacket doing an impression of a whoopee cushion. While the seat pocket was completely redundant, containing no literature of any kind whether of an informative or even merely entertaining nature, the tray table did eventually come into its own as the stewardess served my meal. It immediately became apparent that a working seat pocket and an absent tray table would have been a far more preferable arrangement as I considered the plate in front of me. Half a slice of bread, about twenty cold tinned peas, a serving of cold tinned stewing beef (I think), a small piece of a Spam-type substance and a standard Russian biscuit looked up at me. With no in-flight entertainment on the menu I looked out of the window.

Below, the taiga stretched to the horizon, a continuous wild region of big animals, huge rivers and tough people. In nine hours we would have crossed the country again, reviewing from an aerial perspective what it had taken us five months to experience on two wheels. As I was now experiencing Aeroflot's quicker, but more removed, version of the same trip, I knew which one I preferred.

SPONSORS OF THE TRANS-SIBERIAN CYCLE EXPEDITION

AAMK Innovation Centre

Mobil

Kodak

Michael Henderson

Karrimor

The North Face

Phil Corley Cycles

The Outdoor Shop

Texaco

G. Allawi

Neste

Brooke Bond D

Rohan Designs PLC

Evans, Waterloo

Brownridge